Royal Mail Guide to Direct Mail for Small Businesses

The Marketing Series is one of the most comprehensive collections of books in marketing and sales available in the UK today.

Published by Butterworth-Heinemann on behalf of The Chartered Institute of Marketing, the series is divided into three distinct groups: *Student* (fulfilling the needs of those taking the Institute's certificate and diploma qualifications); *Professional Development* (for those on formal or self-study vocational training programmes); and *Practitioner* (presented in a more informal, motivating and highly practical manner for the busy marketer).

Formed in 1911, The Chartered Institute of Marketing is now the largest professional marketing management body in Europe with over 24,000 members and 28,000 students located worldwide. Its primary objectives are focused on the development of awareness and understanding of marketing throughout UK industry and commerce and in the raising of standards of professionalism in the education, training and practice of this key business discipline.

Books in the series

Royal Mail Guide to Direct Mail for Small Businesses

Brian Thomas

BUTTERWORTH
HEINEMANN

Butterworth-Heinemann
Linacre House, Jordan Hill, Oxford OX2 8DP
A division of Reed Educational and Professional Publishing Ltd

Ɒ A member of the Reed Elsevier plc group

OXFORD   BOSTON   JOHANNESBURG
MELBOURNE   NEW DELHI   SINGAPORE

First published 1996

British Library Cataloguing in Publication Data
A catalogue record for this book is available from the British Library

ISBN 0 7506 27476

Designed and produced by Co-publications, Loughborough <copubs@aol.com>

Printed and bound in Great Britain

Contents

Foreword

Here, at last, is a book on direct mail which is aimed at the person running a small business.

Many earlier books have started from the premise that the reader has thousands of pounds to spend on advertising and is merely looking for ways of spending the budget more cost-effectively.

However, *Royal Mail Guide to Direct Mail for Small Businesses*, part of The Chartered Institute of Marketing Practitioner Series, shows, by example, how highly effective direct mail campaigns can be targeted at small audiences without spending a huge amount of money.

Small businesses continue to face extreme competitive pressures and therefore require a professional approach to their marketing activities. Time and time again we see examples of highly creative pieces of direct mail from small businesses which, if targeted correctly, continue to win new business, generate customer loyalty and lead to repeat business.

In a highly practical way this book leads you through the processes of identifying customers and prospects, building your own lists, writing and producing your own mailings and planning and monitoring your campaigns.

The author, Brian Thomas, has had a wide ranging career in direct marketing during which he has been involved in the planning and despatch of more than 700 mailings. He has run major direct marketing agencies and has also been the leading CIM lecturer in direct marketing for more than 15 years. In that time he has trained many thousands of students, passing on his enthusiasm for the benefits of direct mail.

Combining this knowledge with the resources and wide experience of Royal Mail has enabled us to produce this practical DIY manual for managers of small businesses.

At Royal Mail we are dedicated to helping small businesses make the most of all aspects of written communication. You represent a large and growing percentage of our business and by demonstrating the effectiveness of direct mail we hope to help you continue to grow and prosper in the years to come.

Good luck and good responses.

Adam Novak

Adam Novak
Director and General Manager
Royal Mail National

Preface

WHO IS THIS BOOK FOR?

You are a small business owner or manager. You want to build your business, but you do not have millions nor even thousands of pounds to spend on advertising and marketing.

Despite this, you need to advertise. Not, perhaps, to build broad awareness but to deliver relevant and timely selling messages to existing customers and to encourage new prospects to become customers. There are many advertising options open to you and these are described later in this book.

Your prime requirement is to achieve the best return for your budget, and you will find no method of advertising more cost-efficient than direct mail. However, to deliver the best return on your investment, your direct mail must be highly targeted.

> *Without careful targeting, direct mail is expensive and, sometimes, intrusive.*

This book is a practical, *how to do it* manual for direct mail. It will tell you when direct mail is the right solution to your marketing problem and also when it is not appropriate.

It will show you *how to use direct mail strategically, rather than tactically*.

Anyone can send out a 'mail shot'. However, to benefit fully from the strategic advantages of direct mail you need to think hard about:

- Your target market – who and where are they?
- Your product – is it appropriate for all customers and prospects, or should you consider developing alternatives for different groups?
- Your offer – what can you say to arouse the interest of your reader?
- Timing – people buy products at the time which is appropriate to them, not when it fits your sales plan. You therefore need to time your mailings carefully.

▷ Your presentation – how can you present your sales proposition so that it will be immediately clear to the reader?

The strategic advantage of direct mail is that you can vary the contents and the timing according to the specific needs of your reader. This makes it a very powerful form of advertising indeed.

Clearly, to be able to use direct mail strategically, you need information. It is not enough to know the names and addresses of your customers and prospects. You also need to know about their varying needs and wants; how and when they reach buying decisions; and how much they already know about your product or service.

HOW TO GET THE MOST OUT OF THE BOOK

Chapters are grouped into parts, designed to lead you through the process of planning and managing a successful mailing campaign. There are six parts:

1 **Introduction** – how direct mail fits into the marketing mix, and why it has become such an important advertising medium.

2 **Information** – the sources and applications of information about your customers and prospects.

3 **Communications** – the development of your offer and how this can best be communicated to your customers and prospects.

4 **Services** – how to find and select outside suppliers; the briefing process; a review of the many services provided by Royal Mail.

5 **Campaign planning** – how it all fits together; a summary of the planning and management of a mailing campaign.

6 **Appendices** – legal aspects of direct communications; backup information supporting various chapters; useful addresses and recommended further reading.

At the end of each chapter you will find a short section headed '*What to do now*'. As far as possible I have made these sections relevant to the chapter content. This means you can pick up the book for advice on, say, mailing lists and find the relevant action point in the same place.

You can therefore read it as a book, or use it as a reference aid – to help you get the best of both worlds, I have included cross-references where appropriate. There is also a comprehensive index.

SELF-TEST QUESTIONNAIRES

Where relevant, I have also included a self-test questionnaire.

These exercises and projects can be used for general practice, or adapted to your own situation for yourself or your colleagues. You will find my comments, answers or suggested approaches to these exercises in Appendix 4.

TERMINOLOGY

It is difficult to write a book about a specialist subject without using specialist terms. I have tried to keep these to the minimum, but where it is unavoidable, you will find a full explanation of the term in the glossary.

CAUTION

All the test results quoted in this book are true. The circumstances, however, can never be totally replicated and inclusion of a result is not intended to imply that the same will always happen.

Circumstances will vary from area to area, market to market and even from month to month.

Readers must therefore use the results quoted as a guide and not a guarantee. You must always test your *own* product in your *own* marketplace, to establish a set of norms for your *own* business.

Part One

Introduction

1 Direct mail and other advertising methods

What is direct mail? Let's start with a definition:

Direct mail is a form of advertising which delivers targeted, individually addressed communications to customers and prospects through the postal system.

In other words, direct mail is an advertising medium. It is obviously not the *only* advertising medium, nor will it always provide a solution to your advertising problem. When used correctly however, it is the most powerful and memorable medium available.

In this chapter we will look at the various advertising options available, indicate how and where each could be used, and consider how you can use them together to create a powerful integrated campaign.

TWO KINDS OF ADVERTISING

There are broadly two kinds of advertising: advertising which uses mass media such as television and press and advertising which is more tightly targeted, using media like direct mail and the telephone.

Mass media advertising is used in several ways:

1 **Awareness** – to create awareness, encourage trial and stimulate demand among a very wide audience e.g. when selling a mass market product such as washing powder or cat food to a mass audience. The objective is to encourage people to remember the name and select that brand when shopping. Awareness, or 'image' advertising emphasizes *brand values* and *positioning*.

2 **Reinforcement** – to generate a background of confidence in a company so that other more targeted selling methods, such as mailing or face-to-face selling, are more acceptable and thus more successful.

3   As part of an *integrated campaign* – which leads the prospective customer through several stages from first interest (awareness of the product), through information gathering, to demonstration and sale.

A good example of an integrated campaign would be one run by a company such as Ford, to generate sales of a new car.

A number of media types may be used, as follows:

▷ National television and press advertising creates awareness and stimulates interest in the new model.

▷ This national campaign features a telephone number and an address so that interested prospects can send for an information pack.

▷ The information pack is mailed to each respondent and will include the address of a local dealer. The dealer will also have been sent details of local respondents. Dealers can then 'follow-up' the information pack with a letter or phone call.

▷ Prospects still interested at this stage telephone or visit the dealer to discuss options and perhaps arrange a test drive. This is the start of the face-to-face process when prospect and dealer discuss credit terms, trade-in prices and, hopefully, close the deal.

As we can see there are several stages in this process and several media may be used:

▷ Television
▷ Radio
▷ National newspapers and magazines
▷ Mail – response packs and perhaps targeted mailings to dealers' own prospect lists
▷ Local press – more often used by the dealers themselves
▷ Directories such as Yellow Pages – featuring details of local dealers
▷ The telephone
▷ Face-to-face selling.

The final selection of media will depend on the precise objectives of the campaign and on the basis from which we start. Let us consider two examples.

1

Starting from scratch – this campaign starts from the position that, even though we may have identified a target group in terms of income and lifestyle, we do not know which of the many motorists in this group will be interested in this model. Neither do we know which are thinking of changing their car in the next few months.

We therefore need to use mass media advertising, offering the 'hook' of an information pack, to persuade those interested to write or telephone to identify themselves.

Once we have identified the interested minority, we can switch to targeted media such as direct mail and face-to-face selling, to complete the task.

We may also be able to find some rented lists of good prospects and these can be added to our file of prospects.

Each medium has a role to play and each supports the others. It is not a case of one medium being better than another; simply that some are more appropriate for the specific task in hand.

2

Starting from a better position – the above campaign would be appropriate when we do not know who our potential customers are. Now, let us see how this might vary when we already know the names of the interested prospects.

In this part of the campaign we are not seeking new prospects, but contacting our own previous buyers and enquirers. We can also include in this category any relevant names we can get hold of through dealers – people who have called in to enquire about new cars; those who have their existing cars serviced by this dealer and so on.

Does this mean that we do not need to use the mass media? Yes and No.

In this case we do not need it to generate the names and addresses of our prospects, but it still has a useful role to play. National advertising creates a background of confidence mentioned earlier (page 3 – Reinforcement) so that our targeted communication, probably a mailing or telephone call from the dealer, will be better received.

So, depending on our starting point, we may or may not consider direct mail suitable for the initial communication phase. Sooner or later however, it will be one of the few logical methods of continuing the dialogue.

THE ESSENTIAL STEPS IN DEVELOPING A CAMPAIGN

1 Specify your objective, i.e. why are you running a campaign?

- ▷ to encourage enquiries from new prospects?
- ▷ to generate sales from previous enquirers?
- ▷ to persuade previous customers to buy again?
- ▷ to continue to sell on a regular basis to existing customers?

Clearly, each of the above objectives will require a different strategy.

Make sure your objectives are realistic:

- ▷ If you sell office supplies, such as copying paper and pens, you may very well be able to make sales directly from your advertisement or mailing.

- ▷ If, on the other hand, your product is more complicated and expensive, such as an office computer network, although you may be targeting the same person, you should not expect to make sales immediately.

Products like this take longer to sell and the buyer needs much more information and probably a demonstration too. In this case, your objective would be to generate leads which you could then follow up by mail, phone, or with a personal visit.

Once you have fixed on your objective, the most important factor is targeting.

---

2 Identify your target audience and where to find them

▷ Who are the prospective buyers?
▷ Where are they?
▷ What is the best way of locating them?
   ❑ are they already on your database?
   ❑ is there a rented list available?
   ❑ are they listed in a directory?
   ❑ do they read a specific magazine?

The answers to these questions will help you decide how targeted your initial approach can be.

For example, if you sell a specialized accessory for anglers, you could perhaps rent a mailing list of people interested in fishing, or advertise in a specialist publication such as *Angling Times*.

If your product is one with a much wider appeal, say to all people who own their own houses, you will have to consider a less targeted approach to start with.

---

3 Select your general communications approach e.g.

▷ mass media advertising such as
   ❑ television
   ❑ radio
   ❑ newspapers and magazines (national and local)
   ❑ outdoor advertising such as posters and bus sides
   ❑ directories

▷ targeted communications such as
   ❑ direct mail
   ❑ door-to-door distribution
   ❑ telephone
   ❑ personal visits

▷ a combination of the above options.

4 Decide on the best timing.

Next, you must spend some time establishing the correct timing, ideally for each individual prospect. If you know the right time it is easier to make a highly specific approach – it is also more likely to be relevant to the prospect

---

EXAMPLE

If you sell an accountancy service to help small businesses prepare their year end accounts it will be easier to sell to a company whose year end is approaching.

Let us suppose you have established that your service is of most interest to businesses with a turnover between £150,000 and £500,000 and that you have obtained a list of such businesses from a list broker.

There are two possibilities:

1 You know their year end date – you can therefore target the right businesses from within your list, mailing each business, say, two months before their year end. In these circumstances you can offer the service direct, asking for a decision right away.

2 You don't know their year end date – in this case you have a different problem. How to get them to express an interest now, when the subject is not at the top of their agenda, and how to find out when their financial year ends.

In the first instance you will want to start the selling process right away and your objective will be to identify and follow up leads immediately. In the second case you will have to be a bit more imaginative, e.g. you could produce a booklet called, say, *Accountancy Requirements for Small Businesses*.

This would not give away all the details of your service, but would contain general advice on the things the manager of a small business needs to know. The booklet would, of course, mention the service you provide.

Your mailing would offer this booklet FREE to interested enquirers. In return for the booklet, you could ask each respondent to 'swap' some general information about their business and to tell you when their financial year ends.

This programme would have two benefits:

1 You would have identified the target audience and established the correct timing for each company.

2 You would have generated goodwill through the provision of free advice, making your later approach more acceptable.

As we can see, before you even consider developing promotional messages, you need to spend some time thinking about your target audience and how they might go about deciding whether to buy the sort of product or service you provide.

5 Produce your outline creative briefing plan – having decided on the right media and timing, you can now start to gather information, think up offers and so on, in preparation for briefing your creative team.

6 Arrange your media:

  ▷ book advertising space
  ▷ assemble mailing list.

7 Produce your advertising material:

  ▷ organize design and copywriting, where relevant
  ▷ arrange for artwork
  ▷ write your letter and order your envelopes and so on
  ▷ arrange for print, assembly and postage.

*Don't forget to include a way for your prospect to respond
– coupon, reply paid envelope, telephone number and so on.*

8   Deliver your message.

9   Prepare to handle your replies – if you are asking people to send for
more information, you will need to estimate how much response to
expect. You can then produce enough 'response packs' to satisfy
demand. It is important to avoid keeping people waiting. This is a
good rule in any circumstances, but it is vital when responding to
enquiries. Your prospect may have sent off for details of two or three
alternatives. The first one to respond has a better chance of collecting
the order.

If you are generating leads for a sales person to follow up, speed is
equally important. Leads should be passed directly to the sales person
with any supporting information, e.g. what the respondent asked for,
any special requests, and so on. The sales person may acknowledge
the lead by telephone when making an appointment, but if this cannot
be done quickly a written acknowledgement is advisable.

10   Record the details for measurement and evaluation – your future
campaigns will be easier to plan, and more likely to succeed, if they
are based on previous experience. You should consider developing a
guard book. This is a large binder containing copies of each of your
advertisements and mailings with details of costs, responses and,
where relevant, conversions. Figure 1.1 shows an example.

Details in the results box will, of course, vary according to the activity,
e.g. advertisement, mailing, telephone follow-up campaign. You may
wish to add in other costs such as a sales person's time, and so on. Figure
1.1 shows a calculation of *cost per £ sales*. Some prefer to use a cost to
sales ratio – the choice is yours. Whatever you decide, the important
thing is to have a basis for comparing results and selecting the best, most
cost-effective, approaches for redeployment in future campaigns.

Figure 1.1

Maintain a guard book of your advertisements and mailings, together with details of results

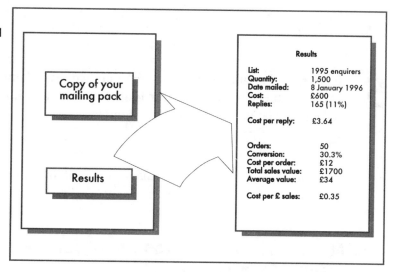

Copy of your mailing pack

Results

Results	
List:	1995 enquirers
Quantity:	1,500
Date mailed:	8 January 1996
Cost:	£600
Replies:	165 (11%)
Cost per reply:	£3.64
Orders:	50
Conversion:	30.3%
Cost per order:	£12
Total sales value:	£1700
Average value:	£34
Cost per £ sales:	£0.35

DO YOU WANT TO MAKE PROFIT NOW, OR LATER?

Another issue to consider in the planning stage is the question of investment. In other words, are you aiming to make profits from your initial mailing, or to invest in new customers with a view to making money later?

Before you can decide, there are several factors to consider:

1 Is your product the sort which people buy once only or regularly? For example, a carpet cleaning service could be sold to the same person more than once. A conservatory is likely to be a once only, or very infrequent, purchase. Similarly, office stationery is a regular purchase, whereas new office furniture is not.

2 If you sell a 'one-off' product, do you have a range of other products which will appeal to the same buyers?

3 Will your product live up to your promises? In other words, will your buyers feel they have been given good value for money and thus be inclined to buy again?

4 Do you have sufficient funds to be able to wait 6 or 12 months for payback?

5 Is it likely that other equally good, or perhaps even better, products will enter the market in the near future? In this case, it is important to recognize that your opportunity is limited.

Clearly, if you can afford to wait for your profit you can recruit more customers, simply by making them a better offer.

WHAT EXPERTISE DO YOU NEED TO PLAN AND IMPLEMENT YOUR ADVERTISING?

There are many advertising tasks which are better left to professionals. For example, the production of a television commercial or a newspaper advertisement requires specialized skills and specialized equipment, which most of us do not possess.

Other aspects, such as media planning and buying, require experience which the average business person does not have. It is therefore recommended that when considering press or broadcast advertising (even when using local newspapers or radio stations), you seek professional help in planning and producing your advertisement.

In practice, you will find many local papers and stations have a department which can help you produce advertising of reasonable quality at a moderate cost.

With direct mail, although good creative work can undoubtedly increase the attention value, it is not so important and there is a very good reason why this is so:

In all forms of advertising the issue of targeting is the most important. However, in some forms of advertising, creativity is an integral part of targeting. For example:

In mass media (TV, press and so on) targeting is achieved in three ways:

1 The selection of the **right medium**, i.e. should you use *The Times* or the *Sun*? And the right section within the medium i.e. sports section, business section, TV programmes and so on?

---

2 The selection of the **right time** – newspaper audiences can vary according to the day of the week, TV and radio audiences vary dramatically according to time of day and programming schedules.

---

3 The selection of the **right audience** by use of your theme and its presentation. In other words, the final stage of targeting in these media, is your headline or attention-grabbing illustration or device.

The quality of your creative treatment is clearly crucial in this third aspect of targeting.

In direct mail, targeting is much simpler – assuming you have the necessary information you write to the decision maker, so the quality of the creative has a lesser role in the targeting process.

This means that with direct mail it is much easier to 'do it yourself'. This is not to say you should ignore creativity. A good creative idea can make a major difference to response, but nevertheless the penalty for being less creative can be small. In other forms of advertising it can mean that no-one even notices your advertisement.

What this is leading up to, is that, happily for those with limited budgets, simple direct mail letters, with low cost leaflets produced on your own desk top computer, can be highly successful. There are several examples of this in the colour section.

These comments are not meant to imply that you should not give lots of thought to your mailings – simply that a good strong idea (or offer), clearly presented and placed in front of the right audience at the right time will give you a good chance of success.

DIRECT MAIL AS AN ADVERTISING MEDIUM

What are the strengths and weaknesses of direct mail as an advertising medium? First the strengths:

▷ **Personalization** – personal communications are always more powerful.

▷ **Targeting** – we use information about individuals to select those for whom the offer will be relevant. The same information also helps us to identify those for whom the message will not be relevant. This benefits us in two ways:

   ❑ we reduce annoyance by not mailing people who would find the message an irritant
   ❑ we save money by reducing our mailing quantities

▷ **Flexibility** – having information about individuals gives us another opportunity – we can vary the message and offer to the precise requirements of an individual person or 'cluster' of people. Thus, we can tailor the message according to whether we are writing to a chief executive or an office manager; a plumber or a heart specialist.

▷ **Relevance** – the above features make good direct mail more relevant to the recipient than other forms of advertising.

▷ **Retention** – research shows that messages delivered by direct mail are retained longer than with other forms of advertising. One major airline found that spontaneous recall of its mailings was 74% three months after the last mailing was received. A mail order company experienced more than 60% recall six months after the mailing was despatched.

To achieve such high recall rates with television or newspaper advertising would cost millions of pounds.

▷ **Creative freedom** – there are almost no limits on creativity in direct mail – apart from the requirement of all advertising to be legal, decent and truthful. We can use colour, sound and movement (via tapes and videos), give demonstrations and use a variety of memorable involvement devices.

> **Impact** – a large sample of business people, when asked which of their mailings they opened first, said 'those which are bulky or look most interesting'.

> **Acceptability** – research shows us that direct mail is welcomed by a high percentage of consumers and business people – 'providing it is relevant and interesting'. In recent research 70% of people said they 'look forward to receiving the post'.

> **Testing facilities** – direct mail is an excellent 'test-bed' enabling us to make comparisons of lists, offers, timing, creative themes, response devices (stickers, vouchers, cards, Freefone telephone numbers, fax numbers, and so on).

> **Do-it-yourself** – most other media require specialist skill in design, layout and writing, because they need to catch the eye against the many competing calls for attention.

In direct mail this is not quite so important – if you place the right message, in front of the right person, at the right time, you will receive attention.

This is not to say that you do not have to work hard at direct mail – merely that this is one form of advertising which is easier to do successfully yourself.

Now the weaknesses:

> **Cost** – despite the cost-efficiency of direct mail, it can be expensive to produce, sometimes costing perhaps fifty to a hundred times as much 'per reader' as a press advertisement.

However, the much tighter targeting capabilities of direct mail can reduce most of the wastage and thus deliver a cost-per-reply or cost-per-order which can be lower than press. To do so however we need to have enough information to enable this precise targeting.

Direct mail is often not the most cost-efficient way to prospect for new customers.

> ▷ **Image** – there are many people, and not a few newspapers, who deliberately decry direct mail as 'junk mail'. In fact, junk mail is not synonymous with direct mail, but with badly targeted direct mail. Despite research which tells us that the majority of people find direct mail welcome, many still receive badly targeted mailings. We must therefore do all we can, to reduce this and keep annoyance and costs to the minimum.

STRENGTHS AND WEAKNESSES OF OTHER MEDIA OPTIONS

In Appendix 3 you will find a detailed review of the strengths and weaknesses of the other advertising methods available.

 ## THE POWER OF TARGETING – EXAMPLE

Some years ago, one of my clients, a major office products manufacturer, decided to test direct marketing for the first time. He asked us to produce a mailing to encourage trials and subsequently direct orders for his new 'state of the art' typewriter. This was his first venture into direct mail, as all sales had previously been made by the sales force following up leads generated by trade press advertising.

The client told me that he had lots of names and addresses of previous buyers and we therefore produced a high quality mailing, including a large full-colour leaflet demonstrating the many new features of the typewriter.

Unfortunately, my client forgot to 'sell' this new idea to his sales people and the first they heard of it was when their marketing department asked them for a list of their contacts.

By a strange coincidence, all of the sales people managed to 'lose' their contact lists and we were faced with a potential disaster – a large pile of expensive mailing material and no names to send them to.

All we had was the list of addresses to which the company had previously mailed invoices. Not the decision makers, and sometimes not even at the same address.

In desperation we came up with a stop-gap solution – above the envelope window we printed the words:

The mailing contained a good offer – fifteen days' free trial of the new machine and the response was excellent. So good, that the company ran out of demonstration machines and had to set up a waiting list!

Note – we were not able to run a comparative test to a sample with names, so we will never know whether that would have produced even more response. However it does show, that even targeting by function can be successful.

EXAMPLE

More recently, a company selling specialist supplies to schools encountered a problem in trying to keep up-to-date lists of named teachers with specific responsibilities. Their solution? – to address the mailings by function – *Teacher in charge of Wet Playtime* and so on. This approach has been highly successful.

CASE STUDY: CAN DIRECT MAIL HELP A SMALL BUSINESS GROW?

Ask Kevin Lunt. At the age of 23 Kevin became head professional at the brand new Great Hadham Golf Club. He didn't know any of the members but the club had excellent facilities including a covered driving range.

Kevin had some innovative ideas for coaching and decided he had to communicate these to the members as quickly and efficiently as possible.

He wrote a mailing to all 700+ members, telling them about himself and his coaching ideas. He had devised several schemes for different groups including ladies, beginners and junior members. He offered reductions for block bookings and also had facilities for video analysis.

Response was so good that Kevin had to hire an assistant right away.

So being able to define his audience accurately, and then producing some interesting offers, enabled Kevin to get the Kevin Lunt Golf College off to a flying start.

However, when it came to his pro-shop, he still had the problem of competing against the powerful advertising of the large golf discount stores. Fortunately, he was then able to use the power of the relationship to good effect. His database now numbers 2,500 and he mails the local golfers with news, views and competitive offers.

A recent database mailing generated 25% response and Kevin says:

As far as I am concerned, direct mail is an unbeatable vehicle for getting lots of information across. It is the driving force behind establishing – and maintaining – customer loyalty.

WHAT DOES DIRECT MAIL COST?

Table 1.1 looks at the costs of producing a direct mailing using a variety of sources from doing the whole job yourself, to the use of a professional, specialist, direct marketing agency.

The left hand column assumes that you produce the entire mailing using your own PC and printer. The £50 cost against artwork and print in this column is a nominal allowance for stationery, laser toner, envelopes and so on.

The comparisons therefore are:

▷ **Do-it-yourself** – you do the whole job yourself, finding addresses from your telephone directory or Yellow Pages. Note though, that no allowance has been made for the cost of your time.

▷ **Local resources** – you may pay a part-time worker to collect names and addresses for you. Alternatively, you could place small advertisements in local newsagents and on supermarket notice boards. The £50 allowance would cover the cost of your part-timer entering the names onto your PC.

▷ Under 'Copy and design' and 'Artwork and print' I have included allowances for you to pay your local printer, who may be able to offer a simple copy and design service. I have also assumed that you will use a commercial printer, rather than your own desk-top printer.

In each of the first two columns we have assumed that you will assemble and 'fill' (enclose) the mailing yourself.

▷ **Professional agency** – in addition to costing out the 1,000 quantity, I also show the costs for mailings of 10,000 and 100,000. There are two reasons for showing these figures: (1) to demonstrate that with small quantities, the use of fully fledged agencies will rarely be cost effective, and; (2) to show how, as your business builds and your mailing quantities increase, the cost of professional expertise can be spread, and thus become more cost-effective.

Table 1.1
Comparison of
possible costs –
mailing of
1,000, 10,000
and 100,000

Item	D-I-Y	Local resources	Professional agency		
Quantity mailed	1,000	1,000	1,000	10,000	100,000
List rental	—	£50	£100[†]	£1,000[†]	£10,000[†]
Copy and design fees	—	£250	£2,500[††]	£2,500[††]	£2,500[††]
Artwork and print	£50	£500	£4,000[††]	£10,000[††]	£15,000[††]
Lasering enclosing and so on	—	£50	£250	£500	£2,500
Postage[‡]	£190	£190	£190	£1,425 (25%)	£14,250 (25%)
Total cost	£240	£1,040	£7,040	£15,425	£44,250
Cost per thousand	£240	£1,040	£7,040	£1,543	£443

[†] List rental charges will vary according to the quality of the list and the amount of detailed selection you wish to make (see Chapter 6 – page 106). I have used a typical cost of £100 per thousand for demonstration purposes.

[††] These costs are not intended to be definitive, but are included to show the sort of money you may be faced with. Some direct marketing agencies will charge more for the design of a mailing (few will charge less!). A good alternative is to seek out freelance copywriters and designers, many of whom are former agency people in any case.

[‡] Postal costs vary according to the class and type of service you use. For demonstration purposes I have used the normal second class rate for the smaller mailings and assumed Mailsort 3 discounts (25%) for the larger quantities.

See Chapter 11 for more details of Mailsort and other Royal Mail services.

As the table shows, the most cost-effective way of organizing a small mailing is to do it yourself as using professional direct marketing agencies will rarely be cost-efficient for very small mailings. However, once mailing quantities go over 10,000, the costs of professional design and artwork are more easily absorbed into the overall cost.

HOW MUCH RESPONSE DO YOU NEED?

This, of course, depends on whether your objective is to 'break even', i.e. to get your money back without making any profit, or to make a profit on your first transaction.

The simple calculation of break even is:

$$\frac{\text{total costs}}{\text{profit per sale}} = \text{number of sales needed to break even}$$

In Table 1.2, I have taken the typical costs from Table 1.1 and calculated the level of response you will need from each of the above mailings to break even at two different levels of profit (£25 and £50 per sale).

Table 1.2
Orders and replies per '000 mailed and % response needed to achieve break even

	D-I-Y	Local resources	Professional agency		
Quantity mailed	1,000	1,000	1,000	10,000	100,000
Cost per thousand	£240	£1,040	£7,040	£1,543	£443
Profit per order £25					
Orders	10	42	282	62	18
Replies	30	126	846	186	54
Response %	3	12.6	84.6	18.6	5.4
Profit per order £50					
Orders	5	21	141	31	9
Replies	15	63	423	93	27
Response %	1.5	6.3	42.3	9.3	2.7

Note – some numbers have been rounded, so are not necessarily exact.

This is a common form of costing in direct marketing, on the basis that if you can achieve break even on a prospecting activity (mailing new names) you are building up a valuable resource for future sales and profits. As mentioned earlier, this will depend on your funding and your profit targets.

The figures in Table 1.2 have been calculated on the basis that:

▷ One in every three replies results in an order (thirty replies = ten orders)

▷ Profit per sale is calculated after allowing for reply costs (postage and/or telephone charges, response packs, brochures, catalogues and so on).

This comparison shows that simple DIY direct mail can be produced economically and with such a cost structure, the responses needed for break even are quite modest.

These calculations also show that, depending on the profit and conversion levels, using some additional 'local' help could be cost-effective for small mailings.

Clearly using a professional agency would not be cost-effective for a mailing of 1,000 pieces, but the examples at 10,000 and 100,000 show how the agency costs can be spread over a larger quantity to achieve cost-efficiency.

SHOULD YOU TRY TO MAKE MONEY IMMEDIATELY?

The calculations in Tables 1.1 and 1.2 are based on break even – the costing method you might use if you have sufficient funding to allow you to develop new customers over a period of time.

In these circumstances the objective for your prospecting activities will not be to make a profit. Indeed the reverse may be true – you may even be prepared to lose money on the initial transaction with a new customer, in order to generate the maximum number of responses.

Note that neither approach is more 'correct'. The decision on which approach to take will be made according to the considerations listed on pages 11 and 12.

THE BENEFITS OF INTEGRATION

There are major benefits to be gained from the integration of two or more media. Many of the successful examples involve large scale mailings and television campaigns and are thus beyond the scope of this book.

However, we should not ignore the lessons because some of these can be adapted to a smaller environment. Indeed let us look at some examples and see how some of these techniques could be used by a small business.

DIRECT MAIL AND TELEVISION

Several advertisers have had success with this combination:

▷ A major publisher found that supporting bulk mailings with thirty-second television commercials substantially increased response to the mailings.

▷ A credit card company found that response to mailings increased dramatically when the mailings were despatched during their TV awareness campaigns.

▷ In 1971, while an advertising manager for a mail order company, I found I could increase response to my Sunday newspaper advertisements substantially by running seven-second television spots directing viewers to the relevant papers.

DIRECT MAIL AND THE TELEPHONE

More and more companies, especially those selling to businesses, are testing this technique, which involves following up every mailing addressee with a telephone call – ideally within three days of the mailing arriving.

This sounds like a costly exercise and indeed it is. If a direct mailing costs us, say £350 per thousand and self-made telephone calls cost us say, £2 each, i.e. £2,000 per thousand, to do this exercise would increase our costs by a factor of almost seven. How can this be justified?

The answer is 'response' – a couple of examples are given opposite. On the other hand, a case study where the telephone is *not* used is given on page 26.

USING THE TELEPHONE IN ADVANCE OF YOUR MAILING

When the value of a response justifies the cost, the telephone can also be used for list cleaning and checking, or pre-qualifying your addressee before you mail.

With one of my clients in the office equipment field, we find that telephoning our best customers in advance of a promotional mailing, also increases response dramatically.

SUMMARY

This chapter makes the point that, while direct mail will almost inevitably enter your planning sooner or later, it is not always appropriate when your first step is prospecting for new customers.

Every medium has its strengths and weaknesses. It is not a case of good and bad media, but simply which is the most appropriate for the specific task you are tackling.

Direct mail is an extremely powerful advertising medium, but it is also costly. To make it work cost-efficiently you must work hard to target the right people, with the right message, at the right time.

One of the main advantages of direct mail is that you can do it yourself more easily than you could produce a newspaper advertisement or a radio commercial. This makes small mailings a very practical proposition for any marketer.

EXAMPLES

1 A PC software company, seeking to generate leads from small businesses, carried out a test programme to rented lists:

Sample (a) received a mailing which included an 0800 response number.

Sample (b) received the same mailing but every addressee was followed-up by telephone within three days of the mailing being received.

The results were startling:

	Responses
Sample (a) - direct mail only	100
Sample (b) - direct mail with telephone follow-up	1,250

The addition of the telephone call multiplied response by twelve-and-a-half times.

2 Using the same technique, a UK charity multiplied response by thirty-five times.

This technique is especially interesting for the small business, because it can be tested so easily and so cheaply. Even fifty or a hundred calls will tell you whether this is appropriate for your business.

Timing is crucial, however, do not wait for a week or two. Make the calls while your mailing is still in their minds, or at least on their desks.

CASE STUDY – THE ULTIMO STORY

In 1992 Ted Rowland set up Ultimo to distribute the exclusive Rogier hand-made Belgian chocolates throughout the UK.

Having no names and no available lists of 'chocoholics' to rent, he started with advertisements in weekend supplements. Realizing that the fanatics represented only part of the potential, Ted offered to customize and personalize any of his wide range of wrappers and boxes, thus widening his appeal to the business and personal gifts market.

This campaign was a great success and soon Ted had built a database of several thousand names.

He now mails more than 4,000 customers and regularly attracts response of 20% or better – even though his mailings do not include any personalization – not even a letter.

This emphasizes a point made several times in this book, that if you offer the *right product or service*, to the *right person*, at the *right time*, 90% of the job is done.

Ted is very aware of the importance of good timing, making sure that his customers have details well in advance of special occasions such as Valentine's Day, Mother's Day and, of course, Christmas.

All orders are sent by first class post, ensuring that everything arrives on time and in good condition.

Planning a campaign comprises ten essential steps:

1 Specify your objective
_____

2 Identify your target audience
_____

3 Select your communications approach
_____

4 Decide on the best timing
_____

5 Write your creative briefing plan
_____

6 Arrange your media – i.e. develop your list
_____

7 Produce your material – print letters, buy envelopes and so on
_____

8 Despatch your message
_____

9 Prepare for your replies
_____

10 Record the details for measurement and evaluation.
_____

Finally, remember that integrating media multiplies their power. You can make 1 + 1 = 3.

WHAT TO DO NOW

Contact:

▷ For help and information about direct mail call Royal Mail on 0345 750750.

▷ The **Institute of Direct Marketing** (IDM) – for details of membership and training courses.

▷ The **Direct Marketing Association** (DMA) – for details of membership.

The relevant addresses are given in Appendix 2.

Self-test questionnaire

? Imagine you are an insurance broker and you want to find new local customers for your car insurance products. You have no in-house list of prospects.

How would you go about this task?

Spend half an hour thinking this through then check the answer in Appendix 4.

2 Why direct mail works so well

In this chapter I will consider some of the reasons why direct mail has become such an important advertising medium. One of the main reasons for the success of direct mail, is the ability it gives us to offer solutions to specific problems – an advertisement can do this in a general way, but cannot vary its message for specific segments of the audience

Before the advent of mass production, sellers of goods and services knew many of their customers by name; they knew their likes and dislikes; when they were more likely to buy things; and how much each customer could afford to spend. Luxury products were made to order for the privileged few. The basic necessities were bought from the corner shop, where the owner knew each customer personally

PRODUCTS, SERVICES AND EVEN SELLING METHODS WERE 'TAILORED' TO INDIVIDUAL NEEDS AND TASTES

Mass production created a need for mass distribution, which in turn led to mass-media advertising. Then in the 1950s, along came the concept which has led mass advertising for forty years – the USP or *unique selling proposition*.

This phrase, coined by Rosser Reeves in the 1950s, spawned thirty years of advertising based on the premise that if you can find something to say about your product which is, or sounds unique, you will create a market from people who want a reason to buy.

Nowadays, the USP is looking a little threadbare and the reason for this is that mass markets are breaking down. Some of the contributory factors are:

▷ mass advertising no longer has the power it once had

❑ there are many more commercial television and radio channels which means greater 'fragmentation' of broadscale advertising messages

❏ newspaper readerships are declining

▷ customers are more selective

❏ many people deliberately avoid products which are sold in a traditional mass market way, seeking out instead those which suit their precise requirements or, perhaps, fit their 'lifestyle'

❏ even when they buy the same product as their neighbour, they do not necessarily do so for the same reasons

▷ customers are more knowledgeable

❏ this is true in both business and consumer markets

This is not to say that mass-produced products will not sell – simply that often the buying decision is made on a more personal basis. It follows that selling messages will be more successful when they fit the situation of the individual.

Today a business needs to develop a number of selling propositions – ideally still unique to the product, but varied to match the needs and aspirations of the various sub-sections of the audience.

> *In other words, we need the ability to run a business like the old-time corner shop – knowing customers by name and offering them selected products according to their individual tastes and needs.*

This is one of the main reasons why direct marketing has become so important today. And the main medium for communicating direct marketing messages is direct mail. There are several good reasons why this is so:

▷ **direct mail can be targeted precisely** – you only need to speak to those for whom this specific message is relevant

▷ **direct mail can be varied at will** – in theory, every individual on your list can receive a unique message. In practice, to make the process more manageable, customers are 'clustered' into groups with similar needs, buying cycles, levels of knowledge and so on

▷ **direct mail can be timed to suit individuals** – as we discussed in Chapter 1, each prospect can be sent a relevant message at the appropriate time – we do not need to compromise as in general advertising.

WHAT IS JUNK MAIL?

Let's not fool ourselves, junk mail does exist. In fact, there is a lot of it about. However junk mail and direct mail are not synonymous – that is to say, not all unsolicited direct mail is junk. Junk mail is badly targeted, irrelevant direct mail.

Junk mail is what my bank sends me. I am self-employed, so I have four bank accounts: one for my business; one for VAT; one for tax; and a personal account.

When my bank decides to 'do a mailing' they send me four identical copies. I've got four account numbers – I must be four people! This sort of logic wastes lots of money and gives direct mail a bad name.

There is a good example of the dangers of junk mail in Chapter 6 – see 'The importance of de-duplication' starting on page 107.

> *A survey completed in the early 1990s by Kingston University showed that more than 75% of people liked receiving direct mail 'providing it was relevant and interesting'. Unfortunately when asked 'Do you receive too much direct mail?' almost 70% of the sample said 'Yes'.*

So, although surveys like the above tell us that direct mail is acceptable to most people, there is obviously still a lot of badly targeted mail.

THE FOUR MAJOR BENEFITS OF DIRECT MAIL

1 **Impact** – no other advertising medium can deliver a message with more impact – advertisers have experienced spontaneous recall of 60 and 70%, several months after a mailing has been received.

EXAMPLE – DISTRIPHAR UK

Distriphar UK offers agency distribution services to pharmaceutical companies – a fairly straightforward proposition one might think, except that Distriphar is a subsidiary of Roussel, itself a large pharmaceutical group.

This means that the selling message is complicated and sensitive, and must be very carefully targeted.

Account manager, Neil Ashcroft, came up with a first class solution which did not cost the earth – in fact, apart from the letter and the response form, he used items which were already in stock.

Neil wrote a powerful, personalized letter to 100 managing directors of companies in the pharmaceutical industry, and added a single page fax order form, produced on his own PC.

This imaginative and inexpensive mailing produced 26% response.

Neil's mailing highlights a good money-saving method – you can use a variety of existing material and draw it together into a cohesive mailing with a good, relevant letter.

---

2 **Relevance** – because you can vary your message according to the specific information needs of your reader, no other advertising can be more personal and thus more relevant – see the example in Chapter 3 – page 47.

---

3 **Involvement** – because prospects can touch, feel, and 'experience' your message, you can get them involved. This makes your message more memorable. Involvement devices can include sound (audio tapes); vision (video tapes); smell (micro-encapsulation giving 'scratch-and-sniff' experiences); and other physical involvement devices such as rub-offs, hats, executive toys, and so on.

A word of warning about 'gimmicks' – make sure you don't leave a lasting impression of your involvement device rather than your product. This has happened on many occasions.

4 **Cost-efficiency** – ask a traditional media buyer to judge the cost structure of direct mail against the costs of press or broadcast advertising and the answer you will get is that mail is too expensive. This is because traditional media people tend to consider the *cost* rather than the *effect* of media expenditure. They compare media in terms of cost per thousand (copies, readers, viewers and so on) and on this basis there is no doubt that direct mail is very expensive. Compared with a cost of perhaps £7 per thousand television viewers or £10 per thousand newspaper readers, a direct mailing costing say £350 per thousand seems ridiculously extravagant. It is only when we start to compare media on the basis of *responses* that direct mail starts to make economic sense.

Direct mail delivers much higher response because it is much more targeted than other advertising media.

EXAMPLE

A direct-sell television campaign reaching 8,000,000 households costs, say, £120,000, (including the cost of producing a 'budget' commercial) - typical response rate would be 0.02% i.e. 1,600 replies @ £75 each.

A lead-generation advertisement in *The Sun*, reaching 4,000,000 households costs, say, £32,000 (including artwork, and so on) - typical response rate would be 0.03% i.e. 1,200 replies @ £27 each.

A direct mailing to 5,000 well-targeted prospects costs, say, £1,750 including postage - typical response rate would be 5% i.e. 250 replies @ £7 each.

These figures are hypothetical, but not untypical. Of course, some TV and press campaigns have achieved much higher response rates than those quoted above, but this is not usual.

It is, however, not at all unusual for direct mailings to deliver quite astounding response rates. There are several cases of mailings producing responses much higher than 50%.

WHAT IS A GOOD RESPONSE RATE ANYWAY?

This is one of the questions most often asked by newcomers to direct mail and in truth, there is no satisfactory answer. It is quite common to see, in the trade press, published surveys stating things like:

The average response rates to direct mail in 1995 were:

▷ consumer mailings   8%
▷ business mailings   11%

SUCH STATISTICS ARE LARGELY IRRELEVANT

Unfortunately, such statistics have little relevance to an individual mailer because response rates will vary according to several factors. Volumes also vary dramatically, causing disproportionate effects to the averages.

The hypothetical, but entirely typical, example at the top of the page opposite shows the dangers of such reports.

As you can see, although the *average* response may be 11%, the huge mailing offering the free drink voucher has had such a major effect that it gives an entirely false picture of the remaining mailings.

Without the drinks mailing the average response in this survey would have been perhaps 3%.

It is important to stress that neither of these averages gives a true picture – the truth is there is no norm and no true average possible.

EXAMPLE

An industry survey quotes the average response rate of consumer mailings as 11% – a detailed analysis of the statistics shows:

▷ four mailings from insurance companies averaging 1% response

▷ six mailings from credit card companies averaging 2.5% response

▷ four mailings from publishers averaging 4% response

▷ one mailing from a soft drinks company offering a free drink voucher to teenagers – mailed to 10 million households – 55% response.

WHAT CAUSES A GOOD OR BAD RESPONSE?

Response is a function of the five factors mentioned earlier:

▷ **List quality**

❑ how well have you targeted the true prospects?

❑ do you have a relationship with them. This is one of the major factors in increasing response – see the two examples over the page.

▷ **Offer** – how attractive is your offer? Offering a free gift in return for a name and address can easily produce 50% response. If you asked someone to fill in details of their financial arrangements to apply for a credit card you would perhaps expect around 2% response. Some insurance companies would be pleased with a 0.25% response rate to a 'cold' list.

On the other hand, a customer satisfaction survey to existing customers will often produce a very high response – my personal best with such questionnaires is 80%+.

A MAJOR OIL COMPANY

Wishing to find out how loyal its shareholders were, the company sent them a questionnaire, at the same time inviting their participation in the latest promotion. The same mailing was sent to a sample of customers who had previously participated in the company's promotions.

Questionnaire responses were:

▷   shareholders   42% responded

▷   customers   26% responded

So, a major factor affecting response is 'what are you asking readers to do?' Asking for an order reduces response. Offering a free gift or even a free information pack increases response. If you are selling direct, response will vary according to how good your price is, whether your prospects have recently received a competitive offer and so on.

CROSS-CHANNEL FERRY COMPANY

This company sent a questionnaire to two samples; one group who had sent for the past year's brochure but never booked; a second group who had used the service in the past year. Again the results (almost identical) show the power of the relationship:

▷   bookers   46% responded

▷   non-bookers   26% responded

➤ **Timing** – how relevant is this offer to the prospect today? If you mail a 'cold' list of motorists with a car insurance offer only one-twelfth of them are likely to be in the market this month, therefore your response will be low. If you know when their renewal is due and you only mail those for whom the timing is right you can expect a much higher response.

➤ **Creative execution** – how well have you presented your message? Although it is not the most important aspect, good creative work, especially clear, easy to follow copy and layout, can make a major difference to response levels.

➤ **Response devices** – have you given prospects every possible method of responding? Have you made it easy for them by paying the postage, filling in the reply form, and so on? Don't forget the phone and fax options too.

Every one of the above factors will have an influence on the number of replies your mailing attracts.

During my career in marketing, I have been involved in the planning and despatch of more than 700 mailings. These mailings generated responses ranging from 0% to 94%. The client whose mailing achieved 94% was naturally delighted, but I have had lots of responses in the 1 to 5% range where the client was equally happy.

Thus, we can only answer the question 'What is a good response rate?' after studying the five factors above and by asking some additional questions such as:

➤ **What is the competitive situation?** If we are one of several companies making similar offers to the same list, our response will be lower than if we are the only supplier.

➤ **Is the daily news good or bad?** For example, the advent of the Gulf War ruined many well-planned campaigns.

➤ **What is the state of the economy?** The recent recession caused reductions in response for many mailers.

SUMMARY

Direct mail offers a number of advantages over most other media:

▷ **Targeting** – it can be targeted very precisely – we can speak to as many or as few prospects as we wish.

▷ **Precision of message** – we can vary our message as often as required. This means we can make our advertising highly relevant to each individual.

▷ **Highly responsive** – response rates to direct mail are normally many times higher than those from most other media.

▷ **Cost-efficiency** – well-targeted mailings can be much more cost-effective than other forms of advertising.

▷ **Timing** – a mailing can be timed to arrive when a prospect is ready to buy – difficult with a short press or television campaign.

Junk mail is not synonymous with direct mail – junk mail is badly targeted and irrelevant. Avoid it like the plague – it costs you money and annoys your prospects.

Average response rates are meaningless and serve only to confuse. You need to establish the right level for your own business, your own marketplace, your own offer and allowing for competitive activities.

The five factors affecting response rates are:

1 **List** – the quality of the data, and your relationship with those listed.

2 **Offer** – how attractive this is to the prospect.

3 **Timing** – how relevant it is today.

4 **Creative factors** – how clear is the message? How well does your mailing stand out against others received on the same day?

5

Response devices – make it easy – give all the options.

HOW TO GET THE MOST FROM YOUR DIRECT MAIL

It will be clear from the above that, to get the most out of direct mail, you need to know quite a lot about your prospect. If you are to take advantage of the precision of direct mail you need to be able to:

▷ Target the right sub-group from within a list.

▷ Identify the key buying or interest 'triggers' for the readers – these can vary for different people on the same list.

WHAT TO DO NOW

Reply to some advertisements:

▷ consumer marketers look in national newspapers and magazines

▷ business marketers – add business journals to your list.

Study the contents of their fulfilment packs – wait to see if they follow you up by mail or phone.

Start a *guard book* of your own and competitive mailings – see example in Chapter 1 – pages 10–11.

Contact your Royal Mail account executive. Ask for details of despatch and reply services and for copies of Royal Mail's many helpful booklets on direct mail.

Self-test questionnaire:

1 What are the five major benefits of direct mail?

(a)

(b)

(c)

(d)

(e)

2 What are the factors affecting response to a mailing? List them in order of importance.

(a)

(b)

(c)

(d)

(e)

Check your answers in Appendix 4.

Part Two

Information

3 Understanding your customers

When Henry Ford was planning the launch of his Model T he was asked by one of his employees 'What colours shall we offer our customers?'

His famous answer was:

They can have any colour they like, so long as it is black!

In the days when the motor car was an exciting new invention to most people, it was not necessary to offer refinements to sell as many as you could make.

The fact that this strategy worked in 1907 does not mean it was the correct one; and it would certainly not work today.

MORE CHOICE AND MORE KNOWLEDGEABLE CUSTOMERS

Today's customers are more selective and better informed. They are also faced with a much greater choice of options in every field.

Even 12 years ago, as my partners and I found to our cost, a good sales person could sell a computer system to a business without any guarantee that it would do the job required. Few customers knew what computers were capable of, or even what their own precise requirements were. Computers were shrouded in jargon and most of us were at the mercy of the specialists.

Since then, thanks to the developments in Apple Macs, PCs, server-based systems, and to the user-friendly software produced by companies like Microsoft and Lotus, we have all become more computer-literate.

In parallel with these changes on the customer side, selling companies are becoming much more aware of the importance of developing long-term relationships, by offering first class products, added value and strong after-sales support services.

The value which is placed on these relationships has been demonstrated in recent years by several surveys from leading research and consultancy companies.

THE VALUE OF SEGMENTATION

However, given today's marketplace with its shrinking margins and greater competition how can you afford to give your customers even more attention? The answer is by segmentation. If you build a computer database, you can segment customers and prospects and 'tailor' your customer management according to past and potential value.

The following diagram shows how a customer file could be segmented, with account management structured according to the value of customers in each segment, as shown in Figure 3.1.

Figure 3.1
Segmenting a
customer file

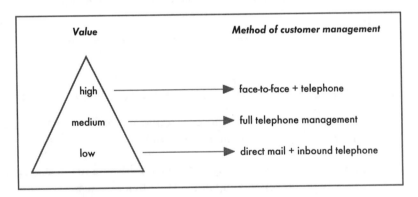

Segmenting customers like this, enables you to allocate resources in a sensible way. You can make perhaps thirty or fifty telephone calls for the same cost as a single sales call, which makes high quality customer management a cost-efficient option for medium-sized accounts.

PREFERRED BY CUSTOMERS TOO

The good news is that customers seem to like it too – a major European business-to-business supplier transferred hundreds of medium-sized accounts onto its new telephone account management (TAM) system, despite opposition to the new system by customers and sales people.

One year after the change was made, a customer satisfaction questionnaire asked: *If you could go back to the old system of face-to-face representation would you do so?*.

The answer was a resounding *'No'*. Customers found they preferred the convenience of speaking to their account manager at any time, rather than waiting for the traditional salesperson's visit.

This change in customer attitudes is also borne out by the results in Table 3.1.

Table 3.1
Results from
research
findings of
Andersen
Consulting

What business customers value most				
	Ranking			
	1970	1980	1985	1990
Contact with outside salesperson	1	3	5	5
Frequency and speed of delivery	2	1	1	2
Price	3	2	3	4
Range of products	4	5	4	3
Contact with capable inside salesperson	5	4	2	1

Over the twenty years of this survey, the importance of having direct contact with the company has increased from fifth place to first place.

ARE BUSINESS CUSTOMERS DIFFERENT TO CONSUMERS?

The answer to this question is *Yes* and *No*. A business decision is more likely to be made on a rational rather than an emotional basis, but the same basic process applies:

▷ **Need arousal or awareness of need** – your prospect has a problem needing a solution. This could be a requirement for a better office computer system (business decision) or for a replacement for a car which keeps breaking down (consumer decision).

▷ **Information search** – reading advertisements and mailings;

collecting magazines and newspapers articles; discussing with friends or contemporaries in other businesses; sending for information packs.

▷ **Consideration of options available** – reviewing the material gathered, discussion with partners in the decision-making process, considering price and payment options, balancing price and performance and so on.

▷ **Detailed trials and negotiations** – at this point the serious buying behaviour begins. Prospects organize demonstrations or trials, ask for specific quotations and start to negotiate on price, guarantees, service contracts and delivery, and so on.

▷ **Purchase** – the deal is completed and the product is delivered.

▷ **Post purchase behaviour** – customers evaluate the product; does it do what was expected? Do the suppliers live up to their promises regarding service (e.g. helplines)?

The above process could equally be applied to the choice of a new car or a computer system. A washing machine or a photocopier.

What then are the differences you need to take account of?

THE DECISION-MAKING PROCESS

Firstly you must make yourself aware of the decision-making process for your product in your marketplace.

A decision to purchase a consumer product, even a new car, is likely to be made by no more than two or three people – and it is highly likely that they will share the same lifestyle and, perhaps, the same aspirations and attitudes.

In business the *decision making unit* (DMU) can consist of several people, at different levels in the business, with varying degrees of authority.

It may also include outside consultants. A further complication is that not all the decision makers will necessarily be at the same site.

When selling anything other than low-priced items it is necessary, in order to make relevant offers to business people, to understand these decision-making units and either identify the key member of the unit, or go the whole hog and mail each of them.

You may feel that this latter route would be too costly for those with limited budgets, but there is an important principle here.

▷ One of the main benefits of direct communications is that you can target a specific individual with a relevant message.

▷ If you take the trouble to identify the various members of the DMU you will find that, although they are considering the same product or service, they are not looking for the same things.

▷ They will not therefore be considering the factors on the same basis.

▷ To be sure your communications are relevant, you need to understand their needs and concerns and answer their questions

EXAMPLE

Product – A new, more powerful office PC network

Prospects – decision-making unit comprises: managing director, financial director, IT director, office manager.

Their concerns:

MANAGING DIRECTOR

▷ What will this system give us that we don't have already?

▷ Why do we need it?

▷ What does it cost and is it a good investment?

▷ Will the users and their managers like it?

FINANCIAL DIRECTOR

▷ What does it cost – can we negotiate a discount – any chance of part-exchanging our present kit?

▷ Can we lease and will this be more attractive?

▷ Why do we need it – what can it do better for the extra money?

▷ Will it cost us money to retrain staff?

▷ What sort of guarantee will we get?

IT DIRECTOR

▷ How does it compare with the Digital/Hewlett Packard and so on model?

▷ What is the chip/RAM/storage capacity?

▷ How many terminals can it support?

▷ What software will run on it – what will they give us?

▷ Will I have to provide more training for the users?

OFFICE MANAGER

▷ Not another computer system – we've only just got used to this one!

▷ Will I understand it – will I be made to look silly by the youngsters?

Once you start to think about these concerns it becomes clear that there will be several questions to answer. If you don't know what the questions are, you need to find out by:

▷ talking to customers, face-to-face or by telephone

▷ reading customers' letters

▷ sending customer questionnaires

▷ talking to salespeople – they are closer to customers than anyone.

SENDING THE MESSAGE – TWO POSSIBLE APPROACHES

1 Tandem mailing – using all your artillery

If you can identify people and their concerns and you have the budget to do it, you could mail all the decision-makers, sending each a unique letter answering their likely questions. A common leaflet or brochure would usually be adequate, although you may wish to send a more technical leaflet to an IT manager, for instance.

This is a very powerful approach which has worked well for some mailers. It is, of course, expensive and is more appropriate when selling a higher priced product.

---

2 An alternative approach – identifying the key decision-maker

If you do not feel you can afford to mail more than one person in the same company, you will have to find a way of identifying the key person in the decision-making unit and delivering the most powerful message you can.

The key person will not necessarily be the final decision-maker – it could be the person most likely to drive the decision, an IT manager for example, who may recognize that a new computer system is necessary.

In order to achieve the objective, the IT manager will have to persuade the financial director to support the financial case, the managing director to support the business case, and perhaps, even the customer service manager who may need convincing that the temporary disruption to customer service backup will be worthwhile.

Here is a possible approach:

▷ You could identify the key decision-maker by phone or via a sales person and try to decide *not only which questions this person will ask, but those they will have to answer, too.* You could then answer these in your letter

▷ You could follow the same procedure but, instead of writing a very long letter, enclose some additional pieces to help your target support the case e.g.

❑ a leaflet entitled *'Why buying XYZ is the right financial decision'* to be handed to the financial director

❑ another entitled *'How XYZ helps the Customer Service Department'*

and, if your key decision-maker is not the IT manager,

❑ a further leaflet *'The technical argument for the XYZ system'*.

The objective of this approach is to give your targeted contacts all the support they need to make a convincing case to their colleagues in the decision-making unit.

This approach can ensure your mailings have a very powerful impact. Clearly it can only work if you gather and organize the necessary information – and this is where your customer database will prove its worth.

THE CUSTOMER DATABASE

This topic will be covered at length in Chapter 5, but a brief introduction is relevant at this point.

It will be clear from the above examples, that a large amount of customer information is necessary if you are to make your mailings relevant and interesting. However, before you go out data-hunting, it will pay you to examine the information you already have – it may not be stored in a computer, but most businesses have lots of customer data in one form or another.

The important thing is to find a way of assembling and accessing all this existing information. In short, *what you need is a customer database*.

DISPELLING THE MYSTIQUE

Until very recently, there has been great mystique surrounding computers, and many businesses, particularly small ones, have been very nervous about getting involved in what appeared to be a large 'black hole'.

Nowadays, however, the problem is much simpler. Not only are computers much smaller and cheaper, but the software available is very user-friendly.

Thanks to the much simpler software now available the average business person can understand and use a marketing database with just a few days' training.

Furthermore, the power of the PC is now so great that most small businesses can set up and run a marketing database with an investment of less than £2,000. And this includes additional applications such as word processing, spreadsheets, presentation software etc.

Once you have organized your existing customer information, you are in a position to identify the gaps in your knowledge and set about filling these.

WHAT ARE THE SOURCES OF ADDITIONAL INFORMATION?

> **Response data** – when you advertise for prospects it is generally a good idea to offer something to encourage people to respond – a brochure, a leaflet, a catalogue, and so on.

This is a golden opportunity to ask for some basic data. Nothing too detailed. You will not get someone to divulge their annual salary in return for an information pack, but they will probably be happy to tell you how many PCs they have, or when their financial year ends.

People are more inclined to part with information if they can see that it has a relevance to a future relationship. Thus the question 'How much do you earn?' will be seen as relevant if you lend money, but irrelevant, and impertinent, if you are offering a carpet cleaning service.

If you really do need lots of personal or semi-personal information, you may need to explain why you need it, and also to reassure people that it will not be divulged to anyone else.

You may also find it helps to include a reassuring statement such as, *There is no obligation to complete the following questionnaire, but if you do so, it will help us to develop better products in the future.*

▷ **External databases** – additional information about consumers can be obtained from bureaux holding the electoral roll. You can identify multi-family households, families with children living at home and so on.

Another source is the lifestyle database companies. They hold lots of very detailed information about shopping, holidays and other family purchases and investments. You can have your own data enhanced and also rent names and addresses of new prospects with similar profiles to those of your own best customers.

If you are selling to businesses you can obtain additional information from Companies House. This tends to be raw data about financial performance and company size.

A better source of such data may be one of the several companies who take Companies House data and enhance it with narrative, trend commentary and so on. Typical suppliers of this sort of information are Dun & Bradstreet, CCN and Market Location.

▷ **Market research** – there are many types of research and many existing sources of research data. The two basic types of research are:

❑ **desk research** – where you look up existing sources from reference libraries, and so on. You can find information about most markets and market segments; details of the number of competitors you have, their turnover, marketing expenditure, and so on.

❑ **original research** – is the name for research which you organize or commission yourself, asking customers, prospects, or members of the public what they think about a product or service, existing or potential. There are three basic ways of conducting such research – face-to-face, telephone and post.

These are listed in order of *cost and effectiveness* – you will always get a higher number of completed questionnaires when using personal interviewers and there is an additional benefit in the fact that a trained researcher will form a very good opinion as to the truth of the answers.

> *Face-to-face research is, however, highly expensive and can also be very time-consuming.*

Telephone research is cheaper and offers some of the benefits of the face-to-face technique – a high percentage of completed questionnaires, a trained opinion as to the truth of the answers, and so on.

> *Telephone research is also very expensive compared to the postal questionnaire.*

Perhaps the ideal solution for a small business is to use a postal questionnaire. This is surprisingly responsive but it does involve a bias. Some people are just not prepared to complete questionnaires and your response sample will thus lose a segment of potential customers. This may not be a major problem, but it is important to take into account when evaluating responses.

HOW MUCH RESPONSE FROM A POSTAL QUESTIONNAIRE?

Having pointed out the potential drawback above, you could reasonably expect to receive up to 20% response to a postal questionnaire sent to a cold list; 20 to 35% from people who enquired about your products but never bought; and between 35 and 80% from established customers. These latter rates (enquirers and customers) will depend on your relationship and on existing opinions and attitudes towards your business.

There are a few additional things you can do to increase the response to a postal questionnaire:

1 **Establish the relevance of the survey to the individual** – make sure you tell people why you need the information. Show how this is relevant to them e.g. it will help you to develop products which will more closely satisfy their needs.

2 **Offer something in exchange** – if you have a booklet which gives useful information this can be 'swapped' for some details about the customer. In this case the number of questions should be small.

3 **Consider a gift** – sometimes a free gift can increase response, but this will not always make a huge difference – perhaps up to 20% increase i.e. from 20% to 24%. Be careful not to insult people. A free pen should be sent *with* the questionnaire – not offered as 'a valuable free gift' in return.

4 **Make it interesting** – more effective than the free gift can be the 'special interest' question. If you know something about their interests you can perhaps include a couple of questions which will make the questionnaire more interesting to the reader – you may not be at all interested in the replies to these questions, but the reader will see the entire questionnaire as more relevant.

CASE STUDY – SILVER DIRECT

This company, which sells silver goods by mail order, sent a postal questionnaire to previous customers.

Questions were mainly about product preferences, customer lifestyles and interests.

The company also included a colour leaflet of current products.

The results were impressive:

▷ 55% returned the completed questionnaire

▷ 10% placed new orders

DEALING WITH CUSTOMER QUERIES AND COMPLAINTS

One of the most important aspects of customer management is the way you deal with complaints. Here are a couple of examples:

CAR RENTAL COMPANY

A major car rental company discovered that those who had complained were better long-term customers than those who had not.

FMCG COMPANY

An FMCG company discovered, during a routine customer satisfaction survey, that only 40% of those dissatisfied were registering a complaint. The remaining 60% did not because they had no name to write to and no confidence that a general letter to 'the management' would receive attention.

The company's complaints handling procedure was good and 90% of those who complained were converted back into satisfied customers; indeed, like the car rental company it appeared that these were better long-term customers than the average.

However, because of the large number not registering their dissatisfaction, the overall statistics were unfavourable – their research told them that, on average, a satisfied customer told three people about the experience whereas a dissatisfied customer told eleven.

Working this through for a hundred dissatisfied customers showed the following picture:

▷ forty complained – thirty-six satisfied – four remained unhappy

▷ sixty did not complain – sixty remained unhappy

i.e. a total of sixty-four remained unhappy, therefore:

▷ thirty-six told three people = 108 positive mentions

▷ sixty-four told eleven people = 704 negative mentions.

The company took rapid action and tackled the problem by printing their telephone number on every pack with a message saying *If you have any queries or suggestions, please call this free telephone number*.

One year, and 500,000 telephone calls later, they repeated their satisfaction survey and found that out of every hundred dissatisfied customers now, ninety were registering their complaints, and still 90% of these were being satisfied by the way their complaints were handled. The statistics now looked very different:

▷ ninety complained – eighty-one satisfied – nine remained unhappy

▷ ten did not complain – ten remained unhappy

now only nineteen remained unhappy, therefore

▷ eighty-one told three people = 243 positive mentions

▷ nineteen told eleven people = 209 negative mentions.

Now while 209 negative mentions was still less than satisfactory their revised strategy made a major difference to the amount of business they were losing and also gained them a large amount of valuable 'word of mouth' publicity.

A COMPLAINANT'S JUST A FRIEND THAT YOU DON'T KNOW

Several companies report that former complainants turn out to be very good customers and it seems that a customer who complains is really saying *'I'd like to have a relationship with you people if only you would get your act together'*. Here's how you can do just that.

The lesson here is to make sure that your customers have a channel to let you know when they are unhappy. Many companies run customer satisfaction surveys to a sample of their file and whilst this can be a valuable gauge of service and delivery levels, it will not highlight specific cases of dissatisfaction.

If you positively encourage your customers to let you know their concerns there will be two main effects:

▷ You will have a pile of complaints to deal with – most of which can be turned into future selling opportunities.

▷ You will pick up cases of dissatisfaction at a very early stage – when it is still relatively easy to put them right. This will help to build your business faster and more profitably.

SUMMARY

Customers today are more knowledgeable, more demanding and therefore more cautious in their buying decisions.

It is vital to develop relationships with your better customers and to segment your customer files so that you can balance the level of service you give with your potential return.

Many companies today use face-to-face sales people only to service and develop large or potentially large accounts. Medium sized accounts can be profitably and satisfactorily serviced on the telephone.

Customers are busier too, so the business lunch is no longer relevant for many executives.

Although the psychology and the essential process is the same, selling to business people is different to consumer selling.

Business buying decisions tend to be made by groups, called decision making units or DMUs, each member of which may have a different point of view and a different range of questions.

To sell successfully to these people you need to understand their concerns and address them in your mailings. Sometimes multiple mailings are valuable in addressing the individual issues.

Market research is a very important tool for direct mailers. Without a detailed understanding of customer needs, wants and attitudes you cannot write a relevant letter. Relevance is one of the crucial factors in deciding whether your mailing will be read.

Although face-to-face and telephone research are more powerful than postal questionnaires, the postal survey is still highly valuable – response can be very high – *as much as 70 or 80% is not uncommon, provided the recipient sees the survey as relevant.*

Complaints should not be avoided, but sought. This is not to say you should try to give customers cause for complaint – simply that you should make it easy for those who are dissatisfied to be able to air their grievances.

Good complaints handling is one of the major factors in developing customer loyalty.

WHAT TO DO NOW

Collect some customer questionnaires from mailings and Sunday newspapers. Study these to identify the sort of questions companies ask.

Ask yourself: *'How many of these questions could I answer about my own customers?'*

If your answer is *'Not many'* then you should consider finding out more about your customers. It will definitely help you to write more relevant mailings.

You will find some suggestions for additional reading in Appendix 2.

4 Targeting and segmentation

First of all, what is meant by the term segmentation?

Segmentation is the breaking down of large customer and prospect files into smaller groups (segments). There are two main purposes of segmentation:

▷ To enable an advertiser to target those likely to be interested in a specific offer.

▷ To permit companies to more closely tailor products, offers and messages to the recipients.

An example of tailoring an offer follows.

An oil company, considering customers of its petrol stations, may segment them into say, high-mileage company car drivers; owner drivers; drivers with children; households with one car: multi-car households, and so on.

Such segmentation would enable the company to decide who to mail and which details to send about a new collector scheme.

A driver who fills up once a month is probably not likely to be interested in collecting vouchers towards a gift - the promotion would be over long before enough had been collected.

On the other hand, the high mileage driver who refuels several times each week would not only be interested, but also able to save towards a more costly gift. Families with children may be more interested in gifts appealing to children, and so on. Households with several cars may wish to accumulate their vouchers and, again, qualify for a higher value item.

SEGMENTATION ENABLES SELECTIVITY

In Chapter 2, I pointed out that direct mail is not competitive with mass media in terms of cost per thousand. Despite this, its greater selectivity makes it the most cost-efficient choice in many cases.

You can only achieve this selectivity if you have information. The ideal starting position is to know who will be interested and when they are likely to be in a buying situation. Targeting is thus not only about people, but also about their situations.

Let's start with finding the **right people**. How can you decide who to select from a list or audience? There are several ways:

1 **Database analysis** – this is best of all. If you have a database of existing customers and prospects, you will:

▷ be able to identify who bought or enquired about this product
▷ have additional data about their characteristics, buying methods, timing, and so on, drawn from previous transactions or questionnaire research. This will enable you to:
▷ draw up profiles of your best customers and use these to identify good segments of other lists or target audiences. Profiling is explained on the next few pages.

CASE STUDY – TIME & SPACE

Ed Stratton was a part-time musician and a full-time sound engineer with Capital Radio. His hobby was sound sampling. Over the years, as a dedicated collector of odd soundbites, Ed had painstakingly accumulated well over 10,000 electronic 'noises' ranging from a dog barking to a range of individual violin chords.

Ed extracted the top 1,000, transferred them to CD and began to target recording professionals, musicians, DJs and fellow home enthusiasts.

Orders poured in and Ed soon built up a large database of customers and enquirers. He now mails this two or three times a year with a catalogue containing very detailed reviews.

Ed says:

'This direct mail package has been a winning formula for Time & Space. Our Winter 1993 catalogue brought in a 15% response on a mailing of 7,500 – our subsequent conversion rate was 87%. And Winter 1994 was even better with orders up by 50%.'

Time & Space now has a turnover of more than £1 million, representing 99% of the UK market. Expansion may be a problem, but it's the sort of problem most of us would like to have.

2 **Testing** – this involves mailing a rented list, or running an advertisement in a mass medium and analysing the replies. Testing is explained in more detail in Chapter 9. Respondents can be 'profiled' enabling you to target more of the same. The example on the next page shows the value of this technique.

3 **Research** – by postal questionnaire or more often by telephone, asking companies or individuals 'Who in your company will be interested in this product?' can be highly beneficial.

When you use this approach, make sure you ask someone who really knows the answers. Some companies have started by simply asking the telephonist or receptionist but this will not always work.

Whereas receptionists will know the answer to: 'What is the name of your marketing director?' they will not always be able to answer the question: 'Who is responsible for executive health insurance?'

When it comes to identifying the members of a decision-making unit for, say, a new computer system, the best person to ask is usually the managing director's secretary, or at least the secretary to a senior manager.

4 **Intuition** – sometimes called judgement. Unless this is based on some evaluation of real events it remains guesswork. Assumptions can be dangerous – as the following example shows.

A company selling a fleet management service on the platform of potential cost savings, started by sending mailings to rented lists of fleet managers. The mailings were not a success. Some follow-up research confirmed what common sense could perhaps have told them - fleet managers are not interested in a service which makes them redundant.

A short direct response advertising campaign produced some highly relevant information - almost all of the replies received from the advertising were from financial directors or managers.

The company then rented lists of senior financial executives and found that this tighter targeting meant they could now generate leads cost-effectively through cold direct mailings.

As this example shows, there is no substitute for careful evaluation based on sound information.

THE USE OF PROFILING

The above technique is called profiling – identifying a characteristic (in this case job title or function) which appears to be common, or more prevalent, than the average amongst customers and prospects. This factor can then be used to select a sub-group of prospects or customers who are more likely to be interested in a specific product, offer or message.

PROFILING FACTORS

Business profiling can relate to company size, annual turnover, geographic location, financial year end, job function of contact, number of locations, even the number of coffee machines or company cars – there are many possibilities.

Similarly consumer profiling can relate to household composition (children/no children), property type (large/small, garden/no garden, Acorn or Mosaic type), geographical location and so on.

If you are able to isolate such factors, they can be very helpful in targeting the right segments of a market, reducing wastage and thus your costs.

Sometimes the targeting factor is very simple, as we can see in the following examples.

CASE STUDY – RUSCO INTERNATIONAL

Geoff and Sue Andrews set up Rusco when they spotted an opportunity in the travel market. Although most of the large tour operators were sending many thousands of British tourists to Spain every year, they had not considered the thousands of British people living in Spain.

These people make regular trips back to the UK and no-one was catering specifically for their needs.

Geoff and Sue concentrated on building a database of British people with properties in Spain – their unique targeting factor. They then started using direct mail to let their prospects know what they had to offer – essentially cheaper flights to Alicante.

They launched the Rusco Travel Club offering their members further discounts for more frequent flights, travel insurance, airport car parking, car hire and attractive hotel deals.

From this base they have expanded into other destinations and their database now numbers 16,000 people. Geoff now mails all members a quarterly brochure and they handle around 20,000 bookings every year.

Think about your own business – can you identify some factors which will help you select those prospects likely to be better customers for you?

USING OUTSIDE HELP

If you need help in profiling your customers and, indeed, in finding more of the same type, there are several organizations who can help.

If you are a consumer marketer, you can use the lifestyle database companies who will take your customer list, identify the relevant characteristics for you, and often add additional data from their own records. They can also offer you additional names and addresses of people on their databases who match your customer profile.

Many companies who have mailed such lists have had great success.

Business marketers will find that companies such as CCN and Dun and Bradstreet can offer a similar service for them.

WHAT IF YOU HAVE NO CUSTOMERS?

Even if you have no existing customers you may be able to identify certain characteristics which signify a higher propensity to buy.

EXAMPLE

Let us assume you are setting up a business offering short term rental of mobile telephones for business travellers – only certain types of people will want such a service:

▷ Head office executives who make occasional trips to sales territories or branches could be good prospects.

▷ Companies expanding into Europe whose UK sales or management executives visit European locations on an occasional basis could be good prospects for Euro-digital mobiles.

▷ Field sales people are likely to have permanent mobiles and are probably not such good prospects.

As mentioned earlier, if you really have no information to help you target prospects you will probably need to use direct response advertising to generate enquiries. Once you have some enquiries, you can analyse these and this will improve your targeting in the future.

A FURTHER EXAMPLE OF PROFILING

Here is an example of a company which encountered a problem of cost-efficiency in marketing expenditure during the recent recession. A basic profiling exercise helped them return to profitability.

They were selling, via direct mail, a high-tech product to businesses. Their mailing responses were insufficient to show a profit although their reputation was good and their product quality excellent.

They profiled their buyers via a postal questionnaire and discovered some highly significant information:

▷ 60% of their sales came from companies with more than 200 employees

▷ 20% came from companies having between 100 and 200 employees.

What made this especially significant is that these companies (i.e. those with 100 or more employees) made up less than 15% of their database.

They developed a new marketing programme:

▷ targeting the larger companies

▷ using more powerful promotions – direct mailings followed up quickly by telephone calls

▷ reducing their expenditure to the remaining 85% of the database.

The results:

▷ sales increased by 10%

▷ marketing expenditure reduced by 15%.

ARE SEGMENTATION, PROFILING AND TARGETING RELEVANT TO A SMALL BUSINESS?

Some people assume that these techniques are only relevant to a large business, but as the examples earlier in this chapter demonstrate, *the opposite is nearer the mark. When funds are limited it is even more important to target carefully and gain the maximum value for every pound you spend.*

Remember too, that profiling and targeting are not just for prospecting – you can increase the profitability of your existing customer activities by careful segmentation – targeting those most likely to be interested in a particular offer, or at a particular time.

ANOTHER ASPECT OF PROFILING AND TARGETING

Let's look at the *ladder of loyalty* – a device first used in the 1950s by an American salesman to categorize his customers. There are various versions of this but the process remains the same.

Figure 4.1

The ladder of loyalty

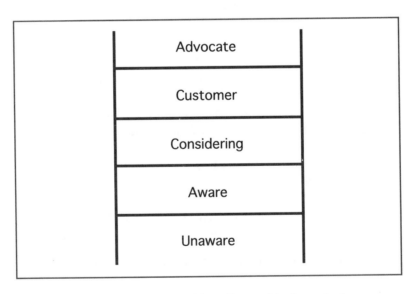

The salesman used the ladder to help him allocate his time, devise appropriate contact strategies for individual prospects according to their potential, and to help him decide what and how much he needed to tell people about his products.

The ladder can be just as useful in helping you decide what and how much to tell the people to whom you are writing.

WHAT DO THE DESCRIPTIONS MEAN?

On the bottom rung are the people who are totally *unaware* of your product or service – in some versions of the ladder these people are called 'suspects'.

The next rung *Aware* contains those who know that your product exists, but who have not yet developed an interest in it. Perhaps they do not realize quite how well it will satisfy their needs? Again, other versions of the ladder name this group 'prospects' – the reason mine does not is explained below.

Next we have those who are *Considering* your product. These could also be called 'non-converted enquirers'. It is important to realize that they may be considering several other products as well as yours.

Customers have placed at least one order with you. Assuming they are satisfied that you have delivered what you promised, these people are potential advocates.

Advocates are regular customers who are so pleased with your product or service that they tell their friends and colleagues. Advocates should be nurtured carefully – they are worth far more to you than the profit from their orders.

WHERE DO PROSPECTS FIT IN?

Some versions of the ladder of loyalty have a hierarchy which is a little different. These ladders still have advocates at the top but descend through various descriptions such as *clients – customers – trialists – prospects to suspects* on the bottom rung. Now while 'suspects' is a good alternative for 'unaware', the term 'prospects' can have several meanings.

In fact any person on any rung could be described as a prospect for something. Those on the bottom rung are prospects for an initial order; Advocates are prospects for a repeat order. The term *prospect* is therefore used throughout this book as someone who has the potential to buy from your next mailing.

HOW DOES THE LADDER HELP?

Clearly, if you are writing to someone on the bottom rung, it will be necessary to tell that person everything about the product. After all, they are probably not even aware that the product exists, and even if they are, they have not seen its relevance to their needs.

The *aware* segment *do* know about your product, though they may not know enough to make them prefer it to competitive offerings.

Those *considering* your product are probably not in need of basic product information – they already have this. However, they may still need some additional detail relevant to their specific situation, and a rationale for preferring your product to a competitive product.

Customers may not need additional product information, although this will not always be the case. Research shows that in many fields customers do not get the best out of products they buy because they are not totally aware of their true range and capabilities. A good example of this would be a sophisticated software package containing features which many buyers do not understand and thus will never use.

At the top of the ladder are the *advocates* – customers who are so impressed by your quality and service that they tell their friends and colleagues about it. You do not need to explain what the product does to these customers – in fact they would be insulted if you did!

Communications to advocates should be to say *thank you for your business*, give information about new developments, or make special offers to encourage continued business and recommendations.

TWO KEY CONSIDERATIONS

From the above descriptions two things emerge:

1 People will need different information and different amounts of information according to their place on the ladder.

---

2 The same person could be on different rungs, according to the specific product you are promoting.

Even this is an over-simplification. An advocate who has regularly bought Product A from you, may not be aware of Product B and could thus be classified as unaware. However, there is a strong relationship already established and, hopefully some information on your database which will help you to sell product B to this person. In this sense they should be classified much higher than the average suspect.

The important thing is that you should use these descriptions to help you identify the right people, the right messages, and the right timing for a specific product or offer. Do not forget however, the huge value of the relationship you have with *existing* customers.

USING THE LADDER

The ladder is a useful device to help you highlight the differences between various types of people or companies and help you produce appropriate communications for each – communications which will be seen as relevant because they recognize the status of each person and deliver relevant messages.

You can categorize your own prospects according to their positions on the ladder of loyalty. If you are setting up a new business then most of your names will be on the bottom rung – or will they?

Sometimes, as in the case of the company mentioned on page 62, the application of a little common sense can help you reduce uncertainty and target those more likely to be good prospects.

Common sense is also a useful ally when deciding how tightly to target best prospects. 100% response to a mailing may be highly interesting, but if you have mailed only forty people you will not build your business very quickly.

So, while it is important to try to improve cost-efficiency, you must also keep an eye on the overall number of sales needed to cover costs and make a contribution to your profits.

SUMMARY

What makes direct mail the most cost efficient advertising medium is targeting.

Precise targeting relies on good information about:

> who will be interested in your proposition

> where these people can be reached

> when they will be in a buying situation.

The best way to obtain this information is by analysis of your own database – ideally your own data will tell you who bought what, how you can contact them and when they last bought.

Once you are able to define different categories of customer you can segment them into discrete groups. The next step is to start profiling by identifying the relevant characteristics of the people and companies in each segment, e.g. large companies, people with gardens, and so on.

These profiling factors can then be used to select appropriate advertising media and precise segments of external mailing lists to improve your targeting and thus the cost efficiency of your prospecting activities.

Profiling and segmentation are not *just* for prospecting. Careful segmentation of your customers can help you to achieve greater relevance in your mailings and thus higher response rates.

Some marketers use a device called the *ladder of loyalty*. This is used to rank your customers and prospects according to their value and their attitudes towards you.

Personalization of messages can make you look very silly if you treat an old customer like a brand new one.

Powerful targeting, segmentation and personalization techniques thus require a high degree of discipline, too.

EXAMPLE

Customer Thomas who has just bought Product A does not need a mailing telling him why he should buy this product – he will probably be annoyed if you send him such a message. He may react well however, to a mailing which tells him how to get longer life out of it, or perhaps to one which explains how buying Product B will enhance his enjoyment of Product A.

Equally, a customer who has been buying from you every month for the last two years, does not need to be told who you are or how you do business.

A device or process like the ladder thus helps you to achieve greater relevance in all your customer communications.

With the power of computer-driven information in your hands, you can deliver powerful, personalized mailings to each of your customers and prospects.

Such powerful mailings are very memorable and effective – but only if you get them right.

WHAT TO DO NOW

Consider your own customers

▷ can you rank them according to their value to you?

▷ where do they fit on the ladder of loyalty?

Try to work out how many you would have on each rung of the ladder and then consider how easy or difficult it would be for you to mail different messages to the various segments.

Read the trade press – *Precision Marketing* (especially its feature *Precision Marketplace*), *Direct Response,* and other publications. Send for information packs from companies offering profiling and segmentation services.

Visit the various direct marketing fairs and exhibitions. You will find masses of information and plenty of people only too willing to explain their services to you.

5 The marketing database – your own private advertising medium

In this chapter, I will first deal with the benefits of developing your own database, then look at how a database can help you build your business, and finally discuss basic hardware and software issues.

Before we start talking about the database, let us just remind ourselves of the value of customer information.

RELEVANCE IS THE KEY TO EFFECTIVE COMMUNICATIONS

And information is the key to achieving relevance. The more you know about the people on your customer and prospect files, the more relevant your communications will be.

Good up-to-date information enables you to segment customers into value bands and behavioural types, so that you can approach the right people, at the right time, and make offers which fit their circumstances and intentions.

> *Not all customers are equal. To build your business cost-effectively you need to be able to identify those customers with whom you are more likely to be able to develop long-term profitable relationships.*

You do not need to ignore the others, but segmenting customers into groups with similar potential value will enable you to match expenditure to the likely return. You can thus devise customer development plans which have relevance to the real potential buying behaviour of each segment or 'cluster'.

The more information you want to keep, the greater the necessity to have an efficient means of storing and retrieving it. This means you are going to need a marketing database.

WHAT EXACTLY IS A MARKETING DATABASE?

A marketing database is a collection of information which helps you to spend marketing budgets more efficiently and develop better, more powerful relationships with your customers.

It is not a computer; nor a piece of software. In fact you don't even need to have a computer to have a marketing database. A pile of bits of paper with customer names, addresses and details of the products they ordered is a database – though not a very efficient one.

> *The information on a scrap of paper will give you a snapshot of an individual customer, but to develop your business cost-efficiently, you need to be able to analyse and accumulate data from many customers and this is where the computer is invaluable.*

A computer is extremely efficient at sorting, collating and assembling scraps of data into meaningful information which will help you build a profitable business.

THE BENEFITS OF BUILDING A COMPUTER DATABASE

Computerizing your data enables you to:

1 **Analyse behaviour** and group customers into 'clusters' with similar buying patterns. This enables you to anticipate needs, decide who to communicate with, when to do so, and what to say. This will…

2 **Make your communications more relevant**, increasing their effectiveness. This enables you to…

3 **Increase the productivity of your marketing budget** through better targeting and selection, which in turn reduces wastage and customer irritation. Many companies find that the first time they de-duplicate their records, they reduce their mailing costs by 25% or more.

4 **Improve customer care** by matching resources to customer requirements. This will increase customer loyalty.

5 **Develop more appropriate products and services** through the dialogue you have with customers.

6 **Improve your forecasting and measurement capabilities**, making all your marketing activities more accountable.

7 **Extend your markets** by opening up previously unprofitable segments, using lower cost alternative sales and communications channels. See the account management model in Chapter 3 – page 44.

8 **Make prospecting more cost-effective** by enabling you to develop customer profiles – these will improve targeting and help to reduce wastage.

9 **Provide colleagues and management with accurate up-to-date reports** on all aspects of the business.

10 **Distribute the same, up-to-date customer information to each customer contact point**, improving the effectiveness of all customer contacts. This increases your professionalism and thus makes customers regard you more highly.

EXAMPLE

At the start of my Database Seminars I find it helpful to ask each delegate *Why are you here?* This helps me make sure that all relevant questions are covered during the day.

One day a delegate answered *'I don't know why I am here. We make specialized precision engineering tools to order for scientists, and at any one time we have only fifty or sixty active customers'.*

> I replied, *'Let's suppose I am Professor Thomas from Brussels and I telephone you to ask when my order will be shipped. What do you do?'*
>
> My delegate said *'I transfer you to the Managing Director, he is the only one who knows the up-to-date status of each order.'*
>
> I then said, *'What if the Managing Director is out, or in a meeting? Wouldn't it be better if you could simply key my name or reference number into your PC and immediately see the details of my order on your screen?'*
>
> *'Ah,'* he said, *'now I know why my Managing Director sent me on this seminar!'*

This true story demonstrates the problem that many people have when coming to grips with the idea of a database for the first time. They can see how a database can be a good source of mailing lists, but fail to appreciate the wider benefits that a business can gain by consolidating data then distributing it around the business.

By helping to organize your customer information, your database becomes a strategic partner in the management and development of your business.

THE VALUE OF DEVELOPING CUSTOMER RELATIONSHIPS

There are several good reasons why you should use your database to develop relationships with existing customers:

1 **It is easier to sell to existing customers** – various researches in recent years suggest that it costs between three and thirty times as much to achieve a first order as it does to obtain a repeat order.

2 **Orders from existing customers are often larger** – the same research suggests that new customers tend to place smaller 'trial' orders at first.

3 **The database is a private medium** – you can communicate with your customers in private without your competitors seeing your 'advertising'.

4 **You can time your communications to fit your customers' needs** – your offers will be more effective if they are received at the right time. The database makes this much easier to achieve.

5 **You can restrict your offers only to those who will be interested** – this makes your mailings more cost-effective and less intrusive.

6 **You can vary your offers according to customer value** – when you segment customers into value bands you can make offers which more closely relate to your potential profit. For example, you could make better offers to the prospects with the highest potential.

HOW THE DATABASE WORKS

Some of you will already have a mainframe computer and a large IT department, in which case it makes sense to make use of all that equipment and expertise.

However, it is important to make sure that the in-house IT department has the time and the specific skills to handle marketing requirements. Many small database operations fail to realize their potential because marketing cannot get any priority on the IT department task list.

Most large computer installations were set up for purposes other than marketing and this sometimes shows.

The good news is that only a tiny percentage of present-day marketing applications need mainframes and IT departments. Most can be carried out cheaply and efficiently on a modern desktop PC, or at least a PC-based network.

Further good news is that today's PC software is designed for non-technical people. There is a wide range of business software which can be run under Windows or another *graphical user environment* (e.g. Apple Mac). Most of this software is of the 'point and shoot' variety which does not require the user to be able to write programs to operate it efficiently.

However, although it is not necessary to be a computer expert to operate a database, a basic understanding of what is happening will help to make the most of the system.

So let us have a brief non-technical look at the way a database works.

JUST A FILING CABINET

A database can be compared to a filing cabinet – but a very special filing cabinet.

Each file (or table) contains some information:

- ▷ Customer names and addresses
- ▷ Details of their businesses or households (number of employees, children and so on)
- ▷ Order and enquiry details
- ▷ Stock records, and so on.

The advantage of a computer database is that any record, in any file, in any drawer, can be linked (or related) to any other relevant record in any other file (hence the term *relational database*).

This is done by attaching to each record a unique code or reference number, which enables the computer to identify which bits belong to each other. The relevant records are then drawn together for a specific purpose (e.g. analysis, mailing run, sales prospect list and so on) by means of a 'query' system.

> *What is the benefit of such a system? Would it not be simpler to have a file for each customer containing all the things relating to that customer?*

There are at least two reasons why this would not be a great idea:

1 Some of the files would be very large and it would take ages to find anything.

2 Each time you wanted to produce any sort of analysis you would need to look at every record in every file, extract the relevant details and assemble these into a report. If you then decided to assemble the data in a different way you would have to do it all over again.

EXAMPLE

We are planning to launch a new product, initially to previous customers - not all of them but those who are more likely to be interested.

Let's look at two ways of doing this - without a database and with a simple PC-based system.

We want to introduce the new product (E) in just one area to start with, say Lancashire. We know from our customer research that this product will appeal to those with teenaged children, especially those who previously bought product A or product B. Customers who previously bought both products (A and B) are likely to be even better prospects.

How can we decide who to contact about Product E?

Without a database we are faced with a choice of either:

▷ Sending a general mailing to all previous customers with Lancashire postcodes, or;

▷ Going through all our previous customer files looking for orders for products A and/or B, from customers with Lancashire postcodes, and ranking these in some way for special treatment.

These would then be sent to a typist somewhere for addressing of letters and/or labels.

With a PC database, using simple 'point and shoot' instructions, we could:

▷ Identify all Lancashire-based customers who ordered products A or B - automatically selecting these by post code.

▷ Rank these according to previous order size – this would enable us to make offers appropriate to their previous buying behaviour.

▷ Group together those who ordered both products.

▷ Automatically count the numbers in each category, so that we can order the right number of leaflets, envelopes and so on.

▷ Use mail/merge to automatically produce the necessary letters, incorporating individual pieces of data, where appropriate, to make each mailing more relevant to the recipient.

All of the above tasks, and many more, could easily be carried out on a PC costing less than £1,500 with software which might cost no more than £400.

HOW RECORDS ARE RELATED

To return to our analogy of a filing cabinet, you will remember that the database consists of a wide range of information stored in numerous files (or tables). The records in each table can be linked (or related) to each other (a relational database) by use of reference elements such as unique customer numbers, order numbers, product codes and so on.

This linking of records enables you to carry out a wide range of useful analyses, counting and aggregating information in almost any way required.

Typical tables might be:

1 Customer details – this table might carry basic addressing details such as:

- ▷ unique reference number – necessary to link with other tables
- ▷ name
- ▷ address (house name/number and street)
- ▷ balance of address (district, town, postcode and so on).

This customer record contains only four fields, so obviously this layout would limit you to very simple activities e.g. production of address labels and so on.

The database sorts and analyses by looking for specific information in each field and producing a series of reports (or new tables).

THE DATABASE SOFTWARE DEALS IN TOTAL FIELDS ONLY

It is important to realize that the software deals in total fields only, i.e. if the name field contains 'Jo Thomas' the system can only use this in its entirety.

You may want to address some letters formally ('Dear Miss Thomas'), and some informally ('Dear Jo'). Others will require a safety default because you don't really know whether Jo is male or female ('Dear Jo Thomas' or perhaps 'Dear Manager').

To achieve this requires the elements of the name to be placed in separate fields, and the addition of an extra field containing the salutation.

With this in mind you may now wish to rearrange the fields as follows:

- ▷ customer reference number (or URN – unique reference number)
- ▷ first name(s), e.g. Jo Frances, or perhaps Jo F
- ▷ initials, e.g. JF
- ▷ surname, e.g. Thomas
- ▷ Mr/Mrs/Miss/Ms, e.g. Miss (if known)
- ▷ salutation – for use in personalized letters, e.g. Jo, Miss Thomas and so on
- ▷ Address Line 1 (perhaps a house name)
- ▷ Address line 2

- Address line 3
- Address line 4 (perhaps the town or city)
- County
- Postcode.

This table, or alternatively another table linked by URN, could also carry simple profiling and selection data such as:

- age
- marital status
- household composition – number of children
- hobbies
- type/number of car(s)
- has a dishwasher/satellite TV and so on
- total sales to date
- method of payment.

WHY HAVE SEPARATE TABLES?

If you hold the above details for the majority of customers, you would generally include them in the first table. If you only have this information for say 10 or 15% of customers it makes sense to build a separate table.

> *The reason for this is that if a field (such as 'type/number of cars') is added to a table it has to be added to every record. If you only have data for a small percentage of records, you are using up a lot of space unnecessarily.*

The reason for separate tables can be seen if you consider the difference between name and address records (which are all broadly of a similar size) and sales records, which will be different for each customer.

If 95% of your customers have ordered once, and 5% have ordered more than a hundred times, every record would need to be large enough to carry, say, 200 order details (allowing for future orders). Equally, if you have details of businesses, some having one contact name and others having twenty contact names, it would be very wasteful to allow for all those names on every record in the main table.

2 **Order details** – these could be held in any order (area, product grouping, chronological, and so on) but each order would carry a customer reference number (URN) linking it back to an individual customer in the first table.

3 **Stock records** – this data could again be assembled in any order, with updates fed automatically from the order details table.

And so it goes on, each table or file being related to the others by use of common fields (usually customer record numbers, order numbers or stock numbers).

Each time you want to perform some marketing function, such as producing a campaign or promotion report, or a planning for a new mailing, you can assemble any combination of data by means of the database's query system – a standardized method of asking the right questions.

Now let's have a look at the issue of data.

FINDING AND CAPTURING THE DATA

First a few questions:

- ▷ What data do you need?
- ▷ Where can you find it?
- ▷ How can you capture it?
- ▷ How can you keep it up-to-date?

WHAT DATA DO YOU NEED?

Most companies have more than enough data – the problem is not generally one of availability, but of centralization and management.

One of the key questions will be what should be kept.

If an item of data is to be used for communications it must be kept up-to-date. Any data is better than none, but out-of-date information can be misleading, even harmful. Writing to people who have moved house

> *or left a company may be difficult to avoid, but the impression left by*
> *your mailing will be very bad.*

This is not to say that old data should be destroyed – it will probably be very valuable for analysis, profiling and so on. However, it makes sense to remove old records to an archive for occasional use, rather than have them taking up space and using data processing time on the main database.

A good start may be to:

▷ **Capture data essential for current requirements** – names, addresses, products purchased and so on.

▷ **Collect key profile data** – family size, company size and so on.

▷ **Collect data which will aid future activity** such as cross-selling and repeat purchase stimulation – which offer customers responded to, timing, method of ordering and so on.

▷ **Collect data relating to the marketplace** and to competitors…
  ❑ peaks and troughs of demand
  ❑ competitors' advertising campaigns.

FIRST DEFINE THE USES

A good rule is to define a use for each piece of data before you include it – if you can't think of a reason to keep it, you probably don't need it. If you are really not sure then you can hold a separate file or table of such data so you don't clog up the main database – bearing in mind that if you don't maintain it, it will eventually become out-of-date.

Appendix 3 contains some details of the sort of data you should consider collecting, its possible uses and some suggested sources.

WHERE DOES THE DATA COME FROM?

Unless you are starting up a brand new company there will be lots of data already available. For example:

> **Administration data** – you will have details of previous orders, despatches, invoices, reminders, demands and payments.

> **Servicing data** – there may be records of visits, calls, repairs and returns.

> **Marketing data**

    ❏ names from previous mailings and advertising responses

    ❏ details of mailings and advertisements carried out, promotions organized and so on.

On its own, departmental data is only of use for its original purpose. When different pieces of data are combined and co-ordinated, however, their true value can be realized.

Without data being co-ordinated you can encounter problems such as:

> your accounts person chasing payment from a customer who is unhappy

> mailings being sent to bad debtors

> multiple mailings going to the same person

> sales calls being made to 'prospects' who are not interested, or haven't paid their last invoice.

These and many similar occurrences happen every day in many companies.

THE CONTINUING NEED FOR DATA

Although there may already be quite a lot of data in and around your business, additional data will probably be necessary and there is a continuing need to build and maintain your database.

Here are some other sources of data:

> **Customer and prospect questionnaires** – these can attract quite large responses – 50% or more from established customers and 20% or more from prospects.

> ▷ **Mailings to outside lists** – there is a wide range of lists available for rent – any respondents can be added to your database, subject to the requirements of the DPA (Data Protection Act – see Appendix 1). Some lists can also be bought outright.

> ▷ **Companies House** – a good source of raw data about companies, extracted from their annual returns. You can also buy the same information, but with additional 'narrative', trend analysis and so on from…

> ▷ **Information brokers** – such as Dun & Bradstreet, Market Location and CCN. These companies can provide not only names and addresses, but additional data about size, performance and so on. They will also verify your own records and add any additional data they hold.

> ▷ **Lifestyle database companies** – such as NDL and CMT provide a similar service for consumer records – these organizations have several million names and addresses on their databases.

> ▷ **Responses** from advertising, inserts and other promotions. Again, subject to the requirements of the Data Protection Act, these can be added to your database.

HOW CAN YOU CAPTURE THE DATA?

However much data you already have, it will not all be in a computer and some data capture is inevitable. If you have the capacity to undertake data input in-house, this is the cheapest way.

It is important to avoid duplication of records, so it is advisable to build some form of de-duplication process into the data-entry routine. De-duplication is discussed in detail in Chapter 6

There are several software tools available (e.g. *Quick-address*) to help you check the accuracy of each address on entry. Most of these will save a high percentage of the initial key strokes.

As an alternative to in-house data capture there are many bureaux offering this service and Chapter 10 tells you how to find them.

HOW CAN DATA BE KEPT UP-TO-DATE?

Data decays very rapidly – some 10% of consumers move house every year and up to 40% of business people move (desks at least) every year. It is vital that data is maintained correctly and some of the ways you can do this are:

▷ **Regular communication inviting response** – questionnaires, offers of information and so on.

▷ **Periodic comparisons with outside databases** – e.g. with Dun & Bradstreet, telephone companies, lifestyle database companies or the electoral register.

Every time a contact is made with a customer or prospect, by mail, phone or in person, you should attempt to verify your data.

HOW CAN THE DATA BE USED?

Now that you have collected all this customer information, what can you do with it? Figure 5.1 shows how and where the database can help you manage your business.

This is a very brief overview – those interested in learning more should read one of the books mentioned at the end of this chapter.

HOW DOES THE DATABASE ACHIEVE ALL THESE THINGS?

Essentially through the linking of the various records, as described in the filing cabinet analogy described earlier. For example, referring back to the product launch mentioned on page 79, in which we wanted to identify all Lancashire-based customers who had ordered products A and/or B and where we also wanted to rank them according to the value of their orders, i.e. how many of the products they bought.

Figure 5.1
How and
where a
database can
help a
business

D	**Planning** – the database helps you to define objectives, select customer segments, develop relevant offers and messages, and match costs to potential returns.
A	**Contact strategy** – the process of deciding which medium, or combination of media will be most appropriate for each task and each category of customer. Your database will also help you to identify individuals for the sending of timely communications. Impending renewals, first orders, birthdays or other significant events can all be reasons for a mailing.
T	**Data processing** – the production of disks or labels for addressing your mailing, lists for follow-up activities, 'mail-merging' of letter copy and addresses, counts and reports to aid planning.
A	**Response handling** – one of the key functions of your database is to record response to promotional mailings. This is easier if you use Unique Reference Numbers on your response forms.
B	**Lead management** – helps you to keep track of enquiries (leads) received, follow these through the sales follow-up process and, where necessary, issue reminders for future action.
A	**Order processing** – your system should be able to produce the necessary paperwork for other departments – despatch, invoicing, stock records, and so on. The database will also produce periodic reports to help you manage the campaign. Order status reports allow you to answer customer queries quickly.
S	**Customer satisfaction surveys** – information from questionnaires can be added to customer records helping to make the planning and selection processes more effective in future.
	Analysis – in addition to producing pre-determined reports, a good database system enables you to do *ad hoc* 'what if' analysis.
E	**Data maintenance** – data, especially name and address details, decay rapidly. Frequent contact can overcome this, providing you update records quickly and efficiently.

The process would be as follows:

1 We first ask the database to single out all customer records with Lancashire postcodes. This is achieved by using the database's query tool, e.g. *In the field called 'Postcode' find all the records which contain any of the following – PR – BB – FY – BL – LA* (and so on, covering all Lancashire postcodes).

2 Identify those who also had a record in the sales table indicating an order for products A or B (using the URN attached to the records in both customer *and* sales tables). e.g. *Look in the fields called 'URN' and 'Product' to find records which contain URN's identified in step 1 and which also contain product codes A or B.* This would give us our first report (or new table). Note, though, that this is a temporary table brought about by our query – we would use a different instruction to bring about a permanent link.

3 Instruct the database to rank or separate the records according to sales value, or number of times ordered and so on.

Although very much simplified, this is how a database works. In order to be able to use one properly, however, you will need to read the manual for your chosen software and to develop your skills through practice – more about that a little later.

HARDWARE AND SOFTWARE – A BRIEF REVIEW

Let's now have a brief look at the issues of hardware and software.

HARDWARE

We will start from the assumption that you plan to run your database on a desk-top IBM-compatible PC or Apple Mac. (An IBM-compatible PC is not necessarily made by IBM but runs an IBM-compatible system such as DOS or Windows, as opposed to Apple's MacOS system.)

Although in several respects an Apple Mac is not the same as an IBM-compatible PC, for the purposes of this section and to avoid frequent use of *and/or* references, the expression *PC* means *PC and/or Apple Mac.* Although Apple microcomputers use a different microprocessor chip, they offer similar performance to the Intel chips used in most IBM-compatible PCs. Software availability is also roughly compatible.

Microcomputer technology advances almost daily, so it is necessary to keep up-to-date by reading one or more of the many PC magazines available from newsagents.

Most small business applications can be run on a PC-based system – even very large databases can be held and run successfully on PCs.

> *My son runs a data processing bureau which is entirely PC-based – he and his colleagues regularly run analyses across the forty-four million records in the UK electoral register.*

KEY FACTORS IN SELECTING A PC

There are several factors to consider:

> ▷ hard disk space (storage space)
> ▷ processor (or chip) and clock speed (the speed at which the processor is set to run)
> ▷ random access memory (RAM).

HARD DISK SPACE

The data storage requirement for a reasonably comprehensive database record, including a couple of contact names and some transactional data, is around 700 to 900 bytes – virtually a kilobyte. When planning a database it is prudent to allow additional working space for sorts, selections and so on to be made. Therefore to be on the safe side, you might double the record space to around two kilobytes. (1,024 kilobytes = one megabyte.)

On this basis 500 records will take up nearly one megabyte of disk space. Thus, a modern PC with a spare hard disc capacity of 100 megabytes (after allowing for software and any document or spreadsheet files) would be quite capable of running a database of around 50,000 customers – more than enough for most small businesses.

> *To be on the safe side, given that each new software package seems to require more and more hard disk storage, it makes sense to use a PC with a hard disk of at least 500 megabytes. This is becoming the entry level nowadays, so new PCs will generally be offered with this size of hard disk.*

PROCESSOR SPEED

Most IBM-compatible PCs are driven by a microprocessor or chip in the series 80286, 80386, 80486 and Pentium. Apart from Pentium, these are normally abbreviated to the final three digits so we have a 286, 386, 486 or Pentium PC.

All but one Apple Macintosh desktop computer (the entry-level machine) use a PowerPC microprocessor, in the 600 series. These are commonly known as Power Macs.

Chip technology is moving very rapidly and software is constantly upgraded to take advantage of faster chips now powering most new computers. Current entry level PCs are installed with the 486 chip and this is rapidly being superseded by the lower speed Pentium chip. Similarly, only one Apple Macintosh desktop computer remains which is driven by the older 68040 microprocessor.

> *This is not to say that an existing 486 or 040 machine will not do the job, but each new release of software will be less and less appropriate for such machines. Therefore, if you are planning to buy a new PC it makes sense to select a Pentium or a Power Mac rather than anything less capable.*

Microprocessor chips are set to run at various 'clock' speeds (this will be pre-set in the model you buy). One could therefore buy a 486/33 PC which would run a 486 chip at 33 megahertz – fairly slow by today's standards or a 486/100 – running at 100 megahertz which is fast even by Pentium standards.

Pentium and PowerPC chips are faster again and currently range from the Pentium P60 (60 MHz) to the 133 (133 MHz), and PowerPC 603 (75 MHz) to the PowerPC 604 (132 MHz).

Incidentally, before you throw your 486 or 040 machine off the roof, check with your PC supplier to see whether you can have it upgraded – sometimes this can be quite inexpensive.

Prices change from week to week, so you need to check before you buy. The good thing is that prices always go down, so prices quoted here could be taken as a challenge – you should be able to beat them easily.

As a general guide here are some prices from the October 1995 edition of the magazine PC PRO.

▷   Dell Dimension XPS P133c – a state-of-the-art, top-speed Pentium (133 MHz), with 16 Mb RAM, 1 Gb hard disk, CD-ROM drive, and all the features and software you need – £2,499 + VAT

▷   Dell Dimension 466 DL – a 486/66 PC with 8 Mb RAM, 525 Mb hard disk – no software and no multi-media – £849 + VAT.

Note that Dell computers are used simply to illustrate a point. They are neither the cheapest nor the dearest on offer.

A decent-sized database could quite easily be run on a fast 486 machine, for example the 486/66 machine mentioned above, but first read the section below regarding RAM requirements.

RAM (RANDOM ACCESS MEMORY)

In addition to the storage capacity on the hard disk, a micro-computer uses another kind of memory to run the various applications required. This is RAM or *random access memory*. There is no need for you to know how this works, simply that you need substantial RAM to run modern word processors, spreadsheets and databases — particularly where these are being run simultaneously under a GUI (graphical user interface), such as Windows or the MacOS.

Most fairly fast machines come with 8 Mb of RAM these days. However, depending on the package you choose, this may not be enough to get the best out of your database system.

To be on the safe side, it is better to have more – 16 Mb is preferable. This is important because RAM is expensive – the October 1995 price to upgrade from 8 to 16 Mb is around £200.

Don't rely on the *minimum system requirements* quoted on software boxes. Most software suppliers tell you how much RAM is required to run their programs, but they don't always make enough allowances for system software and any other applications you may wish to run at the same time.

For example if you are running the database in order to produce some mailing letters using a mail/merge program, you will also need to be running your word processor software. Under these circumstances you need plenty of RAM.

This is not to say that your database will not run with less RAM – in some cases you will be able to complete your tasks, but at a slower speed.

In many ways, RAM is more important than processor clock speed and if you are planning to run a database, it is better to choose a Pentium P60 machine (Pentium chip at 60 MHz), or a Power Mac Performa 5200 (PowerPC 603 chip at 75 MHz), with 16 Mb of RAM than a Pentium P100 or Power Mac 7500 (running at 100 MHz) with 8 Mb of RAM.

Windows 95, while being more user-friendly than earlier versions of Windows, is also more memory-hungry. If you plan to run Windows 95 and the new Microsoft *Office 95* integrated package (as I do) you will need a minimum of 16 Mb of RAM. The newest version of the database package *Access 95* needs at least 12 Mb to run efficiently. The situation is similar running the software on an Apple Mac.

WHAT ABOUT SOFTWARE?

There are many database systems available – Access from Microsoft, Lotus Approach, Alpha Five to name but three. Indeed,a recent magazine survey covered more than twenty and this is just the tip of the iceberg.

Beware of systems advertised as 'simple, trouble-free, loads in five minutes' and so on – you will usually be trading-off speed, power and many user-friendly features for apparent simplicity.

Every system has some good features and those produced by the major software houses are all powerful and reliable. I use Microsoft *Access 95* for several reasons:

▷ It is part of the Microsoft *Office 95* package and is thus totally compatible with Windows 95, *Word, Excel, Powerpoint* etc. It links automatically with these other programs and is thus very easy to use. Data can be transferred from one application to another at the click of a mouse.

▷ Although new, it is already widely used and supported and I have no trouble finding other users who can help me if I encounter a problem late on a Sunday evening.

▷ The on-line help is very easy to use and understand.

▷ There are several simple books about *Access* – I find the *for Dummies* series to be particularly good.

WHAT IF YOUR COMPANY ALREADY HAS A COMPUTER SYSTEM?

If you have a large mainframe or mid-sized computer you should start by finding out what this can offer you. If you also have an IT department, they may be able to take this whole problem off your hands.

Let's start by assuming your company has lots of information in its main computer system and what you need is access – not just to mailing lists, but to the range of applications described above. The ideal solution in these circumstances is for you to be able to download data onto a local (probably PC-based) system with its own software, enabling you to analyse and manipulate data as required.

There are several such systems available, but they do require at least some basic computer knowledge and are beyond the scope of this manual. Your IT department should be able to advise on a suitable solution for your requirements.

SUMMARY

Most businesses will benefit from a marketing database by being able to offer:

> **Better customer service** – faster reaction to orders, queries, complaints and so on. This enables you to build...

> **Better customer relationships** – greater understanding of needs and wants, likes, dislikes, good and bad timings and so on. Profits will also be increased through...

> **Increased customer retention** – requiring less money to be spent on less profitable activities such as new business prospecting.

> **Less wastage** – through the ability to select only those customers or prospects for whom an offer is relevant, reducing cost, and annoyance.

The database is, or should be, a strategic partner, centrally involved in each function of the business.

A good marketing database helps you run your business like a 'corner shop' – putting detailed knowledge of any one of hundreds or even thousands of individual accounts and relationships into your hands, in an instant.

Not surprisingly, this is much appreciated by customers and encourages them to continue doing business with you.

PCs are becoming faster and cheaper all the time and you should be able to buy all the hardware and software you need to run a small but efficient database for less than £2,000. If you are prepared to have your database run a little more slowly, you may get away with less than £1,000 if you shop around.

However, take advantage of my hard-bought experience. In the past three years I have bought four PCs, each time thinking I won't need all that speed or storage only to run out of hard disk space, or need a RAM upgrade within months. My policy now is to buy the most powerful machine I can afford.

WHAT TO DO NEXT

Contact the publishers of *The Journal of Database Marketing*. Ask for a back issue to see whether you want to subscribe.

Read the following books:

▷ *Computer Aided Marketing & Selling* – Dr Robert Shaw.
▷ *Access 95 for Dummies* – Scott Palmer[†]

[†] Assuming this book appears – current latest version covers *Access 2*.

Alternatively, buy a similar 'Idiot's Guide' to the system you choose.

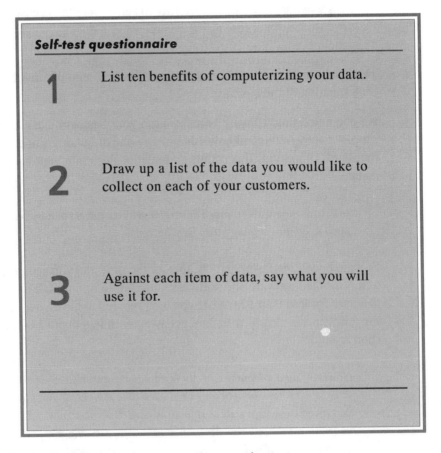

Self-test questionnaire

1   List ten benefits of computerizing your data.

2   Draw up a list of the data you would like to collect on each of your customers.

3   Against each item of data, say what you will use it for.

Check Appendix 4 for answers and suggestions.

6 Mailing lists (rented or external)

There are two kinds of mailing list – those you compile from your own database or other records (internal lists), and those you acquire from outside sources such as list brokers and directories (external lists).

Database selections are covered in Chapter 5 and in this chapter we concentrate on external lists.

WHAT EXACTLY IS A MAILING LIST?

A mailing list is a collection of addresses, usually with names, which has been assembled because of some common factor, and with the intention of being used for the despatch of unsolicited mail.

EXAMPLE – THE INVESTOR REGISTER SHAREHOLDERS' DATABASE
(COURTESY OF DUDLEY JENKINS LIST BROKING LIMITED)

A list of 1,657,041 shareholders, constructed from over 400 different share registers, giving comprehensive coverage across defined sectors.

Selections can be made by:

▷ title (Mr/Mrs/Miss/Ms/Dr/Military title and so on)

▷ type of shareholding (nineteen different types, e.g. USM, property, financial sector, leisure sector and so on)

▷ number of shareholdings (one to nine-plus)

▷ aggregate share value (thirteen categories from £1–£500 to £1 million-plus)

Clearly, some lists will be better than others. One very broad method of making an initial evaluation of the various lists you are offered is to ask *'How did these people come to be on this list'*. This will enable you to separate the lists you are offered into two further categories:

▷ those who *did* something, and…
▷ those who *are* something.

In the first category you may find lists of people who bought a specific product, attended a particular exhibition, enquired about a certain service, or, as in the above example, invested in the stock market. All actions relating to an interest in something specific.

In the second category you may find lists of plumbers, schoolteachers or accountants. Very useful for broad targeting of a marketplace, but without any specific link to a relevant action.

You may find good lists in the second category, but generally lists in the first category are likely to produce higher responses because:

1

You know what they did to get on the list, so you can select people who are more likely to be interested in your offer – for example…

If you sell an investment advisory service you could try mailing people with large houses. This approach is based on the assumption that there will be a high correlation between ownership of expensive property and propensity to invest – not a bad assumption, but nowhere near as good as mailing the investor register already described.

Alternatively, perhaps you sell a software product which simplifies office administration, but which requires a live demonstration to get the selling points across successfully. Let's say you have decided to run demonstrations and seminars in city centres around the country. Once again, you could start with an assumption. You could assume that all office managers would be interested and simply rent a list of office managers, or compile your own from a directory.

However, if you can find a list of office managers who attended the Business Efficiency Exhibition you are more likely to get an interested response because these prospects have pre-qualified themselves by their previous actions.

2 **For the same reason** you can perhaps vary or tailor your offer to make it more relevant to these prospects.

WHY CAN'T I COMPILE MY OWN LIST?

The answer to this question is *You can*, but your success will depend on how well you are able to target the right people. This, in turn, will depend on how wide the appeal is for your product.

The examples in point 1 opposite show how a list relating to an action might be more responsive than one relating simply to a category of job or position.

However, sometimes list building by category alone can be successful as the following case study shows.

 **CASE STUDY – PREMIER GRAPHICS**

Colour business cards are very popular with hotels and restaurants on the South Coast, especially, it seems, with Indian restaurants. In fact more than 300 establishments between Brighton and Bournemouth regularly come back for more.

Repeat business is one of Premier's major strengths – more than 90% of customers repeat and add to their orders.

How do they get new customers? Let Colin Fairall tell the story.

'We used to do a lot of cold calling' he says. *'It was a lot of hard work and very hit and miss. Then we received a special offer mailing from the Royal Mail – buy 1,000 Prepaid Envelopes and get 200 free.*

I was amazed we hadn't thought of direct mail before. Targeting is simple. We use the Yellow Pages to look up companies, hotels and restaurants within a fifty-mile radius, but instead of telephoning we mail tailor-made packages.

Obviously being in the print business we have plenty of cards, brochures and promotional items left over, so we can easily match samples to potential customers.'

How much response do they get? Colin says it varies according to season, but it usually averages around 8% immediately, with more trickling in over a longer period.

Colin says *'The British habit is not to act upon things straightaway. So people can still be responding in six months' time. But then 8% isn't bad anyway'.*

This approach worked very well for Colin Fairall, but even if you have a product which is likely to be of universal interest to an entire category, you cannot always safely make such an assumption.

EXAMPLE

Let us say you are about to publish a new magazine on accountancy. It is possible that mailing a list of accountancy practices compiled from the Yellow Pages would enable you to recruit new customers cost-effectively, without further segmentation.

However, in practice you may find that only 50% of accountancy practices are prepared to take out subscriptions centrally, the other half preferring or expecting their partners/ employees to take out personal subscriptions from their home addresses.

In these circumstances a list of practices which had subscribed to a previous offer by another magazine (even a general business magazine such as *The Economist*) could prove to be much more cost-effective than simply mailing all accountants in the phone book.

THE VARIOUS KINDS OF ACTION-ORIENTATED LIST

Obviously, there can be several types of action, some more relevant than others:

Mail responsive – addresses of people or companies who have responded through the mail to some offer. This may have been to a mailing or an advertisement. In either case, they have shown themselves prepared to communicate with advertisers and suppliers by mail.

This category can be subdivided into:

- **buyers** – people who actually ordered a product or service through the mail

- **enquirers** – not quite so strong as buyers, but at least they expressed a clear interest in a specific type of product

- **attendees** – not generally considered to be as valuable as the former categories, unless of course your mailing is intended to get people to attend an event or exhibition.

SELECTING THE RIGHT LISTS

There are several factors to remember. You should:

- try to identify the precise category of prospect you are seeking

- talk to list brokers, list owners and so on and see what they can suggest for your market

- try to identify the specific characteristics of existing customers and develop a profile of your ideal customer – use this to brief brokers or to select sub-sections of the lists they offer. Profiling is explained in Chapter 4

- ask about test quantities – most lists, apart from those with only a very small number of names, can be rented in part, i.e. you do not need to rent the entire list – there are two applications here…

  ❏ you can test-mail a small number of names before committing to the full list – most lists on the rental market have a defined 'minimum test quantity' (but see section in Chapter 9 about statistical significance)

❏ You can select from within the list those segments which offer the best chance of success, i.e. those which most closely match your 'ideal customer' profile.

Such selections will cost more, but this can be a good investment.

EXAMPLE

In the 1980s a major cruise line used direct mail to attract new prospects for their more expensive cruises. Analysis of responses and buying behaviour revealed some interesting facts:

▷ People who lived in houses with names were three times as likely to buy expensive cruises as those who lived in houses with numbers.

▷ People living in flats were less likely to buy expensive cruises – except for flats in certain postcode areas such as London W1.

To put this in perspective, a rented list would cost around £100 per thousand 'names' (i.e. names and addresses). To select only houses with names could cost an additional £10 per thousand. Thus you would pay a 10% premium for a 300% increase in response percentage.

This does not mean you would get three times as many replies – you would mail far fewer houses but the cost-efficiency would be much greater. You would still need to do the calculations to ensure that you got enough leads or replies to achieve your sales target.

PERSONALIZED ADDRESSING

Ideally a mailing recipient should be addressed by name and, where relevant, title – correctly.

However lists, especially business lists, go out-of-date rapidly – one supplier of business addresses does not offer names because of this.

This company tested a list which had been fully verified by telephone and found that after only one year, 40% of the names were no longer correct.

When there is any doubt about the accuracy of the data, it is better to default to a safe general address and salutation.

It is better to address a mailing to The Financial Director *and start* Dear Financial Director *than to personalize it with an incorrect name or title. Equally, you could start a consumer mailing* Dear Reader *or* Dear Householder *and address it to* The Householder.

Nothing shows up the false nature of 'personalization' more clearly than getting the name wrong. This is especially obvious if you use the name more than once in your mailing.

THE PROBLEM OF GENDER

This can be difficult. If only an initial and surname are listed you have to allow for both sexes. Again, a salutation such as *Dear Marketing Executive* or *Dear Reader* is preferable to guessing wrongly. Even where you have an obviously female first name you are still faced with the problem of marital status – some people resent being mis-titled *Mrs* or *Miss*; others dislike *Ms*. When in doubt play safe.

WHERE DO LISTS COME FROM?

There are several possible sources:

▷ **List owners** – some organizations are prepared to rent their lists direct, as the example on the next page shows.

▷ **List managers** – large organizations may use a list manager who will deal direct with a prospective mailer.

▷ **List compilers** – some organizations will build lists to order. Many list managers and compilers are part of list brokerages.

EXAMPLE – MODULARBUILD

RB Farquhar produces prefabricated buildings, marketing these under the name Modularbuild. The company thought up a novel idea to make their product stand out from the competition.

They decided to produce a booklet *Four Short Stories*, allowing them to explain case studies in an interesting and eye-catching way. Producing the testimonials in this way enabled them to 'humanize' them by showing faces – always a good idea in a mailing.

Their target was architectural practices, but only those with a proven interest in modular construction.

> *They approached the Royal Institute of British Architects, which supplied Farquhar with names and addresses of 5,500 practices claiming to have expertise in designing hotels.*

Their enquiry-generating mailing was very basic, using address labels on an envelope printed with the *Four Short Stories* logo, the *Four Short Stories* booklet, and a reply paid enquiry card. No letter was included at this stage.

> *The response rate was almost 4%.*

The fulfilment pack contained two large colour brochures with a personalized letter explaining Modularbuild in greater detail. To aid recognition, the outer envelope carried a logo *The Whole Story* in the same design as the original *Four Short Stories* logo.

> *Many of the enquiries generated have been converted into substantial orders.*

> ▷ **List brokers** – the most frequent source of rented names.

List brokers act for many list owners and can offer advice and a range of options for most requirements. To locate a list broker you should contact the Direct Marketing Association (DMA), whose address you will find in

Appendix 2. The DMA will be happy to send you a list of member brokers.

HOW TO CHOOSE A LIST BROKER

There are many brokers in the UK and it is useful to have a check-list of questions designed to help you make a choice:

❑ do they have experience in your market?

❑ do they have access to all the lists you might require. If not, can they recommend other sources, or even negotiate the entire package for you?

❑ does your individual contact inspire confidence?

❑ what sort of response did you get to your brief – was it helpful and did it add or suggest anything?

RENTAL COSTS

List rental pricing is normally quoted as a fixed rate per thousand 'names', but negotiations are possible based on volume. It is also possible to negotiate a very good deal as a first time mailer.

The basic rental agreement is for a single use, i.e. you are not permitted to carry out more than one mailing to the names unless you have negotiated otherwise. Any breach of this agreement will be noted and acted upon by the broker or list owner. All rented lists contain a small number of names (called 'seeds') who feed back to the broker information on all mailings received.

Costs are usually quoted for a basic run of all names, or a specified proportion. Simple selections, such as postcode segmentation or *nth name*[†] sortation, will often be provided at the basic rate. Other selections will often attract additional charges.

[†]nth name is a simple method of randomizing selections. If you intend to rent 2,000 names from a list of 10,000 you should specify *every fifth name* – this ensures that any bias based on time or geography is removed from your selection. For example, if the list is kept in chronological order and you ask for the first 2,000 names, your mailing will go to the most recent or oldest customers – hardly an unbiased sample.

A large percentage of lists are held in geographical order and if you ask for the first 2,000 names these will all be based in the same part of the country – again this sample will not be representative of the total list.

These will be added to the basic cost, and typically would be £7–£10 per selection.

PRODUCTION

The physical production of a list on disk, tape or labels will be charged and added to the overall rental cost.

COMMISSION

The broker or manager will receive a commission on the rental price, usually 20% – this will already be built into the price quoted.

WHAT SELECTIONS CAN I MAKE?

There are many options – here are a few examples:

- **nth name** – as previously described, this is a process of selecting an unbiased sample from a list, e.g. to select a sample of 2,000 from a list of 8,000 you would specify *every fourth name*.

- **Geographic** – you may want to make selections based on postcodes, enabling you to concentrate on, or avoid, a particular area.

- **Address factors** – e.g. postcode areas can be analysed – it is possible to select households by Acorn, Mosaic and other categories.

- **Household composition** – families with children, multi-occupancies, single gender households and so on.

- **Buying behaviour** – products purchased, payment method and similar factors.

- **Job title/function** – this can be useful, but caution is needed especially when mailing small companies. Titles do not always accurately describe responsibilities and functions.

- **Names/titles** – some business lists may not include names – in this case there are two options:

❏ simply mail to the title or…

❝ ❏ identify the name, either by telephone or by reference to an outside database such as Dun & Bradstreet.

The second course can be expensive, but depending on the value of a response, it can be worthwhile. Using the telephone gives you an opportunity to identify the others in the decision making unit.

▷ **Industry sector/SIC** and so on – companies can be broadly qualified by industry sector (e.g. heavy engineering) or more specifically by Standard Industry Classification (SIC) code.

▷ **Company size** – may be available by number of employees or annual turnover.

▷ **Financial data** – additional information about companies can be obtained from Companies House or from one of the companies who take this basic data and supplement it with additional detail.

THE IMPORTANCE OF DE-DUPLICATION

If you are planning to mail one or more outside lists, plus your own customers and prospects, it is necessary to identify 'duplicates', i.e. people whose names appear more than once.

Lists from various sources and the names and addresses on your own list, can be run through a 'merge/purge' to highlight possible duplicates, which are then scrutinized and eliminated as necessary.

Your own list should also include addresses you do *not* wish to mail (e.g. people who owe you money, or who have asked not to be mailed).

WHERE TO GET YOUR LISTS DE-DUPLICATED

There are numerous bureaux who can take your own and a selection of external lists and carry out the de-duplication process for you. Most bureaux have very powerful equipment and lots of experience. This experience is very valuable and although a bureau will charge you a fee (generally hundreds rather than thousands of pounds) it can often be cost-effective.

The benefits of de-duplication are not purely financial however, a merge/purge run can save much customer irritation and also tell you something about the potential value of an external list.

For example a prospective list has greater potential:

▷ If it has zero, or very few *internal* duplicates, i.e. addresses appearing twice on the same list. This problem is by no means rare, but if a list is very 'clean', it is likely to be well managed and therefore more likely to be up-to-date.

▷ The higher the duplication with:

❑ your own best customer list
❑ the other candidate lists.

Names which are on all or several lists, are often the best names of all and some mailers actually single these out for special treatment, e.g. better offers and so on.

The addresses on different lists may well not be in the same format and some additional data-processing may be necessary. However, most bureaux cope very efficiently with this problem and a merge/purge run will usually be cost-effective.

> *De-duplication is important even if you are only planning to mail your own customers and prospects.*

Duplication can be very common, even within internal lists unless you have been very careful in checking each new name as it is added.

Some companies keep records by account numbers rather than customer names and addresses and this can lead to a high level of wastage and customer dissatisfaction.

The example opposite illustrates the importance of de-duplication and good database management – unless you check names as you add them to your database, your best customers will appear the most times on your list.

EXAMPLE

A large investment brokerage began to use direct mail regularly and it soon started to receive complaints about junk mail from its customers.

The main reason for the problem was that customer records were kept by account number and no de-duplication work had been carried out.

The brokerage dealt with some twenty different types of investment, therefore a customer investing in more than one type had a separate account number, and thus *a separate customer record for each type.*

A de-duplication run was organized and the brokerage found that its average customer held three accounts – the very best customers had twelve or more accounts.

In short, not only were many customers receiving more than one copy of the same mailing, the best customers were receiving the largest number of copies - more than twelve copies in the worst cases, so the very people they were most anxious to impress were receiving the most junk mail.

A BUYER'S CHECKLIST

When renting lists you need to be aware that, what seems to be a good fit to a list broker, may not always match your idea of precision targeting. You need to ask some questions to ensure suitability.

For example:

▷ **Source of names** – how did these names get onto the list? A list of people *interested in PC software* may have bought an office networking system, or attended a PC games exhibition. Are they there because they *did* something, or because they *are* something? If the list is a compilation, how up-to-date was the source data?

▷ **What did they do?** – are they buyers or enquirers? What do you want them to do?

▷ **Recency** – how recently did they take this action? The more recent the action, the better prospects they will be – unless they have just bought a competitive product.

▷ **Frequency** – how often do they do it?

▷ **Value** – how much do/did they spend? This can help you develop relevant offers.

▷ **Profile** – is there any profiling data you can match against that of your own best customers?

▷ **Other users**- who else mails this list? If it is regularly mailed by a competitor there is a good chance it will work for you.

▷ **How often is the list mailed?** – although it may seem odd, frequency of mailing does not seem to affect response. Indeed, the more frequently mailed lists seem to be the best. This is a 'chicken-and-egg' argument, of course, but a good list broker will ensure that a list is not over-mailed.

▷ **What selections are available?** – if you have been able to identify some key factors, like number of children, or company size, you need to know that the list can also be segmented in this way.

▷ **Updates** – how often is the list checked and updated, and when was the last time?

▷ **Future uses** – what are the conditions for future use? If you plan to follow up the mailing, either by mail or telephone, it is more cost-effective to negotiate the multiple use at the start. Remember, unless you arrange an alternative with the broker, you can only use the names and addresses once. Of course, once they respond to your own mailing, they can be added to your database and mailed without further consultation with the broker – subject to the requirements of the Data Protection Act (see Appendix 1).

▷ **Legal requirements** – you are entitled to expect a list supplier to have taken the necessary actions, but it is worth confirming that this has been done.

The examples of list datasheets over the following seven pages have been provided by Dudley Jenkins List Broking Limited and indicate the level of information you can expect from a list broker.

DUDLEY JENKINS *list broking* LTD

DATASHEET   1400

The Investor Register.
Shareholders Database.

Profile

A comprehensive database built with the direct mail advertiser in mind, The Investor Register is constructed from over 400 different share registers, giving comprehensive coverage across defined sectors. Selection opportunities offered by this impressive database are unique and have been designed for the promotion of almost any consumer product. High volume, credit worthy names are available for advertisers looking for large volumes, and the precision selection possibilities mean that specific, defined target markets can be accurately targeted to maximise response.

Charity rental for this list is £75.00 per 1,000 inclusive.

Reduced rental for volume - 10,000+ at £85.00 per 1,000.
25,000+ at £80.00 per 1,000.

Total Quantity: 1,657,041	DPR Number:	161187
Rental Cost: £90 per 1000	Postcoding Level:	100%
Minimum Order:	Warranties:	Yes
	MPS Cleaned:	Yes

Delivery Time: 10 days - will be charged at cost.

Selections Available

Description	Cost	Type	Notes
Nth	£0	per 1000	
Mailsort	£5	per 1000	
Gender	£5	per 1000	
Multis	£5	per 1000	
Geography	£5	per 1000	
Value	£5	per 1000	
Demographic	£15	per 1000	
Keycoding	£1	per 1000	

Output Media

Description	Cost	Type	Notes
S/A Labels	£5	per 1000	
Cheshire Labels	£0	per 1000	
Magnetic Tape	£20	Flat	

1400	Tel: 0171 407 4753 Fax: 0171 407 6294	Page 1

Figure 6.1

DUDLEY JENKINS *list broking* LTD

DATASHEET   I400

The Investor Register.
Shareholders Database.

Diskette		£35	Flat	

Selections

Type of Shareholding.

USM (unlisted securities)	63,076
Penny Shares	59,325
High performance stock	688,476
Green investors	115,530
Property investors	18,285
Incentive shareholders	68,444
BES (Business expansion schemes)	12,061
speculative investments	17,507
Blue chip	1,038,562
High dividend shares	48,908
Financial sector	68,281
Leisure sector	51,605
Service sector	725,295
Oil & gas sector	150,170
Third market	19,478
Privatisation issues	697,305
Investment trusts	61,420
Commodity investors	20,140
Ethical investors	203,702

Number of Shareholdings.

1	1,033,46	2	167381
3	23,579	4	23,579
5	11,446	6	5,989
7	3,149	8	1,745
9	1,023	9+	1,613

Aggregate Share Value.

£1 - £500	564,291	£501 - £1,000	237,508
£1,001 - £1,500	126,615	£,501 - £2,500	89,977
£2,501 - £5,000	95,890	£5,001 - £10,000	66,492
£10,001 - £25,000	51,935	£25,001 - £50,000	21,453
£50,001 - £100,000	13,104	£100,001 - £250,000	10,198
£250,001 -£500,000	3,572	£500,001 - £1m	1,450
£1m+	693		

Title Selection.

Mr	732,772	Mrs	373,743
Ms	20,197	Miss	60,953
Dr/Doctor	20,176	No title	13,038
Other known females	1,081	Military titles	3,222

I400	Tel: 0171 407 4753 Fax: 0171 407 6294	Page 2

Figure 6.1 (contd)

DUDLEY JENKINS *list broking* LTD

DATASHEET   P000

Pathfinder Companies & Executives Database.
Survey responders.

Profile

A list offering a new approach to business targeting. All data has been
almost entirely response generated through direct mail. Information has
been gained from a comprehensive survey completed by executive
secretaries/P.A.'s. A vast range of criteria is available covering almost
every aspect of business life. All data can be combined with other data
criteria on the Pathfinder database to ensure ultra-precise targeting.

Total Quantity: 35,692	DPR Number:	161187
Rental Cost: £100 per 1000	Postcoding Level:	95%
Minimum Order:	Warranties:	No
	MPS Cleaned:	No
Delivery Time: 7-10 days - will be charged at cost.		

Selections Available

Description	Cost	Type	Notes
Nth	£0	per 1000	
Mailsort	£3	per 1000	
Geography	£5	per 1000	
SIC	£0	per 1000	
No. Employees	£5	per 1000	
Job Function	£0	per 1000	
Influence	£20	per 1000	
Keycoding	£1	per 1000	

Output Media

Description	Cost	Type	Notes
S/A Labels	£5	per 1000	
Cheshire Labels	£0	per 1000	
Magnetic Tape	£20	Flat	
Diskette	£35	Flat	

Figure 6.1 (contd)

DUDLEY JENKINS *list broking* LTD

DATASHEET   P000

Pathfinder Companies & Executives Database.
Survey responders .

Selections

Type of company.
```
-----------------
Manuf-engineering  7,532   Manuf-processing    4,027
Construction       2,102   Wholesale distrib   1,778
Retail distribution1,578   Hotels/catering       478
Transport/freight  1,178   Financial services  2,635
Professional serv  3,993   Services to other   1,685
Locl government      659   Central government    115
Advertising/print  1,261   Other               6,671
```

Establishment Size.
```
--------------------
0-5            4,036   6-10              3,262
11-25          6,173   26-75             7,344
76-100         3,159   101-250           5,585
251-500        3,068   501-1000          1,672
1000-2000        740   2000+               653
```

Head Office @ £110.00 per 1,000   24,259

Sales Force Size @ £110.00 per 1,000 13,686 companies
```
-----------------
1-5            5,149   21-50             1,738
6-10           2,565   51-100              854
11-20          1,932   101+              1,438
```

Import/Export @ £110.00 per 1,000   23,819 companies
```
--------------
Western Europe  21,756   Africa            5,618
Eastern Europe   9,617   South Africa      5,899
Scandinavia      9,329   USA/Canada       13,637
Far East        10,216   S./C. America     6,153
Middle East      8,975   Australasia       8,057
```

Computer Users @ £110.00 per 1,000
```
----------------
Accounting      17,243   Desk top publishing5,713
Stock control   10,756   Design             4,847
Forcstng/budgets11,522   Manufacturing      3,518
Customer records13,655   Word processing   16,361
Personnel        9,912   Networking         4,335
Sales/marketing  9,284   Other              3,036
```

Type of Computer @ £110.00 per 1,000
```
--------------------
PC/Business sys 15,007   Mainframe          9,130
```

Figure 6.1 (contd)

DUDLEY JENKINS *list broking* LTD

DATASHEET		P000

Pathfinder Companies & Executives Database.
Survey responders.

```
Other Facilities @ £110.00 per 1,000
----------------
Vending machine   10,492    Staff restaurant   6,404
Social club        5,441    Private health sch12,110
Pension scheme    15,565    Donate to charity 14,067
```

Job Function	Director	Manager
MD/partner/owner	24,709	-
Publicity/marketing/advert	1,473	1,332
Sales	1,975	1,848
Production/manuafacturing	794	613
Works/factory	199	438
Finance/company secretary	2,985	1,075
Personnel/training	577	1,054
Technical/R & D/design	665	579
Office/administration	320	932
General/commercial	399	1,044
Computer/DP/MIS	212	575
Transport/fleet	86	193
Purchasing/contracts	175	363
Export/import	134	181
Other	2,302	2,883
Totals	37,005	13,110

```
Motoring @ £130.00 per 1,000
----------------------------
Private car                33,178   Company car 41,243
Choice of company car      32,346

Business Travel - method @ £150.00 per 1,000

Business Travel - Frequency per year @ £180.00 per 1,000.
--------------------------------------
By Car/  1 - 10    11,504    By Air-UK/  1 - 10  18,526
        11 - 50    15,209               11 - 50   5,486
         50+       19,128               50+          811

By Rail/ 1 - 10    20,208    By Air-Foreign/1 - 10   18,816
        11 - 50     8,624                   11 - 50  10,135
         50+        1,479                    50+      1,297

Destination of Business Travel @ £160.00 per 1,000.
--------------------------------------------------
Western Europe   12,881   Africa                      841
Eastern Europe    3,718   South Africa                968
Scandinavia       3,423   USA/Canada                7,328
Far East          3,454   South/Central America     1,000
Middle East       1,975   Australasia               1,457
```

P000	Tel: 0171 407 4753 Fax: 0171 407 6294	Page 3

Figure 6.1 (contd)

DUDLEY JENKINS *list broking* LTD

DATASHEET   P000

Pathfinder Companies & Executives Database.
Survey responders .

Usual Class of Travel. @ £180.00 per 1,000.

First class	4,961	Business Class	13,789
Economy	6,504		

Hotels @ £180.00 per 1,000.

Average Number of Nights Stay per Trip	UK	Overseas
1 - 2	34,757	8,290
3 - 5	6,872	11,740
6 - 8	619	3,966
9 - 11	150	1,275
12 - 14	96	955
15+	171	575

Purchasing Influence.@ £120.00 per 1,000.

Stationery/print	14,443	Courier/despatch serv	7,803
Typewriters	14,941	Staff - permenant	29,067
WP equipment	20,277	Staff - temporary	20,264
Computers	24,882	Staff - training	21,361
Computer supplies	14,640	Staff - incentives	17,374
Computer software	17,854	Marketing/PR	18,565
Office furniture	24,384	Premises management	15,307
Fax/photocopy equip	19,074	Company conferences	15,564
Airline tickets	14,015	Car Hire	11,234
Cleaning services	9,953	Vans/lorries	9,564
Catering services	7,482	Car/telephone	15,766
Motor cars	24,924	Portable telephone	11,933
Telephone equipment	20,364	Paging equipment	8,939
Company gifts	18,587	Company insurance	17,485
Hotel bookings	12,003	Vending machines	7,621
Corporate hospitality	14,326	Audio/visual equipment	9,708
Factory/prodc'n equip	13,286	Health & safety prods	12,515
Post room equipment	8,409	Security services	14,407

Geographical Breakdown - Companies.

Avon	594	Bedfordshire	366
Berkshire	1,030	Buckinghamshire	667
Cambridgeshire	534	Cheshire	793
Cleveland	206	Cornwall	133
Cumbria	213	Derbyshire	524
Devon	488	Dorset	517
Co. Durham	255	Essex	956
Glos	409	Hampshire	268
Herefordshire	87	Hertfordshire	975
North Humberside	295	South Humberside	170
Isle of Wight	74	Kent	1,118
Lancashire	1,828	Leicestershire	608

P000   Tel: 0171 407 4753   Fax: 0171 407 6294   Page 4

Figure 6.1 (contd)

DUDLEY JENKINS *list broking* LTD

DATASHEET   P000

Pathfinder Companies & Executives Database.
Survey responders .

Lincolnshire	368	London	4,250
Merseyside	524	Middlesex	921
Norfolk	434	Northamptonshire	388
Northumberland	104	Nottinghamshire	573
Oxon	488	Salop	223
Somerset	266	Staffordshire	497
Suffolk	419	Surrey	1,270
East Sussex	324	West Sussex	459
Tyne and Wear	499	Warwickshire	327
West Midlands	1,911	Wiltshire	383
Worcs	355	North Yorkshire	338
South Yorkshire	669	West Yorkshire	1,360
Wales	1,065	Scotland	2,877
Northern Ireland	420	Eire	63
Channel Islands	34	Isle of Man	19

Geographical Breakdown - executives.

Avon	821	Bedfordshire	516
Berkshire	1,493	Buckinghamshire	1,014
Cambridgeshire	715	Cheshire	1,070
Cleveland	264	Cornwall	180
Cumbria	285	Derbyshire	726
Devon	655	Dorset	750
Co. Durham	343	Essex	1,323
Glos	581	Hampshire	1,824
Herefordshire	129	Hertfordshire	1,423
North Humberside	443	South Humberside	232
Isle of Wight	104	Kent	1,539
Lancashire	2,488	Leicestershire	885
Lincolnshire	518	London	6,120
Merseyside	747	Middlesex	1,467
Norfolk	570	Northamptonshire	534
Northumberland	141	Nottinghamshire	781
Oxon	710	Salop	311
Somerset	336	Staffordshire	714
Suffolk	583	Surrey	2,016
East Sussex	442	West Sussex	683
Tyne and Wear	700	Warwickshire	467
West Midlands	2,672	Wiltshire	544
Worcs	474	North Yorkshire	471
South Yorkshire	929	West Yorkshire	1,889
Wales	1,374	Scotland	3,801
Northern Ireland	559	Eire	27
Channel Islands	39	Isle of Man	23

P000	Tel: 0171 407 4753 Fax: 0171 407 6294	Page 5

Figure 6.1 (contd)

SUMMARY

A very common source of names and addresses is the external list. This may be rented from the owner or, more probably, from a list broker.

To get the best from a broker, you need to have a very clear idea of the target you are aiming for. Good brokers will be happy to discuss your ideas and help you define your target.

There are broadly two kinds of rented list:

▷   Those who *did* something — bought a product, booked a seminar, attended an exhibition.

▷   Those who *are* something — architects, accountants, plumbers and so on.

If you can relate your requirements to your target's previous actions, in other words, if what you want them to do is the same thing they did to get on the list, the first category will be much better for you.

A list which is mail-responsive will be best of all since the names on this list have actually responded by mail, rather than just expressed an interest in something.

Segmentation is often a cost-effective process when arranging to use an outside list. If your customer analysis tells you that only households with young children will be interested in your product, specify this to your list broker. The chances are that the list can be segmented by making 'selections' enabling you to mail only those households which match your criteria.

Selections are just as valuable in renting business lists – you may be able to select by company size, number of locations, date of financial year end and so on.

There will be extra charges for selections, but these are quite small and the increase in cost-efficiency is often very worthwhile.

De-duplication is a very important process for direct mailers. It reduces costs, but perhaps even more important, it prevents customer annoyance. *De-duplication helps you stamp out junk mail.*

WHAT TO DO NEXT

Contact the DMA for the addresses of their List Broker Members.

Write to some brokers for details of the lists which cover your market.

Self-test questionnaire

1   Write a brief, explaining to a list broker precisely who you are trying to reach.

Make up your own headings and sections, thinking carefully about what information the broker will need to produce some good lists for you.

When you have finished, compare your briefing list with the list given on page 215.

Part Three

Communications

7   The importance of an offer

> In this chapter, I will discuss the importance of developing an offer for your product or service.
>
> The offer is the sum total of the ways you present your sales proposition to your customer or prospect.
>
> It is that group of features and benefits which a customer will get in return for giving you an order. Although price offers are very common, an offer does not necessarily include a discount, nor is it necessarily 'promotional'.

Your offer can comprise any combination of elements:

- **The promise of the solution to a specific problem**. If you have the answer your audience is desperately looking for the only offer you may need to make is *Here it is*.

- **A specific (sometimes timed), promotional device** e.g. an incentive or discount.

- **Quality** – the best available. If you use this claim, make sure (a) that it's true, and (b) that quality is important to your prospects. See the Rolls–Royce example on page 128.

- **Value** – best at this price. This works well for many marketers, but make sure you can sustain your claims when the competition reacts.

- **Availability** – only from ourselves. If you have exclusivity on a popular product, you may not need to make any more detailed offer than *now available from…*

- **Free trial or demonstration** – don't take my word for it, try it yourself in your own home (or office). Such an offer is not only attractive, it is very convincing to prospects.

CASE STUDY – TEDDY BEAR TIMES

Publishing director Lyn Vowles calls it *The magazine that's packed full of news and views for you and your bear.* This unusual glossy magazine, published six times a year, was launched eleven years ago and is avidly read by some 25,000 teddy bear fanatics.

Specialist publications are totally reliant on their subscription base for survival – these determine economical print runs and guarantee future income.

When it comes to marketing, subscription renewals have a high priority and Lyn 'leaves no pun unturned' to maintain the warm feeling that exists between the magazine and its readers – mainly females aged twenty upwards.

This year's 'Early Bear Offer' was sent out with a letter beginning *A beary great opawtunity to renew your subscription.* The offers are interesting and very appropriate:

▷ Renew your subscription early and we'll send you this beautiful Colourbox bear. He's called Damien and normally sells for £6.75

▷ Renew early, for two years and get a £5 M&S voucher as well.

Responses were still coming in as this book was written, but suffice to say the publishers are 'very encouraged'.

This example illustrates some important points:

1 offers work better if they have a strong relevance to the recipient

2 double or multiple offers can be very effective

3 extended subscription offers are especially valuable for publishers because they provide

 ❑ very good cash flow
 ❑ reduced costs – no need for renewal mailings next year
 ❑ extended commitment which makes long-term planning easier.

EXAMPLE – RESPISAM NEBULISER

A nebuliser is a unit designed to relieve breathing difficulties in patients with asthma, bronchitis and similar conditions.

When you are selling specialist medical equipment nothing can beat a professional recommendation. The target of this campaign is GPs and the objective is to get them to recommend the nebuliser to their patients.

The suppliers – MG Electric – decided they would initially mail local GPs with a powerful offer.

The pack outlined the unique benefits of this portable unit and offered doctors the opportunity of 'winning' a nebuliser for a free trial period.

The mailing was sent to 422 doctors and they received ninety-five replies – more than 22% response.

Marketing assistant Gillian Hibbins explained *'A sale can only be achieved if a doctor has a patient requiring a nebuliser at the time, so we designed our campaign to keep the product at the front of the doctor's mind'.*

After the initial mailing came a series of follow-up mailings, announcing which practices had 'won' a free nebuliser and enclosing discount vouchers to be given to patients who wanted to buy their own machine. Doctors were also provided with posters for their surgeries, to maintain awareness.

Remembering the value of integration, Gillian issued a press release to coincide with the mailings, gaining valuable additional publicity.

A final word from Gillian *'The campaign has already paid for itself and more orders are coming in all the time'.*

➤ **Reassurance** – if you can feature a well known person or company saying 'This is what it did for me/my company' it has much more credibility than the same claim made by you.

You should always make the strongest guarantee you can. You may be surprised, but very few people will take advantage of you.

Customers respond well to offers of help via telephone helplines, free consultancy, and so on.

➤ **Superior performance and/or technical superiority** – preferably backed up by 'expert' testimony.

You do not always have to think in strictly promotional terms – simply telling the right story, in the right way, to the right person will often be sufficient.

Some of the above offers are very specific and promotional – others can be a part of a promotional message too, but remember that they must also link to your longer term positioning.

What is positioning?

For people new to marketing, positioning can be a difficult concept to grasp. Positioning is not something you do to your product although, depending on the positioning you choose, it may require you to make changes so your product fulfils your claims for it.

Positioning is the overall impression you wish to place in the mind of your prospect once they have read your letter or advertisement.

Whole books have been written about positioning, yet for the new marketer, the concept can be made very simple.

Your mailing will have described the benefits which your product will bring to the prospect, but something more is needed. What can you say that states very succinctly what this product means to the prospect?

Let's start by looking at the positioning of a motor car. Would you write the same advertisement for a Rolls-Royce and a Ford Fiesta? Clearly, the answer is no. Yet they both perform the same job – that of transporting someone from A to B.

If a Fiesta costs £10,000 and a Rolls costs £100,000, why would anyone buy a Rolls? The answer is, that apart from the basic transport function, there are additional factors in play:

- prestige
- power
- luxury
- ostentation

and several more. So a person buying a Rolls-Royce is making statements to the world at large. *I am important. I am wealthy. I am powerful. I enjoy luxury.*

Now, there are other cars available which can match the Rolls-Royce in many departments e.g. speed, acceleration, power, comfort, but they are not Rolls-Royces and the difference is positioning.

Some advertising agency account handlers in briefing their copywriters, are faced with the question *What impression do I want to leave in the mind of my reader?* The copywriter is looking for a positioning statement and in answering this question the account manager is likely to use an analogy. One of the most frequently used is:

If this product were a motor car what would it be?

This simple analogy enables the copywriter to get a good feeling for what is required in terms of quality, reliability, efficiency and so on.

When establishing positioning, it is not enough to simply make a claim. The positioning you choose must be credible, defensible against your competitors and affordable. It must also be marketable.

EXAMPLE

In the early 1990s a well known manufacturer of PCs when asked the above question answered, *Rolls-Royce.*

The company *did* have a reputation for excellent build quality and reliability and, in the booming 1980s, this was enough to keep it at the top of the market.

By the early 1990s two things had happened:

1   buyers were more knowledgeable and capable of comparing alternative PCs

2   the recession had taken hold and companies were much more price conscious.

A potential buyer asked one of its salespersons *'Why should I pay £2,750 for your 386 PC when I can get one from AN Other with the same chip, the same amount of RAM, and the same size hard disk for only £900?'*

The salesperson, trained to sell on the Rolls-Royce platform, sneered at the question and said *'If I drop my company's processor on the floor I can pick it up, plug it in and carry on working. Try that with the AN Other machine and you will need a dustpan and brush – it will fall to bits!'*

The prospect replied *'But I don't often drop computers on the floor and in any case, I have a good insurance policy. What's more I can buy two AN Other machines, keep one in reserve and still have £950 in the bank.'*

The salesperson failed to close the deal and his company got into serious trouble before it realized the flaw in its positioning. It established its positioning as the Rolls-Royce of the PC market in a boom, when buyers put quality ahead of price. It became out of touch with its marketplace and did not notice how customer buying behaviour was changing.

Its Rolls-Royce positioning was credible in terms of what was delivered but it had not noticed that its customers had become more interested in Ford Escorts – rugged, reliable machines with equally good after-sales service, but without the luxury price ticket.

To sum up, the positioning you choose must be:

1   **Credible** – the claims you make must be believable and true.

2   **Deliverable** – you must be able to fulfil your promises or you will never make a second sale and, as we have discussed already, repeat sales are easier to make and tend to be more profitable.

3   **Sustainable** – if you make a claim that you are better value than competitor X, can you sustain this claim if X reduces its prices?

4   **Marketable** – in other words, are people buying what you are selling? In a recession your prospects may have different priorities. You must keep in touch with what is current in your marketplace.

YOUR OFFER SHOULD BE LINKED TO YOUR OBJECTIVE

Is your mailing designed to sell your product direct or generate leads for further action? If the latter, do you want 'loose' or 'tight' leads?

A 'loose' lead is one that has been told very little about the product or the price – just the benefits. Loose leads do not convert as well as tight leads, but you do get more of them. A 'tight' lead is one that has been given the full story at the start – these leads are not so plentiful, but they tend to convert more readily.

For example, a company selling language courses could use an offer which promises *In one month you could be speaking French like a native – send for your FREE information pack*, without giving very much more detail. This would attract a high volume of response, but once the prospects realized that they had to spend £3,000 on a four-week 'total immersion' course, very few would actually buy.

An alternative approach might be to ask a question something like *Would you be prepared to give up an entire month in order to speak fluent French?*

A third approach could mention the £3,000 price tag.

> *The latter two offers would produce much less response of course, but the conversion level would be higher.*

There is no golden rule about loose or tight leads. You must test alternatives and use your judgement to decide which is right for your product and your business situation.

HOW CAN YOU MAKE YOUR OFFER MORE ATTRACTIVE?

One of the key words is relevance – if your offer is seen to be relevant to a prospect's needs or wants, or at the very least interesting, it will be considered seriously.

To achieve relevance you must try to see your product from the customer's point of view. Transport managers do not buy a truck lubricant because it is a high tech product, they buy it because it reduces engine wear and maintenance costs.

In other words, they do not buy features, but benefits. A feature of a gateleg table is that it folds – the benefit is that it fits into a smaller space.

> *If you express to a genuine prospect, at the right time, the real benefits your product will bring, you have the basis of your offer*

PROMOTIONAL OFFERS

To many people the word 'offer' conjures up visions of sale tickets saying *1/2 price* or *50% off* and these are certainly offers of a kind.

Do such tactics work? Are people attracted by such claims or does their suspicion prevent them from 'taking advantage'?

The answers to these questions can be quite surprising to those who have not tested the fine details of offer variations.

EXAMPLE

If we were to test the following two messages at the top of a letter which would produce the most response?

▷ **50% off**
▷ **Buy one get one free**

Well, even for products where one would normally order a single item, the *Buy one get one free* offer tends to produce more response (some companies have experienced increases of 40% or more).

The word free *often has a dramatic effect.*

EXAMPLE

In an advertisement for a new translation of the Bible the following headlines were tested:

▷ **Announcing an important revision of the Bible**
▷ **Most Important Bible News in 300 years**

The second headline produced twice as many enquiries as the first.

The key word here is news.

EXAMPLE

In America, a well-known book club tested the following offers:

▷ **Any four of these books for only $5**

▷ **Any three of these books for only $5 – get one free**

Although these two offers are identical in all but presentation, the second produced twice as many orders as the first.

Again the word free *had a dramatic effect.*

PRESENTATION IS IMPORTANT TOO

So, an offer will be more or less successful not only according to content, but also to presentation.

SHOULD EVERYONE MAKE DISCOUNT OFFERS?

Not everyone can, or should, make discount offers. Sometimes the impression you will want to give, will be one of quality rather than low cost and in such cases, an aggressive price offer could even work against you.

Therefore, when considering your offer, you should also think carefully about how it fits with your positioning.

As we have seen, it is possible to make offers more attractive by offering discounts, or even by simply using words like 'New' or 'Free'.

Do not be put off by the word *free* – it need not imply cheap gimmicks or costly incentives. Many people are attracted by offers of free advice or information.

The example opposite illustrates that another way of improving the attractiveness of your offer, is to study the buying process and see how you can 'break the chain' by getting in first.

EXAMPLE

A few years ago a paint manufacturer attracted a huge response to press advertisements by offering a set of free booklets covering such issues as:

▷ **How to prepare for decorating your home**

▷ **How to select the right paint**

▷ **How to use colours effectively (making low rooms lighter, high rooms more cosy and so on)**

▷ **How to mix and match paints and fabrics**

This campaign enabled them to pre-empt the normal buying process by:

▷ **Identifying those currently interested in decorating**

▷ **Getting colour cards into potential customers' hands before they visited the store**

USING PRIZE DRAWS

These often work well and you don't need to offer a £100,000 prize. Some prize draws have been known to double response – even when the only prize was a free meal for two or six bottles of wine. Bear in mind, though, that it is illegal to place a condition on entry with a prize draw – so you can't say *Only open to anyone who orders this product*. In fact you are obliged to tell people that no purchase is necessary for entry.

The law is clear, but the interpretation is rather vague, so although a prize draw must be open to everyone, not just the people you decide to mail, many mailers get round this by a form of 'weasel' saying something like: *Return this form to see if you have won a prize* or *Call this number to enter the draw*.

The main benefit of prize draws – that they increase response – must be balanced against the impression you will give to your readers.

COMPETITIONS

Where you can introduce a requirement for some skill to be employed you can run a competition, e.g. *Place the following items in the order in which you think the US President would choose them.*

With a competition you are allowed to apply conditions, such as *Only open to customers sending two proofs of purchase with their entry forms,* or *Open to people placing an order between now and the end of January.*

In a competition the prize generally needs to be rather more substantial than a few bottles of wine, given that you are asking for an order and asking the respondents to rack their brains. However, judging by some recent competitions, the amount of brain power required to satisfy the law is fairly minimal, so the amount of work required can be fairly small.

For instance, most people would have no difficulty in matching the Eiffel Tower with Paris, and the Empire State Building with New York!

DO INCENTIVES WORK IN BUSINESS MARKETING?

The answer to this question is, as usual, yes and no!

There are broadly two ways of using incentives:

- in return for a purchase
- in return for a trial.

The former works quite well in consumer marketing, but is a high risk strategy when marketing to large businesses.

There are many businesses which flatly refuse to accept any form of consideration in return for placing orders and, while this can be understood, a sensible seller can often find a way of offering an inducement which does not contravene the regulations in force.

- You could offer an **incentive for a no obligation free trial** – this does not compromise the company executive, but is still frowned upon by many large corporations.

- You could offer an **incentive in the form of free supplies** e.g. rent this photocopier and we will give you a month's supply of paper and toner. This, not surprisingly, is more acceptable to many companies.

You must decide what is right for your product and your marketplace. Remember too, that your promotional strategy will affect your positioning in the marketplace. It would be futile to adopt a high quality positioning and offer a cheap free gift to respondents.

BALANCING RESPONSE, CONVERSION AND LONG-TERM DEVELOPMENT

There are numerous ways of increasing response and Chapter 8 gives details of some techniques which have worked for many marketers. But beware of giving the wrong impression in the quest for higher responses. For example:

▷ The more powerful your claims and your incentives, the more response you will receive.

▷ However, unless your product lives up to the claims, you will suffer in three ways:

 ❑ you will have a higher-than-expected level of returned goods

 ❑ you will have difficulty in selling anything else to these particular respondents

 ❑ disappointed prospects will tell several people of their experience, losing you an unknown amount of future business

If you use a two-stage technique, i.e. sending further information before you ask for an order, your percentage conversion-to-sale will reduce. This is a balancing act – the stronger offer will undoubtedly increase enquiries – you need to identify the point at which you maximize responses while not damaging your conversion rate too much.

Hard-sell techniques generally (but not always) increase response, but you must give some thought to the majority of people who received your mailing, but did not respond:

▷ How many of them read it?

▷ How many intended to respond and forgot?

▷ How many responded?

> ▷ How many read it and, in the process, changed their minds about your company?
>
> ▷ How many of these now think more of you?

HARD-SELL WORKS – BUT...?

Here is another balancing act you must consider – the harder you sell the more likely you are to irritate some of your readers.

One of the most powerful selling weapons is the *door-to-door salesman*, but he also attracts the most disfavour.

Next on the list comes the *telephone salesperson* – the more powerful the technique, the more people resent it being used against them.

This same principle applies in *direct mail*. Some of the world's most successful marketing organizations use very hard-sell mailings, attracting huge responses, but also much criticism.

Here's a final example – a case study showing the value of good, well targeted, relevant incentive offers.

WESTMORELAND GARAGE/COLTSFORD MILL

It's not often you get a free meal for two when you have your car serviced, but if you're a customer of Westmoreland Garage in Bromley, that's exactly the deal.

And why not, when the owner of the garage is also the owner of Coltsford Mill, an olde worlde restaurant in a converted water mill.

Roger Bruce is passionate about direct mail. As he says '*You simply have to keep in touch with your customers or business just disappears*'. And Roger certainly keeps in touch. At the garage, his 8,000 strong database, built-up over twenty years, allows him to mail not only timely, personally targeted MOT and service reminders, but also imaginative special offers every month.

Coltsford Mill boasts ten acres of fishing, five acres of lakes, and is dedicated to hunting, shooting and fishing for plump brown and rainbow trout.

Roger therefore sends frequent, well-targeted mailings featuring corporate hospitality days, trout fishing days, special events, theme days, special menus and numerous offers in partnership with Diners Club.

Until recently, Roger kept the two ventures decidedly separate. But his first attempt at cross-merchandising has worked extremely well, motivating many motorists to sample the delights of dinner at his restaurant. And vice versa.

Asked to qualify the success of his recent joint mailing, Roger got quite excited '*We're barely two months into the programme, yet the response is already around 7.5%. However that's not the true figure, because customers are pinning up the mailing on their notice boards, to redeem against their next service, so the final response could be as high as 20%.*'

SUMMARY

Once you have identified the right target for your mailing the most important element is your proposition or offer. An offer can be defined as:

what the customer gets in return for placing an order.

This definition indicates the breadth of options open to you in constructing an offer. You can offer one or a combination of things such as:

- ▷ **Prestige** – *only this product can make this statement about you*
- ▷ **Problem solving** – a powerful promise, if it is credible
- ▷ **Availability** – *exclusively from...*
- ▷ **Price** – a discount or simply the cheapest price on the market
- ▷ **Value** – not necessarily the cheapest but the best value
- ▷ **Quality** – superior performance or technical superiority – perhaps justifying a premium

▷ **Service** – faster delivery or a higher level of customer care

▷ **Added value** – perhaps a free advisory service?

▷ **Reassurance and security** – the safe option for buyers

▷ **Involvement** – in a competition or prize draw

▷ **Personal gain** – incentives, competitions and so on.

This is not intended to be an exhaustive list – simply an indication of how widely you must think when planning your offer.

WHAT TO DO NEXT

Study the direct mail you have received recently – refer to your guard book. Compare the offers and decide how good they are.

Self-test questionnaire

? Construct an offer for your product or service. Now work out how its content and presentation might differ according to whether you are writing to:

▷ suspects (e.g. on a rented list)

▷ warm prospects – people who have previously enquired or who have been recommended to you by a customer

▷ previous customers who have not bought in the past year

▷ existing good customers.

---

8 How to increase responses through more effective writing and design

A question I am often asked is *'Why do some mailings work well, and others fail to meet their response targets?'*

In earlier chapters, I have emphasized that the three most important factors in the success of a mailing are:

▷ targeting the right person (list)
▷ saying the right thing (offer), and
▷ achieving the right timing.

So, in answering the above question, I am going to assume that your targeting, offer and timing have all been planned correctly.

If you get these three right, your mailing should not be a disaster, even if it does not produce quite the response you hoped for.

The objective of this chapter is to show you how to turn an average response into a good response. And this is where a fourth factor (creative treatment) comes into play.

THE POWER OF GOOD CREATIVE WORK

Once you have the first three factors in place, it is possible to achieve major gains in response through changes in copy style or length, variations in envelope design and other purely creative factors.

STEP ONE – DEFINE YOUR OBJECTIVE

Before you can design a suitable mailing you need to be clear about your objective. Do you want to:

▷ sell your product or service direct, i.e. ask for an order now?

▷ persuade prospects to send for more information?

▷ ask for a sales person to visit?

▷ encourage them to visit a retail site?

▷ invite them to an event?

The answers to these questions will help you decide how much information the mailing needs to contain. You will normally need longer copy to generate a direct order than an enquiry, but you also have to *consider the prospect's knowledge of your specific product and the product field in general.*

EXAMPLE

Situation 1

If you are offering car tyres direct to motorists your copy could be quite short. Prospects will want to know price, quality and any special features which may give your product a competitive edge.

You may, for instance, have patented a unique design which extends mileage or reduces petrol consumption. This will obviously be a major feature of your mailing. But you will not need to explain why car tyres are useful things to have.

Situation 2

If, on the other hand, you are selling a piece of software which increases the capacity of a PC hard disk by compressing data in a new and foolproof way, you are likely to have to sell the concept, as well as the product.

The second situation will require longer copy and perhaps more reassurance than the first.

STEP TWO – THE PACK OUTLINE

Reviewing your objective in this way will enable you to develop a mailing outline under the following headings:

- **Objective**
- **Target audience**
- **Offer**
- **Timing**
- **Creative approach**...
  - ❏ Message
  - ❏ Envelope
  - ❏ Letter
  - ❏ Leaflet 1
  - ❏ Leaflet 2 (if required)
  - ❏ Reply form
  - ❏ Reply method(s)
- **Despatch programme**
- **Response handling**
- **Follow-up**.

Let's work through this outline for the two situations mentioned above:

SITUATION 1 – CAR TYRES DIRECT

Target

- Motorists owning their own cars
  - ❏ rented list
  - ❏ also a two-stage press campaign (enquiry generating).

Offer

- Prize draw – win a new car
- Strong guarantee of quality, longer life and money saving
- Special price for buying two or more tyres.

Timing

▷ Relating to existing mileage and tyre buying pattern

▷ You don't have this for the rented list so you decide to send the one-stage mailing in June to link with many motorists' holiday planning

▷ Press enquirers will have told you their annual mileage when replying. You can adjust your copy, and perhaps your price offer, according to this information.

Creative

▷ **Message** – relating to price offers, guarantee and prize draw. Need for visual demonstration of new design features

▷ **Envelope** – message relating to money saving and prize draw opportunity

▷ **Letter** – laser printed with name and personalized salutation – fairly short – leading on cost savings and prize draw – reply form attached (perforated) to enable laser personalization of both items

▷ **Leaflet 1** – pictures and diagrams showing features and product in use – well known drivers if possible

▷ **Leaflet 2** – testimonials for reassurance. Themes of safety, economy and reliability

▷ **Reply form** – laser printed – attached to letter by perforation

▷ **Reply methods** – reply-paid envelope (Freepost), and telephone number (Freefone).

Despatch programme

Details of quantities, filling and despatch details, any terms negotiated with Royal Mail and so on.

Response handling

Estimates of responses from Press – for production of response packs and planning/handling requirements (data capture, addressing and despatch of packs and so on). Estimates of responses from mailing – for order handling and despatch of products.

Follow-up

Plans for further action to remind non-respondents, non-converted enquirers and so on.

You may also decide to send mailings to company fleet managers, independent garages etc. If so, your offers, timing, creative content and response handling plans will vary to suit the circumstances.

SITUATION 2 – NEW SOFTWARE PRODUCTS

Target

Selected names from the list of people who bought a GUI (graphical user interface – e.g. Windows 95) from you in the past year.

You know from the information they gave you on their previous order forms that they have smaller hard disks i.e. 120 to 210 megabytes. They are thus likely to suffer from a shortage of hard disk space.

Offer

▷ Increase your hard disk space without changing computer

▷ Thirty-day money back guarantee.

Timing

No specific timing constraints – mail a.s.a.p.

Creative

▷ **Message** – *How to increase your available hard disk space without changing your computer*. You will also need some reassurance because of problems with similar products in the past.

▷ **Envelope** – message relating to increased disk capacity and perhaps, thirty-day guarantee. Perhaps you could use part of the quotation from Michael Dell, mentioned later.

> **Letter** – laser printed with name and personalized salutation – at least two pages long – leading on quotation from computer personality (Michael Dell?) about how good and reliable this new software is and how Dell install it as standard on new machines. Laser personalized attached reply form, with bold reminder of 30-day money-back guarantee

> **Leaflet** – pictures showing users and their quotes. Charts showing increases in performance due to being able to keep all files on HD rather than having to use floppies. Quotes from PC magazines who have reviewed the product

> **Reply form** – laser printed – attached to letter by perforation

> **Reply methods** – reply paid envelope (Freepost) and telephone number (Freefone).

Despatch programme

Details of quantities, filling and despatch details, any terms negotiated with Royal Mail and so on.

Response handling

Estimates of responses to ensure handling capacity and stock levels are adequate.

Follow-up

Plans for follow-up of non-respondents. Possible test of telephone follow-up to best prospects (e.g. perhaps those who have ordered more than once previously).

> *The outlines featured here would not be adequate as creative briefs but are simply to help you devise a brief without forgetting any major feature.*

The finished brief will contain much more details about the prospect, the product, the offer and so on. See page 219.

Now let's see how Chris King plans *his* mailings.

CASE STUDY – KING'S COFFEE

Chris King sells coffee to offices, factories and industrial parks in Surbiton and surrounding areas. When it comes to his business Chris has two passions – first class coffee and first class service.

Chris turned to direct mail after receiving a special offer from Royal Mail and he now uses nothing else. One of the things he appreciates is the way someone from the Royal Mail came round to explain the do's and don'ts of using mailings.

As a former accountant he also appreciates the cost-effectiveness of direct mail and the way it enables him to control response.

Chris says *'Like a lot of businesses, we need a constant supply of new leads, but with limited resources we can only properly handle a certain number of enquiries each week'.*

By disciplining themselves to send out a controlled number of mailings each week they gain two advantages:

▷ The quantity of leads received is manageable

▷ Each lead can be followed up quickly ensuring maximum conversion.

They find that promotional offers work well for them. Their current offer of a bottle of champagne to every new customer, is particularly popular.

Their results reflect this popularity – mailings produce up to 8% response and King's are successfully expanding their product range into other drinks, vending machines, various ingredients and a range of janitorial supplies (in case you're wondering, that means toilet rolls, bin liners, kitchen rolls, and so on).

The above case demonstrates a number of important points, but especially underlines the need to estimate responses and ensure you have the means to handle them efficiently.

A badly handled enquiry can do more than lose you a single sale – it may have been your first contact with your biggest ever customer.

145

What do you want to achieve with your mailing? You want to:

▷ **Attract the prospect's attention** – mainly through use of the envelope and letter headline

▷ **Confirm the relevance of your offer** – by immediately relating your attention-getting statements to the reader's situation

▷ **Convince the prospect of the benefits** – by clear explanation, demonstration and testimonial quotes

▷ **Confirm the action required** – by using well-designed forms and clear instructions – frequent reminders can help too

▷ **Close the sale** – by a powerful final paragraph and a PS reminding readers of the major benefits

▷ **Take the order** – by supplying a completed order form, which can be simply signed and returned in a reply paid envelope. Don't forget...

    ❑ the option of a free telephone number
    ❑ perhaps a fax order form as well.

WHAT ARE THE ESSENTIAL PARTS OF A MAILING PACK?

You may find it helpful to think of a mailing as a sales visit. You arrange to see the right person (by selecting the right names), you think carefully about what sales argument will interest that person (the offer), you try to establish an appropriate time for the visit, then you go along and have your discussion.

The face-to-face discussion is your mailing pack and the elements in that discussion are as follows.

THE INTRODUCTION – ENVELOPE AND LETTER HEADLINE

First your envelope:

▷ Is it impressive? It doesn't need to be covered in starbursts and colour pictures but it will need to stand out amongst a pile of envelopes, especially if you are mailing a business person.

⮞ Does it carry a message? An envelope message is not essential but many companies who test the various elements of a mailing continue to use envelope messages, even in business mailings.

⮞ Is the message interesting or intriguing? The purpose of the message is to attract the interest of your prospect. Many people, most of whom I suspect have not tested this technique, make the assumption that an envelope message will signal 'junk mail' and therefore consign the mailing to the waste bin, unopened.

EXAMPLE

One day, when I was running an advertising agency, my media director showed me a large (C4) brown envelope which she, and each of her five assistants, had received that morning. It carried an address label and a long message:

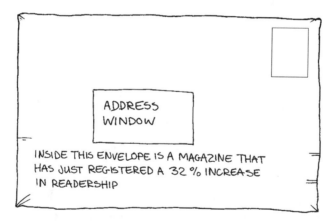

ADDRESS
WINDOW

INSIDE THIS ENVELOPE IS A MAGAZINE THAT
HAS JUST REGISTERED A 32 % INCREASE
IN READERSHIP

On an average day, each member of the media department received between ten and fifteen mailings. Intrigued by this envelope, I asked each of them which of their mailings they had opened first that day.

Without exception they had opened this envelope first. Why?

Because it promised news which would help them do their jobs better.

Those who are not attracted by the envelope message will quickly realize that this mailing is not for them and will of course throw it away unopened. Is this a problem? If they are not interested in your offer and proposition is there any advantage in getting them to start reading your letter, and then binning it? Probably not.

One suspects that people (especially business people) like envelope messages because they save time. It is easy to sort the mail into piles headed 'interesting' and 'bin'. This may be the reason why envelope messages so often increase response.

Your letter – the most important piece

Remembering our analogy of a sales visit, it is quite important not to start off on the wrong foot. Make sure, therefore, that you do not get the name, the gender, or the salutation wrong.

It is surprising how often companies using 'heavy' personalization make a mistake in the name or the gender. There is a popular saying in the computer industry:

To err is human; but to really screw things up you need a computer.

The following example makes this point emphatically.

This letter underlines the fact that the more you use personalization, the more important it is to have good, up-to-date information.

Ideally you will use a list which is up-to-date and correct in every detail, but sometimes this will not be possible.

If you are not sure of the name, perhaps with a list which has not been updated for some time, it may be wiser to play safe by using a generalized salutation such as *Dear Reader*.

Get the opening right

Once you are satisfied about addressing and salutation, you can concentrate on your opening. This is one of the most crucial parts of the letter – unless it says something interesting to the reader the rest of your copy will most likely be ignored.

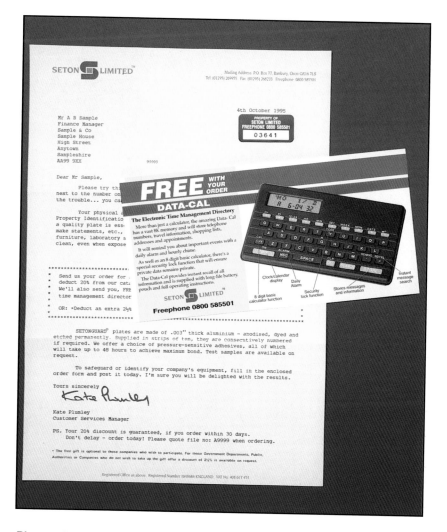

Plate 1 Seton Ltd

I first came across this letter in 1989, when I used it in my seminars to make the following points:

1 The label on the letter attracts attention and is also a good involvement device.
2 The typeface is Courier.
3 The free gift is included in all mailings but with an important disclaimer which reads 'The free gift is optional to those companies who wish to participate. For those…who do not wish to take up the gift offer, an extra discount of 2.5% is available'.

In November 1995 I met the marketing manager of Seton who told me that this mailing is still working well, without any significant changes, six years later.

This mailing illustrates the value of demonstration and involvement and also tackles successfully the difficult issue of free gifts in business mailings.

Plate 2 The Pier – questionnaire mailing

This mailing shows how you can learn a lot about your customers without spending a fortune.

The questionnaire, which contains almost forty questions, was produced on a desk-top PC using only word-processing software. There is an incentive included (but not heavily featured) – a free prize draw for a weekend in Florence.

The letter explains why the information is needed – to enable The Pier to offer better service and more interesting products.

A Freepost reply envelope was enclosed.

Response was more than 40%.

This illustrates the value of the relationship and the importance of giving respondents a good reason for taking the time to complete and return your questionnaire.

Plate 3 Vantage One Direct

Vantage One Direct sell games software and peripherals by mail order. A low-cost mailing, created entirely in-house, was mailed to the in-house customer database, supplemented by a list rented from a relevant magazine. The mailing touched down in November, ideal timing for the Christmas gifts market.

The powerful envelope message was repeated in the letter and again in the PS.

A Freepost envelope was enclosed for the order.

Response was 8.4% and the mailing produced a gross profit of almost £30,000.

A good example of just how much you can do yourself, if you get the targeting and timing right.

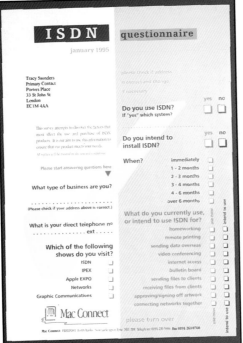

Plate 4 Mac Connect

Selling a complicated technical product like ISDN (Integrated Services Digital Network) can be difficult.

Mac Connect used direct mail with a dual objective:

1 To invite prospects to one of a series of seminars.

2 To clean the database.

The pack – test-mailed to 2000 names – generated ninety seminar bookings (4.5%). 10% of these actually ordered ISDN after the seminar. Mac Connect also received 220 (11%) returns enabling it to clean up its database.

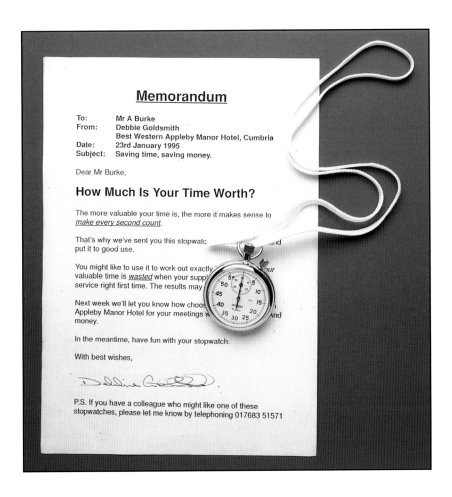

Memorandum

To: Mr A Burke
From: Debbie Goldsmith
Best Western Appleby Manor Hotel, Cumbria
Date: 23rd January 1995
Subject: Saving time, saving money.

Dear Mr Burke,

How Much Is Your Time Worth?

The more valuable your time is, the more it makes sense to _make every second count_.

That's why we've sent you this stopwatc   ...nd
put it to good use.

You might like to use it to work out exactly   ...ur
valuable time is _wasted_ when your supp
service right first time. The results may

Next week we'll let you know how choos
Appleby Manor Hotel for your meetings w   ...nd
money.

In the meantime, have fun with your stopwatch.

With best wishes,

P.S. If you have a colleague who might like one of these
stopwatches, please let me know by telephoning 017683 51571

Plate 5 Appleby Manor

The marketing staff at Appleby Manor identified a problem encountered by many people when organizing conferences – the time wasted in getting details right. They used this to produce an imaginative and successful two-stage campaign. The letter in the illustration was sent first with a stopwatch. Ten days after this 'teaser', prospects received the full mailing.

The entire mailing cost £1,095 and the response rate of 13% generated almost £20,000 of additional income – a return on investment of more than nineteen to one.

The National Autistic Society
276 Willesden Lane
LONDON
NW2

Dear Friend

There are over 30,000 autistic people in the UK.

Autism is a condition that's impossible to detect until the baby is several months old.

To be autistic means it's impossible to recognise emotional differences. For instance an autistic person cannot distinguish between a happy or a sad face, to them it looks the same.

It is also very difficult for autistic people to understand the relationship between all the everyday subjects, we take for granted. In their eyes there is no link between a table and a chair.

The overall effect is than an autistic person is completely isolated in a world where nothing makes sense and this disability makes it impossible to lead a normal life.

Autism can't be cured but it can be helped.

The National Autistic Society was set up in 1962 to cater for the special needs of autistic people; primarily children.

There are now seven schools for autistic children, an adult community and several adolescent training centres, where with understanding and patience, we can help autistic people to come to terms with the very confusing world they live in and develop a particular area of skill, which will help them in the outside world.

All this of course costs money and we desperately need more, to fund our existing schools and to build more adult centres.

Given a little time you'll be able to encompass these pieces of paper into a letter. For an autistic person this would be an impossible task, in fact it reflects the world in which they live.

Asking for money is always difficult, but any amount however small would I assure you be greatly appreciated.

Yours sincerely

Elliot & Harwood

THE BARONESS ELLIOT OF HARWOOD DBE

The National Autistic Society, 276 Willesden Lane, London NW2 9RB. Telephone 01-451 3844.
Registered as a charity with the National Assistance Act 1948 and as a charity under the Charities Act 1960.

Dr K. Mark M. Oliver
31 Saunders Copion
London
Surrey
0372 089

1
2

The National Autistic Society
276 Willesden Lane
London NW2 2YP

THIS IS HOW IT FEELS TO BE AUTISTIC

Envelopes donated and printed by DRG Envelopes. Tel (0442) 42124. Telex 826382.

DRG ENVELOPES
Putting the
message first

Plate 6 The National Autistic Society

As you probably know, autistic people can have difficulty in relating everyday objects to tasks, and in connecting things in a logical way.

This letter demonstrates the problem and involves the reader in a very clever way. I have watched many people read this letter and they all did the same – they studied every piece, sorted them into order and then read them again. Part of the copy reads: 'Given a little time you'll be able to unscramble these pieces of paper into a letter. For an autistic person this would be an impossible task…'

Of all the mailings I have seen this is the one I most wish I had thought of myself.

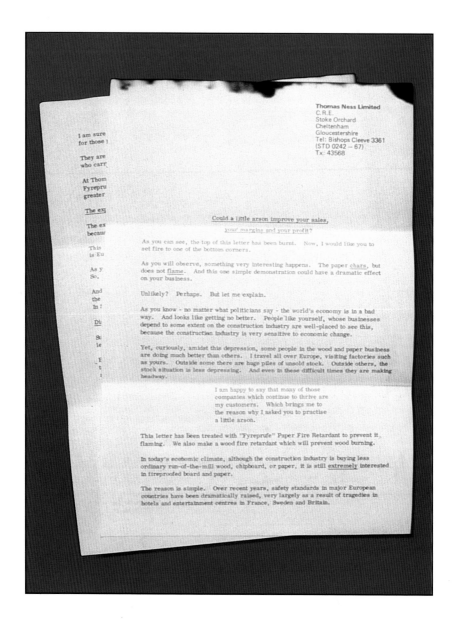

Plate 7 Burnt letter mailing

The product is Fyreprufe, a flame retardant fluid which, when sprayed on wood or paper, prevents them from burning. As you can see, the top of the letter is burnt and the sender asks the reader to set fire to one of the bottom corners of the letter to show how the paper chars but does not flame.

Here again, the lesson is that involvement and demonstration work well.

EXAMPLE

A client of mine, Paul Musson, Vice President of SunExpress Europe, a division of Sun Microsystems Inc., gave me a mailing he had received from a diary manufacturer.

This advertiser hoped to sell Paul a quantity of diaries complete with the Sun name, to be given away to customers. The diary would then act as a semi-permanent reminder of the relationship and, of course, the Sun name.

To emphasize the attractiveness of the diary the manufacturer had printed the company name in gold letters on the sample he enclosed. So far so good.

But the reason Paul passed it on to me, was because this manufacturer, amazingly, managed to get three things wrong at the same time:

▷ He addressed the letter to Mr Paul *Mason* instead of *Musson*

▷ He used the company name of *Sun Microsystems* instead of *SunExpress*

▷ Each time he used the company name both in the letter and gold-blocked on the diary, he mis-spelled it *Su* instead of *Sun*.

He then compounded these errors by 'heavy' personalization as follows:

> *Dear Mr Mason*
>
> *Surprised to see the Su Microsystems name on the enclosed diary? Looks good doesn't it!*

Two paragraphs of selling copy followed and then some more personalization:

> *And so Mr Mason, soon all your customers could be looking every day at the Su Microsystems name and thinking of you...*

So don't take the advice given by a professional copywriter in a trade magazine recently – save your best till last – if you do this your reader will most probably discard your letter without ever realizing that there is something relevant in there.

As a face-to-face salesperson your initial objective would be to attract attention. This also works well for mailings.

If your envelope has attracted the right sort of attention, you should immediately continue on the same theme.

LINK THE ENVELOPE TO THE HEADING

Your envelope message should link directly with the heading on your letter – assuming you have a heading on your letter. And before you dismiss this idea as another 'junk mail' symbol, put yourself in the position of your reader.

You have just sorted your mail and decided, perhaps from the envelope message, perhaps from the general 'feel', that this may be worth reading – what do you do next, read the letter?

Sadly *no* – most people first scan the letter, picking up impressions from words and sections that catch their eye and mentally asking the questions:

- Who sent this?
- What's it about?
- Is it really relevant to my job or my interests?

While scanning the letter they will usually read headings, sub-headings, the signature and a PS, if there is one.

This all takes place very quickly, (perhaps in twenty seconds or less) and before they decide whether to read your letter in full.

This perhaps starts to explain why longer copy letters tend to generate more response – the scanning process 'burns off' the casual reader very quickly, but real prospects will read as much as is relevant to their needs.

This brings us back to one of the central points of this entire process – relevance. When producing direct mailings, you must remember that the readers are not normally looking for entertainment or amusement.

Their primary reason for reading your mailing is to see whether it contains any advantage for them. An important factor in your success therefore is to show the major benefits, quickly and clearly.

Short copy is not important, but rapid explanation is. People rarely select a novel according to how many pages it contains. They are more concerned with how interesting the story is.

EXAMPLE

While on the subject of long copy I would like to introduce you to my father-in-law. Malcolm is seventy-six, has a golf handicap of twelve and is keenly interested in his investments.

I received a mailing from an American publisher suggesting that I invest $125 in a subscription to his investment newsletter. Realizing that this mailing was more relevant to Malcolm than to me, I decided that I would take it for him to read.

This was the critic's classic 'junk' mailing;

- the envelope itself carried about 200 words of copy

- the mailing contained eight pages of reprints of magazine articles, plus

- an order form which carried 250 words of promotional copy

- a reply envelope which was addressed to Virginia, USA, but without any form of postage prepayment

▷   and a letter. But what a letter...

```
Sixteen  pages  of  twelve-point  Courier
typeface,  just  like  this,  with  lots  of
headings,  sub-headings,  numbered  points,
indented paragraphs and even a lengthy PS.
```

Now, as you will have gathered, being an experienced direct mailer, I am not at all worried by long copy. But sixteen pages! Would anyone really read all that? I seriously doubted it.

Thinking about this, I realized I had the perfect test bed – Malcolm! I decided that if Malcolm would read the letter I might be convinced.

I took the mailing along to his house and simply passed it over saying *What do you think of that, Malcolm?* He sat down, put on his glasses and glanced through it – then he read it – *all of it.*

He put it down on his coffee table and I went to pick it up. *Hold on* said Malcolm, and promptly picked up the letter and skimmed through it again.

He asked me to leave it with him and I was fairly confident he would subscribe. I had only one doubt – Malcolm does not throw his money around and he might balk at the price.

Two weeks later I called again and asked him if he had subscribed. 'Of course not' *he replied,* 'do you think I would spend $125 on a newsletter? I got my accountant to subscribe, he's got more money than I have!'

I was telling this story in one of my seminars when a delegate put up his hand to tell us that his company was the UK distribution partner of this publisher and that *they had now abandoned the sixteen-page letter.*

Before I could muster a defensive argument, he went on to say that they had now switched to a twenty-page letter, as they had found more case histories to relate!

This story is not intended to persuade you to try to write sixteen-page letters – simply to point out that if the content is interesting the prospect will read it. If it is not interesting, a single paragraph may be too long.

TECHNIQUES TO MAKE YOUR LETTERS MORE EFFECTIVE

I have just mentioned in passing, some of the techniques used by the American publisher to keep the reader interested. Let's summarize these:

- ▷ **Long copy** – this often works because it answers all the questions that a real prospect might raise in a face-to-face discussion. It will of course be too long for the casual scanner.

- ▷ **Headings** – some of the most successful letters start with a strong headline or statement of benefits. These are sometimes run above the salutation in bold face, as shown in Figure 8.1.

Figure 8.1
A bold
heading

New Anyname Block Paving

30 February 1997

New Anyname Block Paving
– ideal for pedestrian and vehicle
– as used on London's Oxford Street

Dear Mr Thomas,

If you are looking for hardwearing block paving, where better to go than the company who recently paved Oxford Street?

Yours sincerely,

Headlines sometimes stand out better in a box like this one from an estate agent:

```
┌─────────────────────────────────────────────────┐
│                                                 │
│   Free Home Letting Guide and estimate of       │
│      the rental value of your property          │
│                                                 │
│        Telephone 0800 24 92 24                  │
│                                                 │
│      No charge and no obligation                │
│                                                 │
└─────────────────────────────────────────────────┘
```

This is called a Johnson box, named after an American direct marketer who first gave a name to this technique.

> *These headings work (with or without the box) because they quickly tell the prospect whether the letter is relevant.*

▷ **Sub-headings** – long copy works in many cases, but only if it is well laid out with liberal use of sub-headings to help the scanner decide on the relevance of each part. In addition to being helpful in the scanning phase, the 'sub-heads' make the letter look easier to read.

Other successful letter techniques include;

▷ **Indented paragraphs** – these can give long copy an easy-to-read appearance. The indentation does not need to be large – a single 'tab' position is sufficient to make a paragraph stand out and lighten the whole appearance.

▷ Displayed selling points – compare this:

```
In his presentation John Benson will explain how he has
helped the following companies solve major management
problems:

*Barclays Educational Services *Nutritional Fruit Juices
*Oxford Computers *Newcounty Health Authority *Paragon
Tableware *AN Other Motor Company
```

with this:

```
In his presentation John Benson will explain how he has
helped the following companies solve major management
problems:
```

        *   Barclays Educational Services

        *   Nutritional Fruit Juices

        *   Oxford Computers

        *   Newcounty Health Authority

        *   Paragon Tableware

        *   AN Other Motor Company

Note how much easier it is to pick out something of interest from this list when it is displayed in this manner.

The scanner has more chance of seeing something relevant with the second layout.

A SMALL PRIVATE RESEARCH PROJECT

I sometimes use a version of this letter in the letterwriting seminars I do for the Chartered Institute of Marketing. Just before lunch break, I hand out a copy of the letter featuring real company names to each delegate and ask them to read it for a couple of minutes.

The layout is similar to the second example, i.e. the company names are laid out on separate lines. I simply present it as a good clear way of laying out a letter. We then have a general question and answer session, with no mention of this particular letter.

While the delegates are at lunch I collect all the sample letters and replace them with a brief questionnaire. There are only a couple of questions – the first one relates to the headline which I have not shown you. The second asks:

Which companies are featured in the letter you read before lunch?

The answers are very revealing:

▷ The delegate from *Mercedes* said: '*AN Other Motor Company*'

▷ The man from *Hertfordshire TEC* said '*Newcounty Health Authority*'

▷ The FMCG delegate said '*Nutritional Fruit Juices*'.

Each delegate remembered the name of the company most relevant to their own situation.

The advantages of good layout do not only apply to brief product or company names. Below we look at how brief descriptions of situations can be better displayed, again making it easier for a casual glance to pick up something relevant.

Compare this:

```
You will see; a company needing to expand, but
failing to persuade its investors; falling profits
forcing doubtful decisions; why a company with a full
order book still needs to reconsider its marketing;
how a health authority copes with a huge overspend;
when revolution is better than evolution; how
conflicting interests can be healthily aired, debated
and then resolved.
```

with:

```
You will see:
```

O a company needing to expand, but failing to persuade its investors;

O falling profits forcing doubtful decisions;

O why a company with a full order book still needs to reconsider its marketing;

O how a health authority copes with a huge overspend;

O when revolution is better than evolution;

O how conflicting interests can be healthily aired, debated and then resolved.

You may have noticed that the above examples are printed in a typeface which differs from the book text.

```
This typeface is Courier which, for some reason,
seems to increase response to many mailings. Perhaps
it is because it is large and clear, or maybe because
it looks like a typewriter face and thus more like a
letter.
```

No-one really knows why this happens, but if you study the mailings of many major direct marketers who test their responses regularly, you will find that they continue to use Courier. This must be because it still works better for them than Roman or sans serif faces.

While on the subject of typefaces, it is worth considering the results of some research carried out during the 1980s by an Australian journalist called Colin Wheildon. Wheildon was intrigued by numerous references to the serif/sans serif question by David Ogilvy and other well-known advertising figures.

Many experienced direct marketers knew they should not use sans serif or reversed out type for body copy, but did not really know why.

Wheildon decided to put these vague theories to the test, by getting people to read a piece of text and then asking them to answer ten questions about what they had just read.

Before I show you the results of Wheildon's research, however, let me demonstrate what each typeface looks like.

ROMAN OR SERIF TYPE

This paragraph like most of the copy in this book, is printed in Times, a popular serif or Roman face. Many advertisements and newspapers are printed in faces like this one, although magazines tend to ignore the rules and print in 'fashion' type styles. Experienced direct response designers use Roman or serif faces for *all* body copy.

ANOTHER ROMAN FACE

An alternative to Times is another Roman face – Century Schoolbook – a clear attractive face which is easy to read.

SANS SERIF TYPE

This paragraph is printed in Univers, a popular sans serif face, used by many designers in the advertising industry. It is interesting to note that sans serif faces are used much more frequently by designers of traditional (non-response) advertising. Most experienced direct marketing designers know that using sans serif faces can reduce their response, despite the fact that this face actually looks clearer than the Roman type.

The next example shows another style popular with designers, but not with experienced direct marketers.

REVERSED-OUT TYPE

Another form of display to avoid for body copy is this, which is *reversed-out*. We can reverse-out any typeface – this is Times, whereas the paragraph below is Univers.

Some people feel that when reversing out, sans serif faces work better than Roman, but while Wheildon's research supports this marginally (see figures below showing an improvement in good comprehension from 0% to 4%) there does not seem to be any other research to support this so it may be a 'designer argument'.

Now that we have demonstrated various typestyles, let's have a look at Wheildon's research statistics.

The programme took place over a five-year period (1982–86) and groups of adults and high school students were each given an article to read, several pages in length.

The tests were repeated at intervals, with groups being switched from serif to sans serif type. Articles varyied from those of general interest to those of direct interest to the reader.

Participants were supervised while reading and were then asked ten questions about what they had read. In the tests mentioned here:

▷ one group was given the articles set in Corona (eight point on nine point body) a serif face

▷ the other group read the same article set in Helvetica (eight point on nine point body) a sans serif face.

Comprehension was judged on the following basis:

▷ seven to ten questions answered correctly = good comprehension

▷ four to six correct answers = fair comprehension

▷ zero to three correct answers = poor comprehension.

The results are shown in Table 8.1.

Table 8.1
Results of the Wheildon research into typeface comprehension

	Comprehension level		
Typestyle	Good	Fair	Poor
Serif type for body copy	67%	19%	14%
Sans serif type for body copy	12%	23%	65%

After the tests and questionnaires were completed, readers were asked if they had any comments on what they had just experienced. These too, are very interesting. Here is an extract from Colin Wheildon's report:

Comments made by the readers who showed poor comprehension of articles set in sans serif type had a common theme – the difficulty in holding concentration.

An analysis of the comments offered by one group of 112 readers who had read an article of direct interest *to them revealed that of the 112 readers, sixty-seven showed poor comprehension, and of these:*

▷ *fifty-three complained strongly about the difficulty of reading the type*

▷ *eleven said the task caused them physical discomfort (eye tiredness)*

▷ *thirty-two said the type was hard to read*

▷ *ten said they had to backtrack continually to try to maintain concentration*

▷ *five said that when they backtracked to recall points made in the article, they gave up trying to concentrate*

▷ *twenty-two said they had difficulty in focusing on the type after having read a dozen or so lines.*

Some readers made two or more of the above comments.

Yet when this same group was asked immediately afterwards to read another article with a domestic theme, but set in Corona, they reported no physical difficulties and no necessity to recapitulate to maintain concentration.

The conclusion must be that body type must be set in serif type if the designer intends it to be read and understood.

Tests on reversed-out type

Another series of tests examined the effect of reversing out the text people were asked to read. The format of the tests was the same – one group read the article printed in black on white paper. Other groups were asked to read the same article in white on a black background, white on a purple background, and white on a deep blue background. In all cases, the typeface was a roman serif face. The comprehension scores are given in Table 8.2.

Table 8.2
Wheildon's
results of tests
on reversed-
out type

Typestyle	Comprehension level		
	Good	Fair	Poor
Text printed black on white †	70%	19%	11%
Text printed white on black	0%	12%	88%
Text printed white on purple	2%	16%	82%
Text printed white on deep blue	0%	4%	96%

† Very similar to the serif scores in the previous tests (same type style).

To complete this series and to test the school of thought which contends that reversed out type is only a problem with Roman or serif faces, a final set of groups was tested on reversed-out type but this time set in Univers.

The results are given in Table 8.3.

Table 8.3
Wheildon's
results of tests
on reversed-
out Univers
type

Typestyle	Comprehension level		
	Good	Fair	Poor
Black on white ‡	14%	25%	61%
White on black	4%	13%	83%

‡ Very similar to the sans serif scores in the previous series (same type style).

None of this is intended to suggest that you do not use sans serif or reversed-out type for short headings or sub-headings. This can make them stand out well against the rest of the text. The above tests and the comments (mine and Colin Wheildon's) relate to body copy only.

WHY SHOULD A LETTER HAVE A PS?

The PS is another of those 'old-timer's tricks' which just keeps on working. Some modernists describe it as 'hackneyed', 'corny' and so on, but the PS just keeps on going. Why?

There are numerous theories, but no definitive answer, since all of the evidence is empirical.

However, the evidence is emphatic. Siegfried Vogele, the German marketing psychologist, when describing his twenty-five years' research into this subject, says that more than 90% of all recipients read the PS first and that they read it more slowly and carefully than the rest of the letter.

Why should this be so? Perhaps people think that it must be something topical or especially important if the writer added it later? Perhaps they are becoming trained that the PS is a quick reference to the gist of the offer contained in the letter? *Whatever the reason, you should experiment with the PS – it just may make the crucial difference to your letter.*

Incidentally, Professor Vogele says that the PS is less important in very short or in original (i.e. truly individual) letters.

Siegfried Vogele has documented his research and his extensive direct marketing experience in his recent book *The Handbook of Direct Mail.* You will find details of this book and many others in Appendix 2.

> *Before we move on to look at the other enclosures, let us consider why the letter is such an important piece in a mailing.*

If we examine the purpose of each piece in the mailing we can see that each has a job to do:

▷ **Outer envelope** – to reach the right person and, perhaps, to introduce the topic.

▷ **Letter** – to 'sell' the proposition in words, explaining the benefits that this product or service will bring to the recipient. It is the most easily 'personalized' piece and equates to the face-to-face discussion with the salesperson.

In the same way that a good salesperson will adapt the presentation according to the person being addressed, your letter wording and the structure of your argument should be varied, according to the knowledge and interest level of the reader. This is easy to achieve with a letter, very difficult with a brochure or leaflet.

▷ **Leaflets and brochures** – if the job of the letter is to sell the proposition, the brochure's role is to demonstrate it. Pictures, showing the product in use, with captions emphasizing the benefits, make the brochure a valuable addition to the pack.

Don't just use any old captions. On more than one occasion, I have been able to increase the response to a mailing simply by rewriting the captions in the brochure. Even captions about your service need to be thought about carefully. Figure 8.2 shows how captions can make all the difference.

Figure 8.2
Showing how captions can enhance your message

Our brand new high tech assembly line is the most modern in Europe

Our new assembly line has reduced delivery times by four days

The caption on the right refers to the same picture but demonstrates a customer benefit. The one on the left is corporate 'chest beating' – it makes the chairman feel good, but does nothing for the customer.

SUPPORTING PIECES

Like a good salesperson, a mailing needs to be able to overcome uncertainties. The difficulty is that, unlike the face-to-face encounter, you cannot vary what you say according to the reaction of your prospect so you need to find a way of overcoming this problem without adding significantly to the costs.

GET THE RIGHT INFORMATION

First and foremost, use all the resources you have (e.g. telephone, database information and so on) to gather facts and identify concerns and uncertainties before you write the copy.

MAKE IT 'READER-FRIENDLY'

Next, make sure you display the information in the mailing in such a way that you give the reader the opportunity of reading it or not, according to choice.

For example, instead of putting everything into the letter and possibly 'overselling' to someone who is already convinced, you could introduce a couple of additional leaflets e.g.

- **About AB Components** – a leaflet giving some company background for those who like the sound of the product, but have reservations because they have never heard of AB Components.

- **What our customers say about us** – a leaflet carrying testimonial statements from well known or at least, credible customers – to persuade those who like the proposition, but are not sure whether you can fulfil your promises.

Elements like these could, of course, be introduced into the letter and if you are writing to someone you know will need such reassurance, this is probably the best place for them. For a 'cold list' mailing however, where you know very little about your prospect, the separate leaflet method could be a good approach.

As many of the tips in this book have emphasized, the solution to a mailing problem is often to think hard about the person you are writing to. Try to imagine the questions they would ask, then answer those questions as fully and frankly as possible.

USING NEWSPAPER AND MAGAZINE REPRINTS

The American publisher mentioned earlier, enclosed eight pages of reprints from magazines. If you have been lucky enough to get a good review in a paper, you should use it for all it is worth.

The publication has, or is assumed to have, an independent point of view and if they say your product is good, it carries much more weight than the same wording written by you. You are expected to say it is the greatest product ever, so your claims are discounted a little by the reader.

GETTING A RESPONSE

If the rest of your mailing has done its job, your prospect is now in a mood to order, or send for more information. Now your response form comes into focus. The purpose of a response device is to get a response. Obvious you might think, but take a look at the coupon given as an illustration in Figure 8.3.

Figure 8.3
Example of a reply coupon recently received

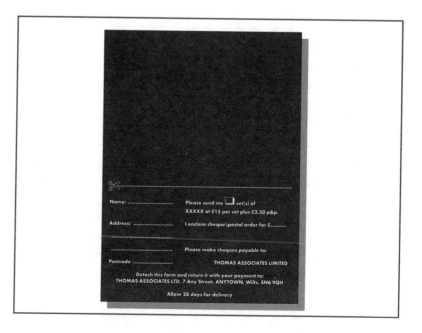

Name: ....   Please send me ☐ set(s) of
                                XXXXX at £15 per set plus £2.50 p&p.

Address: ....   I enclose cheque\postal order for £.........

....

....   Please make cheques payable to:

Postcode ....   THOMAS ASSOCIATES LIMITED

Detach this form and return it with your payment to:
THOMAS ASSOCIATES LTD, 7 Any Street, ANYTOWN, Wilts. SN6 9QH

Allow 28 days for delivery

Now, do you think the designers of this form had response in mind? *Of course not*, they were clearly more concerned with style than the number of replies that would be received!

WHAT ARE THE ESSENTIALS OF A GOOD RESPONSE DEVICE?

1   **First and foremost – make it easy for the respondent** – here's how:

▷ **Give respondents a choice** – post, fax, phone. *Let them decide* which is most convenient.

▷ **Do as much of the work as you can** – apart from the phone and fax options, you should also try to fill in the prospect's name and address. There are at least three good reasons for doing this:

❑ You get more back – perhaps up to 15% more

❑ You will be able to read and process all the coupons you receive. A surprising number of people fail to include their town and postcode and when the item they sent for doesn't arrive, you get the blame!

❑ You can print a customer reference number on the form so you only have to key in a few digits and your computer will automatically pull up the full address. This could save around 60% of your order input time.

---

2   **Repeat your address and the main details of the offer on the order form** – some people will keep just the order form until they have time to send it. If the details are not repeated those who cannot remember will not return it. Others will pass it on to a friend or colleague, who will not always see the full mailing.

---

3   **Pay the postage** – If you use Freepost or the Royal Mail's Business Reply Service, you pay only for those who reply and it's a small extra amount to pay for the details of an interested prospect. You can use a postcard or an envelope, but don't decide on price alone. It really depends on what you are asking the respondent to tell you. If you just ask for their name and address, a postcard may do. If you want them to tell you how much they earn, or how many employees are in their firm, make sure you include an envelope.

DIRECT MAIL CHECKLIST

Here's a summary of the things to remember when designing your mailing:

GAIN ATTENTION

1

Consider your envelope – will an overprint be appropriate?

It is not essential to use an envelope message, but you should always think carefully about how your mailing will stand out against the rest of the mail.

There are many examples of major gains in response due to a relevant envelope message.

One client, a major investment broker, targeting middle-aged men, put the whole story on his envelope, like that shown in Figure 8.4.

Figure 8.4
A long and detailed envelope message

This mailing was one of a series targeted at specific groups segmented by age, lifestyle and investment history. Average response across the series was nearly 7%.

Some successful mailers use size to gain attention – larger, longer, or thicker envelopes tend to work well. Remember the research quoted in Chapter 3. Nearly 2,000 business people answered the question *'Which of your mailings do you open first?'* The most frequently selected answer was *'Those which are bulky or look most interesting'*.

2 **Start with your strongest benefit statement or main item of news**
As with other forms of advertising many people will look at the start or headline and stop at that point if not attracted. Research tells us that news is many times more attractive than humour, curiosity or other gimmicks. Make sure your headline links closely to your envelope message.

3 **Be specific** – it is more credible. Real numbers and facts work better than 'hype'. *One of my clients achieved a sizeable gain in response simply by changing a headline from* 'Save up to £300' *to* 'You could save £294.95'.

4 **Use a headline or overline on your letters** – this is one of the main factors in persuading people to read on. Siegfried Vogele's research shows that the headline is one of the first points of decision by a prospective reader. If it doesn't say something relevant, many simply stop reading.

5 **Try to create visual interest** – but avoid irrelevant gimmicks.

6 **Do not assume others share your tastes** – this is especially important when considering humour. Don't be afraid to test new ideas, but if in doubt, err on the side of good taste rather than bad.

In my seminars I tell the apocryphal story of the car dealer who, having the franchise for a French car, thought up a spiffing idea. He had his envelopes hand-addressed by a small local mailing house who were instructed to add the message: *Inside – a French letter from (name of car company)*. Inside the envelope, as you will have guessed, was a condom and a letter which started *Dear Mr X, I bet that made you smile! Well now that I've got your attention, I'd like to tell you about the new...* and so on. This letter probably amused around 10% of the recipients, another 60% probably thought *How tacky!*. The remainder phoned or wrote to the car company's head office to complain. *The dealer lost his franchise.*

Now I am prepared to believe that the story may not be true, but I told it in Manchester one day and a delegate put up her hand and told us that her boss was about to use the same gimmick in a mailing to his customers. The message is – when in doubt – *don't use humour.* If you must, make sure it is 'harmless' humour.

CONFIRM THE RELEVANCE OF YOUR OFFER

1 **Link your claims to the reader's situation where possible**.

2 **Demonstrate the product benefits** – with displayed facts and figures showing how it fits into the buyer's situation – and where possible with illustrations.

TELL THE FULL STORY

1 **Do not be afraid of using long copy if necessary** – many opponents of long copy have never tested it. (*Remember* – there is no merit in long copy, nor short. Copy should be long enough to tell the complete story and it will vary according to your objective, e.g. lead generation, sales, requests for details and on the information needs of your audience.)

2 **Use sub-headings, especially if the copy is long** – many readers scan these first before deciding whether to read the entire letter. *Make sure they are relevant to the reader*. Use the same approach that I used with the captions a few pages ago, when I replaced *The most modern assembly line in Europe* with *New assembly line means faster deliveries.*

MAKE IT EASY FOR THE READER

1   **Keep to a logical sequence** – after I have written a letter, I write a phrase summarizing each paragraph. I then check these to see that I have made my points in the right order for the reader.

---

2   **Use short words, short sentences and short paragraphs**.

---

3   **Try to involve the reader** – enclosures which *do something* (tapes, videos and so on) often work well.

CASE STUDY – AUDIO MEDICA

How on earth can we entice notoriously busy doctors and consultants to listen to our message, was the problem facing former BBC medical journalist Peter Goodwin.

Peter founded Audio Medica in 1990 to distribute up-to-the-minute information about new treatments and techniques in the medical world.

Realizing how little time doctors and specialists have and how much mail they receive from the many pharmaceutical companies, Audio Medica came up with a new approach – cassette tapes.

Audio Medica tapes feature top consultants and researchers discussing leading edge developments in medicine: cancer research, heart disease, kidney and liver transplants and so on.

Not surprisingly these are very popular with an increasing number of practitioners, as the following comments demonstrate:

▷   *The tapes bring the subject alive*

▷   *Excellent – especially for listening to in the car*

▷   *A major contribution to medical knowledge.*

> Audio Medica's list of testimonials is as thick as Black's Medical Dictionary.
>
> Peter gets new customers by using carefully targeted mailings, followed up in many cases by personal telephone contact. He also appears at various medical conferences around the world, recruiting both customers and specialist participants for future taped discussions.

CONVINCE YOUR PROSPECT

1 **Offer samples, trials or demonstrations**. *Don't take my word for it, try it yourself at my expense* – this is a very powerful offer.

2 **Sell the benefits, not the attributes**. People buy products because of what they do for them, not for what they are.

3 **Use testimonials** – they are always more believable than your own claims. One well-known correspondence school used more than 50 testimonials in their enquiry pack – each time they added some more their conversion increased. They only stopped adding more when they reached the next weight limit.

4 **Quote research data** – it carries greater authority.

5 **Provide reassurance**
  ▷ no obligation
  ▷ strong guarantee.

CONFIRM THE ACTION REQUIRED

1 **Don't be vague** – say exactly what you want the prospect to do.

2 **Consider shorter time closes for offers** – the purpose of a time close is to stimulate action now – the best time closes are no longer than two or three weeks and should be an actual date if possible.

I once, accidentally, ran a time close of three days – the response was three times the normal level.

3 **Repeat the offer on the response form** – remember those who only keep the form to fill in when they have more time.

4 **Fill in as much of the response form as you can** – make it easy for the respondent and yourself.

5 **Give alternative response options** – telephone and fax numbers – perhaps even a fax order form, which just requires a signature.

CLOSE THE SALE

1 **Make sure your letter has a powerful final paragraph** – summarizing the benefits and the action required. It is not that people are lazy, just busy. If they have got to the end of your letter in a mood to buy, don't stand in their way – give them everything they need – at the right time and place.

2 **Try a strong PS** – you may be surprised how well this old chestnut works!

3 **Consider a follow-up** – by mail or phone. If you do follow up, make it earlier rather than later. Most people have already forgotten last week's mail.

Companies who have experimented with the timing of telephone follow-ups find that the best time is within three days of the mailing arriving. There is no reason to suppose that direct mail follow-up should be any different. Opponents of early follow-up point out that you will actually contact some people who will reply anyway –

therefore you are wasting money. Well, yes, but if your response is say, 5% in total, even if you wait for three or four weeks, you will still have to contact 95% of the total, so the saving will be very small. *Not only that, the impact of your follow-up will be much, much less.*

Companies that have followed up within three or four days (usually by telephone) have reported huge increases in response.

EXAMPLE – SOFTWARE COMPANY

This company ran a three-way test:

▷ Sample A – direct mail only – no follow-up

▷ Sample B – direct mail, but adding an 0800 (free) telephone number

▷ Sample C – as sample B, but with every prospect followed-up by telephone within three days of the mailing arriving

Results (indexed)

▷ Sample A   100

▷ Sample B   200 – *the free telephone facility doubled response*

▷ Sample C   2,800 – *the telephone follow-up multiplied response fourteen-fold.*

This is not an isolated case – there have been numerous tests in the past few years showing that a rapid telephone follow-up acts to multiply response levels dramatically.

A traditional direct mail follow up, arriving some ten to fourteen days after the initial mailing, would normally increase overall response by between 25–40%.

I am not aware of any recent tests of rapid mail follow-up, but I believe it should be tested – I see no reason why it would not work better than a reminder arriving two weeks later.

How much of the mail you received two weeks ago is still on your desk – or even in your filing cabinet?

SUMMARY

When seeking ways of 'tuning up' mailings, we keep coming back to the same basic fact.

The three most important factors in the success of a mailing are:

- ▷ **targeting the right person** (list)
- ▷ **saying the right thing** (offer), and
- ▷ **getting your timing right**.

If these three are achieved successfully, your mailing should not 'bomb'.

If they are not, the finest creative work in the world will not save you from disaster.

The first step is to set a clear objective – having a single-minded objective will make your letter, or even your creative brief, much easier to write. The objective is the first stage in developing a pack outline – the remaining stages are:

- ▷ **target audience definition**
- ▷ **establishing your offer**
- ▷ **identifying the best timing** – for each customer, or group of customers
- ▷ **working out your creative approach** – long copy or short, how many pieces, reply methods and so on
- ▷ **planning the despatch programme**

▷ **setting up your response handling system**

▷ **planning any follow-up**.

It is vital to be able to handle your response efficiently. This may be your prospect's first experience of your company. If it is handled badly, you may never get another chance. Worse still, the disillusioned prospect may tell many others about their treatment.

Once you have developed your mailing outline, you can concentrate on creating a powerful, relevant communication. Your mailing has to:

▷ **attract attention** – using your envelope and letter opening

▷ **quickly establish the relevance of your offer** – by relating your product benefits to the reader's situation

▷ **convince the reader of the benefits of your product or service** – by clear demonstration

▷ **confirm what action you expect** – by clear directions

▷ **close the sale** – where relevant – with a powerful final paragraph and PS

▷ **take the order** – where relevant – by making it as easy as possible for the respondent.

The essential elements of a mailing pack are:

▷ **the outer envelope** – your selling message starts here. Not always with a printed message, but at the very least by making a good impression on the recipient.

▷ **the letter**...

❑ **your letter headline** – linking to your envelope message where relevant. Stating very simply and quickly what will be the major benefit of reading this letter. This is one of the crucial 'decision points' in a letter – when the reader decides whether to carry on reading or not.

❑ **the salutation** – no complicated rules here – get it right or play safe. Wrong or mis-spelled names, wrong gender, wrong title

– any of these can spell disaster for your mailing before it is even read. *Dear Reader* is better than *Dear Wrong Name*.

❑ **your opening paragraph** – don't waste the reader's time by waffle – tell them the news right away – they may not get as far as your third or fourth paragraph if not.

❑ **tell the full story** – if this can be done in two paragraphs, fine. If it takes three pages, that's OK too. But if you use long copy, break it up with sub-headings, indented paragraphs, bold face emphasis and so on.

❑ **think about the typefaces you use** – better not to use sans serif or reversed-out type for body copy but OK for headlines of only four or five words, but if your headline is longer it's better to use roman type.

❑ **try a PS** – critics think this is old-fashioned, but it still works well for many mailers.

❑ **leaflets and brochures** – the letter sells, the brochure demonstrates – a good salesperson does both – make sure your mailing does too.

❑ **testimonials** – whether these are in your letter, your brochure, or printed as separate pieces, they are valuable additions to your armoury.

❑ **reply methods** – your prospect will decide on the right response method. Your job is to offer all the options you can – postage paid, with a free telephone number and free fax number would be ideal. If possible, address the response form so your prospect simply has to tick, sign, fold, enclose – make it easy.

❑ **consider a follow-up** – you should test mail and telephone and experiment with the timing. Those who have tried rapid (three days) follow-up rarely go back to a more extended period.

WHAT TO DO NEXT

Become a direct mail collector. Get yourself onto as many lists as you can by responding to advertisements, mailings and inserts.

Study what other mailers are doing. Use *The Rule of 3* to decide whether other companies' mailings are working.

THE RULE OF 3

1   If you receive a mailing once, it may be a test.

---

2   If you receive it again, after a period of time (to make sure you are not duplicated on the list), it may have worked, or something may have gone wrong with the first test.

---

3   If they mail it a third time, again after a period has elapsed, the mailing is working – or the marketing manager is a moron!

Self-test questionnaire

1   Collect some mailings and evaluate creative techniques used. Do they attract you?

2   List their good and bad points — then compare them with the checklist which begins on page 167.

3   Now write a mailing for your own product or service. Review it against the checklist. Rewrite it until you are satisfied it tells the full story, in the right sequence.

9 Direct mail testing and measurement

Testing is one of the most important weapons available to the direct mailer. Research can give you good ideas and some valuable feedback on how well your messages are understood, but it is very difficult to quantify without spending a lot of money.

Research can often tell you *why* something happened, but only testing can measure precisely *what* happens in terms of response and sales when you vary your list, timing or creative approach.

Testing is fascinating, but this interest is not academic – a well-planned test programme will enable you to generate more sales and make more profit.

This chapter discusses the advantages and limitations of testing. You will read about a number of testing techniques, but it is important to remember that testing is not an exact science. Testing will certainly help you reduce uncertainty and risk, but it should be used as an *aid* to judgement rather than a *replacement* for it.

You must be particularly cautious when dealing with small numbers.

With direct mail you are targeting individuals, or at least small well-defined segments of a market so you are uniquely equipped to:

▷ Control your messages very precisely
▷ Test alternative messages to the same or other segments
▷ Measure response and thus learn what works best.

TEST OBJECTIVES

A test programme has only one strategic objective – to help you spend your marketing budget more cost-effectively. There are three ways in which this objective can be achieved. You can improve:

➤ **Quantity** – a test can establish which list, offer, timing pattern, creative treatment, response device and so on produces the most response.

➤ **Quality** – alternatively you could test to identify how to attract a better quality of respondent – e.g. one who converts more easily, who places larger orders, or remains a customer for a longer time.

➤ **Cost efficiency** – here you will be looking primarily to reduce the cost per lead, the cost per conversion, or perhaps the cost per £ of sales revenue.

These three subsidiary objectives are not mutually exclusive. A test programme can be designed to measure and improve more than one. In fact they are all interconnected – for example:

➤ If you increase quantity of replies your cost per response will reduce.

➤ If you improve the quality of response (e.g. by attracting people who convert more easily, or place larger orders) your cost per sale, or per pound of sales, will reduce.

➤ If you can reduce your costs by better buying, you can maintain the same response levels and still reduce your cost per response.

Although many test programmes concentrate on new business activities, e.g. lead generation and conversion activities, they are not restricted to these areas. It is just as important to test alternative approaches to existing customers – in many cases the payback from a successful test to customers will be much higher.

WHERE TESTING FITS

Planning test programmes is part of the development of contact strategies.

During this process you should consider all of the information and resources at your disposal, then decide on the ideal way to deliver a relevant message to your customer or prospect. Testing is designed to confirm or question your judgement, without risking the entire budget in the process.

WHAT ARE THE MAIN FACTORS TO TEST?

Tests can be constructed to answer a number of questions relating to:

> ▷ **List selection** – you can compare the results from one mailing list or list segment, with those from another.

EXAMPLE

This can be a crucially important test. A few years ago, one of my clients asked us to identify the ideal lists for the launch of a new subscription product targeted at professional people at their home addresses.

We produced ten lists which, according to their descriptions, seemed to be equally good.

The test results showed that the best list was six times as effective as the worst.

> ▷ **Offers** – as we have seen, various offers can be tested against each other. An offer can be an incentive, or simply the way you present your product or service benefits. Varying types and levels of offers or incentives could be tried according to the objective, e.g. to increase response, or achieve a higher conversion rate by attracting a better quality or a more committed respondent.

The way in which the offer is presented can also be important. You could test the effectiveness of an expensive incentive versus an inexpensive one. Or the merits of prominent versus discreet display. Offers are discussed in detail in Chapter 7.

> ▷ **Timing** – another important aspect is to test the effect of varying the timing of communications, perhaps relating to buying patterns or, in the case of businesses, their financial year end.

> ▷ **Creative aspects** – you can test the effects of changing a headline, the style or length of copy, or a completely redesigned mailing package.

> **Response methods** – e.g. coupons versus telephone numbers versus fax numbers. You can measure the effect of paying for the reply postage or telephone call, and the effectiveness of pre-printing the addressee's name on the response form.

There may be additional factors worth testing from time to time, but your main testing programmes should concentrate on one or more of the above. They are, incidentally, listed in order of importance. In other words, a successful list test will usually produce a greater return than an offer test. An offer is more important than creative treatment and so on.

Responses vary widely at different times and in different markets – the only way to establish a norm is to try some tests yourself and build experience.

EXAMPLE

Although I have stressed that creative tests are not the most important, it is still possible to achieve a sizeable uplift in response by changing the creative approach. To demonstrate this point the following test results have been achieved in recent years:

> Rewriting the opening sentence of a letter in a complex mailing package increased response by 25%.

> Changing the sequence of paragraphs in another letter increased response by 40%.

These worked because they placed the relevant benefits in the right place for the scanning process, see page 150.

AN IMPORTANT REMINDER

Make sure you do not concentrate too much on response data to the detriment of longer term interests.

It is very important that you continue to monitor the performance of respondents by source, to ensure that a promising looking approach is not simply attracting a high volume of low grade prospects.

HOW DOES DIRECT MAIL TESTING WORK?

In many ways direct mail is the ideal test medium – you can:

▷ Select matched test cells from a list.

▷ Ensure that the quantities and the timing are precisely controlled.

▷ Vary the length, size, design, and so on of your packages, to a degree controlled only by the size of your budget and the number of names available.

You can also vary your message:

▷ By segment (perhaps making one offer to a large company and another to a smaller prospect).

▷ By individual (by say, varying the copy according to whether you are communicating with a company chairman or an IT manager).

SAMPLE SIZES

With direct mail, as with all forms of testing, you must be sure to use samples which are large enough to make the results reliable. This aspect is discussed in detail later in this chapter.

DESIGNING A TEST PROGRAMME

Having discussed the benefits of testing, we can now consider the procedure for designing, implementing and measuring tests:

1 **Establish your control** – a control is your best performing package, insert or advertisement (or at the least, one which you know has worked previously to this market segment). It is the approach you would use if you were unable to test alternatives. *Control is the 'yardstick' against which all other tests are measured.*

2 **Decide on your tests** – there are numerous possibilities but as discussed earlier your test priorities should be:
   ▷ list
   ▷ offer
   ▷ timing
   ▷ creative aspects
   ▷ response methods.

Table 9.1
Example test
strategy
statement

TEST STRATEGY STATEMENT

Project: Spring 1996 new customer recruitment mailing
Issued: 15 September 1995

Control: C4 window envelope with two-page letter, standard brochure and reply card

Test	Objectives	Method
1 Format test: C5 vs C4 envelope	To reduce pack costs whilst maintaining the same response	All internal elements to be same as control pack, folded to fit C5 envelope
2 Free gift added – low key presentation	To improve response by offering a free gift, without affecting the basic tone and structure of control pack	Mention free gift in the letter copy and the PS
3 Free gift added – heavy emphasis	To improve response by offering a free gift, featured heavily throughout the pack	Include separate four-colour free gift 'flyer'; refer to gift in letter copy and PS; include on order card with illustration
4 New creative approach	To find a totally new approach which will produce more response than control	All new elements – design to be briefed and discussed

Analysis of previous results will help you decide which new tests look the most promising.

At this point, it is advisable to produce a simple test strategy statement like the one below. This will have many uses, including briefing, estimating costs and obtaining quotations, and evaluation.

This should be shown to colleagues and suppliers as early as possible – it will stimulate discussion and often produce helpful suggestions for improvement.

An example of a test strategy statement is shown in Table 9.1.

TESTING LISTS

Where several are available, your test strategy should also include the testing of lists. Matched samples of each of your candidate lists should be mailed *with the same pack.* This is very important – to mix alternative creative themes or presentations within a list test would leave you with no readable results.

TEST DESIGN

Tests can only be designed to examine either:

▷ One element in the mailing e.g. envelope design, letter copy and so on, or

▷ The total package.

In the first case, the cause of any difference to response can be identified – in the second it cannot.

> *Therefore, an important rule when constructing a test strategy is – if you want to measure a specific factor, you must make sure that no more than one variable appears in any single test cell.*

There are two major exceptions to this rule:

1 **Where you decide to break away from earlier thinking as in Test 4 of Table 9.1** - however you should always have a control to measure against. Without the control you will never know whether the good or bad result was caused by the creative treatment, the timing, a competitive offer or some other outside factor.

2 **Where the quantity of names, or the available budget, make multi-cell testing impossible.** In this case, you are obliged to adopt a 'total package' approach – you will still know which test cell created the most response, but not necessarily why (i.e. which of the altered elements caused the change).

THE STATISTICS OF TESTING

SAMPLE SIZES

As mentioned earlier, testing is designed to help you make sound judgements, but it is not an exact science. Test results will help you reduce risk by following the route which offers the greatest *probability of success*.

That word *probability* is very important – no test result can offer an absolute guarantee that, when repeated, the same mailing will produce the same result.

With direct mail the sample sizes are crucial and because of this it is necessary for you to understand a little about statistics. This is so that:

▷ You will know how many people you need to mail in order for a test result to be 'significant' and therefore a reliable predictor of what will happen when you 'roll-out' the chosen mailing to the full list.

▷ You can decide, after the event, whether a particular test result is reliable.

Direct mail tests are conducted on samples from the various lists available. For comparative tests to be reliable, you must ensure that you are testing 'like with like' – in other words, the samples used for each test cell must be:

▷ Matched with each other in terms of composition and characteristics.

▷ The same size, or at least of a known size, so that you can allow for size variances in evaluation.

▷ Entirely typical, and a known proportion of, the universe they represent, so that you can predict the eventual performance of a 'roll-out' from the test data.

▷ Large enough to give a 'statistically significant' reading.

To ensure that samples are truly representative of their total 'universe', they would typically be systematic i.e. one in *n* samples. In other words, to select a sample of 3,000 names from a list of 12,000 you should instruct the computer to select every fourth name – this ensures randomization across the list, eliminating bias caused by keeping the list in say, chronological or geographic order.

This is a very important point – the simplest way of extracting 3,000 names from a list of 12,000 would be to take the first 3,000 records. If you used this method with a list held in chronological order, you would extract the 3,000 newest or oldest names which would not, of course, be typical of the list as a whole.

There are three basic statistical concepts involved in planning tests: confidence level, limit of error, statistical significance.

1 **Confidence level** – This is the number of times out of 100 that one could expect the test result to be repeated in a 'roll-out'. The levels commonly used in direct mail testing are between 80% and 95%.

2 **Limit of error** – Statistics is not an exact science and a test result is subject to a plus or minus correction according to sample size and response level. A 2% response from a sample of 5,000 names is subject to an error limit of 0.4%. This means that if you are comparing responses from two test cells, each of 5,000 names, you have to allow for this error before you can make meaningful comparisons. For example:

▷ Cell A (5,000 names) – produces 110 replies, i.e. 2.2% response.
▷ Cell B (5,000 names) – produces ninety replies, i.e. 1.8% response.

If you accept these response numbers without question you would say that response from cell A is 22.2% better than that from cell B (which of course is true) – *but applying the limit of error required for these statistics (cell size and response percentage) produces a different picture.*

A response of 2.2% from a sample of 5,000 is subject to a limit of error of 0.41%, and a response of 1.8% to a limit of 0.38%.

Applying these factors to these test results shows that when 'rolled out' to the larger lists:

▷ List A (test cell A = 2.2% test response) is actually likely to produce a response between 1.79% and 2.61%.
▷ List B (test cell B = 1.8% response) is likely to produce a response between 1.42% and 2.18%.

In other words, as cell B at best (2.18%) would be better than cell A at worst (1.79%), the apparent 'result' is not reliable.

3   **Significance level** – explained most simply with a question – 'Is the difference observed sufficiently large for it to be outside the variances expected due to the limits of error?' If the answer is 'yes' the result is significant, if 'no' it is not significant.

The formula for establishing minimum sample sizes and evaluating the significance and reliability of a test result is complicated and there is no need for us to go into great detail here.

You do not need to master any complicated formulae but it is important for the sample size to be large enough. After the event, you also need to know whether a result is significant and Table 9.2, although very basic, gives a quick idea of how reliable a result is likely to be.

Table 9.2

Significance factors in split-run testing (with 95% confidence level)

Total response Test cell A + Test cell B	Significance factor (% for result to be significant)	Number of responses in 'winning' cell	Number of responses in 'losing' cell	% difference
50	64.24	33	17	94%
100	60.00	60	40	50%
500	54.47	273	227	20%
1,000	53.16	532	468	14%

Thus if the total response to both halves of a test is fifty replies, there will only be a significant result if the 'winner' has produced at least thirty-three of those replies (i.e. the winner is 94% better than the loser).

Table 9.2 makes the point that the smaller the number of responses *(a* function *of sample size and response percentage)* the greater the difference needed *for the result to be significant.*

Two examples show how this table is used.

EXAMPLES

Example 1 – The mailing test cells produce 100 replies in total:

▷ **Mailing cell A produces sixty-one of that total (61%).**

▷ **Mailing cell B produces thirty-nine (39%).**

This result is significant, *but only just.*

Example 2 – With the same total of 100 replies:

▷ **Cell A pulls fifty-five replies (55%).**

▷ **Cell B pulls forty-five replies (45%).**

This result is *not* significant.

You can consider 'significance' to be synonymous with reliability – in other words in Example 1 you can rely on cell A producing more replies than cell B (give or take certain required tolerances) nineteen times out of twenty (note the table sub-heading – 95% confidence level).

The result in Example 2 is not significant, despite the fact that mailing A produced 22% more replies than mailing B.

Although the first of these two examples is statistically significant you should be very wary of making major plans from such small test results.

As the above examples show, a fairly high level of response is needed to enable you to rely on small differences with any confidence.

Don't stop monitoring

Measurement of response is only the start, of course. You must continue to monitor the on-going behaviour of respondents to ensure that an apparently successful new idea is not simply producing a large volume of poorly qualified enquiries.

Benefit testing – an alternative approach

As we have seen, most testing is based on volume response and is organized by exposing either:

> Alternative offers or creative treatments to matched samples of the same mailing list, or

> The same offer to alternate lists.

This approach requires sizeable samples or test cells, and sizeable budgets. For those whose markets or budgets are not so large there is an alternative, sometimes referred to as benefit testing.

This is really a form of telephone research involving, typically 100 to 150 calls. It will not predict precise responses, but it will often tell you which of a number of 'benefits' are likely to be most attractive to the audience. As a by-product, this method also shows whether the audience understands what each statement means.

Benefits can be offers or headline statements and the technique works as follows:

1 **Sample selection** – identify a sample and 'qualify' each of the names (i.e. make sure they are typical of the audience you are seeking) to ensure the statements will be relevant.

2 **Benefit wording** – statements must be clear and unambiguous (a small pilot will confirm whether this is so), and should be the ones you will use in the mailing, when the research is completed. In other words, you should write or brief your creative people to write a series of alternative statements, so that the one which scores best can be used. To rewrite the lines after the research will invalidate the results.

Typical statements for a diesel fuel might be:

▷ *Will not congeal, even in sub-zero temperatures*
▷ *Diesel with the smell removed.*

These examples are not 'copy' but the sort of wording you could use to brief a copywriter.

3
Making the calls – telephone each person asking for their help in a research study, e.g. *I am going to read out a number of statements about a new diesel fuel – after each statement will you please tell me, by giving it a score out of ten, how important this feature would be to you in deciding whether to buy this new fuel?*

The statements are then read out, one by one, and the scores noted. You can then move to phase 2: *I am now going to read out each statement again. Can you please score them in the same way, but this time on the basis of how unique each is, i.e. do you think this is an unusual feature or would it be readily available in existing products?*

4
Assembling the results – you will often find one or two statements scoring highly on both tables. This, or these, are the ones which will work best in your mailing.

This technique has been used successfully by numerous businesses where test volumes or budgets are restricted.

EVALUATION OF MAILINGS AND CAMPAIGNS

Evaluation is the precise measurement of marketing activities with a view to deciding which should be continued, which amended and which abandoned. In this way you can evaluate your direct mailings before making any major investments.

A clear understanding of the inter-relationship between costs, revenue and activity – combined with careful analysis of performance – is crucial to the success of your marketing activities.

Bringing the information generated by these analyses to the decision-making process, means that everything you do can be budgeted, measured and evaluated. It means that all activities are highly *accountable*, but this is no bad thing – although your activities can also be measured by others in your business, it also means that by studying the results of your activities you can improve your performance.

Accountability

Unlike general advertising, most direct mailings are designed to elicit a response from the recipient and they can thus be measured very exactly. This enables you to identify good and bad lists, creative treatments and, indeed, types of prospect very quickly and without spending large amounts of money.

This aspect appeals to all marketers, not just those with small budgets.

Should I be selling products or developing relationships?

As already mentioned, developing relationships is one of the key concepts of direct marketing – in fact direct marketing is often called 'relationship marketing'.

However, you are in business to make money and it is important to find the correct balance between investing in new customers who will become profitable later and getting a satisfactory return on your expenditure in time to stay in business.

This balance is a critical success factor and the point of balance will vary according to the nature of your business. Consider the example on the opposite page.

If you are just setting up in business, you are likely to have only limited funding, so you will not be able to afford to go flat out for later payback. However, some element of investment is probably advisable. In order to reach sensible and affordable decisions, it is necessary to make constant comparisons between these options.

EXAMPLE

Company A has a small range of products which it sells through single product advertisements in national newspapers. Once a customer has bought they are sent a catalogue or leaflet carrying details of the other products in the range.

▷　Prime objective – to make a profit from the orders received from each advertisement.

▷　Secondary objective – to build a 'list' and make subsequent sales (and more profit) from future mailings to these customers.

Question

Should this company stick to its policy of making profit from the first transaction or could it do better in the long-term by 'breaking even' on the first sale, thus generating more customers for its list?

Answer

We don't know! It is likely that in most markets the 'investment route' will eventually yield more profit, but only a carefully planned programme of testing and evaluation will enable the right balance to be found.

EASY WAYS TO MANAGE NUMBERS

In marketing, we often find ourselves looking at numbers at two extremes: on the one hand we talk of mailing quantities, or customer databases which can run into many thousands, or even millions, for example: *the UK electoral roll contains 44 million records.*

On the other hand, we may be looking at the response to a newspaper advertisement, which may be a fraction of 1%, e.g. *0.003% response from the Sun newspaper equals 1,200 replies.*

It is important, therefore, to find a way of presenting and comparing extremes of data that is immediately informative, so that two quotations or two results can be compared, with only a quick glance at the figures.

To make this possible we use a series of 'standard measures'.

THE STANDARD 'PER THOUSAND' MEASURE

One answer to these numerical extremes is the standard 'per thousand' measure. Thus print costs are measured 'per thousand' units, lists in 'per thousand' names, and so on.

STANDARD PRODUCTION MEASURE

In the area of production, most suppliers now quote on a 'per thousand' basis, but if you are comparing two quotes, make sure you are comparing like with like, as in the example below.

COMPARING SUPPLIER QUOTES

You have received two quotes for different mailing quantities, one of 15,000 mailings and one of 22,000. The cost of the first mailing is £7,495, and the second £9,650. How do you compare these quotes?

Converting them into cost per thousand shows:

▷ **Quote No 1** $\dfrac{£7,495}{15,000} \times 1,000 = £499.67$ per thousand

▷ **Quote No 2** $\dfrac{£9,650}{22,000} \times 1,000 = £438.64$ per thousand

It is now easy to compare the quotes.

STANDARD ANALYSIS MEASURES

The commonly used measures for analysis are either *per thousand* based, or *per order/sale* based. By using these measures you can quickly compare campaigns in terms of the response or sales you receive *per thousand companies mailed.*

Here are three simple calculations which occur frequently in marketing evaluation:

Cost per thousand

$$\text{Cost per thousand} = \frac{\text{Total cost}}{\text{Total quantity}} \times 1{,}000$$

or

$$\text{Total cost} \div \frac{\text{Total quantity}}{1{,}000}$$

Response per thousand

$$\text{Response per thousand} = \frac{\text{Total response}}{\text{Total mailed}} \times 1{,}000$$

Cost per order

$$\text{Cost per order} = \frac{\text{Total cost}}{\text{Total orders}} \quad \text{or} \quad \frac{\text{Cost per thousand}}{\text{Orders per thousand}}$$

POSTAL COSTS – A COMMON MISTAKE

Be especially aware of confusion when comparing postage costs on a per thousand basis. It is easy, when carrying out rough calculations at speed, to calculate a postage cost of 19p per item as £19 per thousand. This is not correct – 19p per unit is £190 per thousand.

ALLOWABLE COST-PER-ORDER – WHERE IT ALL BEGAN

One of the simplest measures used to control direct order marketing activity is the *allowable cost-per-order*, an approach which has been around for many years.

Allowable cost-per-order is reached by building a mini profit and loss account for an average sale, *including* the desired profit, but *excluding* promotional costs.

The result is the amount you can afford to spend to secure a sale – the allowable selling or promotional cost or the allowable cost-per-order.

Calculating the allowable cost-per-order		
Selling price (including c & p)		£150
Cost of product	£50	
Order receipt, processing, handling and so on	£15	
Carriage and packing	£ 5	
Total costs	£70	£70
Contribution		£80
Profit required		£45
Allowable cost-per-sale		£35

This costing shows that you can afford to spend £35 to obtain each order and that each sale will give you a profit of £45 to help fund business management and growth.

You can use the allowable cost-per-order to calculate the required response rate from your mailing, for example:

▷ Cost of mailing to 2,500 prospects, say £1,250, including print, postage and so on.

▷ Dividing the £1,250 cost by the £35 'allowable cost' shows that thirty-six orders will be needed, i.e. a 1.44% response from the 2,500 mailing.

You then need to use your judgement to decide whether this is achievable. Ask around – if you know someone who is selling a non-competitive product of similar price and interest level to the same market, they may be prepared to tell you what response they get. Don't assume you will get exactly the same, but you will at least get an idea of the approximate range of response you might expect.

You can take this costing a stage further by calculating how many orders you will need to 'break even', i.e. to get the investment back without any profit. In the above model, you would simply divide the £1,250 cost by the £80 'contribution', to show that sixteen orders would recover the mailing costs.

This demonstration has deliberately been kept very simple. Even this approach should be tailored to your own business to allow for such things as breakages, returns, bad debts and so on. Remember to put in all costs including, where relevant, design, photography, artwork, printers' charges, any response costs (postage, telephone and so on).

Although the allowable cost approach is very simplistic, it does help to give a better feel for the point of balance between acquisition and retention.

If you feel confident you can make future sales to your new customers – *and you have sufficient funding to enable you to wait for profit* – you can be more relaxed about the amount of profit achieved from the first sale.

The allowable cost approach is very useful, but it has limitations, too:

1 It requires sales to be estimated in advance to establish the unit cost.

2 It assumes that product cost is fixed, i.e. it will not change with volume of sales.

3 It leads to decisions being based, not on profit maximization, but on profit satisfaction – thus it can become a self-fulfilling prophecy.

4 It does not take into account any future purchases by a new customer – it can therefore sway your judgement, perhaps, in the wrong way.

ALLOWABLE COSTS – A MORE FLEXIBLE APPROACH

This problem is easily addressed. All that is required is to re-run the numbers based on different prices.

All other things being equal, a lower price will produce a higher response rate and a higher price will produce a lower response rate.

You must then judge whether the response rates required to make the desired profit are reasonable or not.

Calculating allowable costs and required response using different prices

Mailing quantity	5,000	
Mailing cost	£1,750 (@ £350 per '000)	
	Price A	*Price B*
Price	£79.50	£59.50
Direct costs	£37.50	£32.50
	£42.00	£27.00
Required profit	£20.00	£15.00
Allowable cost	£22.00	£12.00
Response needed to cover mailing cost	80	146
Response percentage required	1.6%	2.92%

TAKING A WIDER VIEW

One of the problems of simple allowable cost calculations is that they overlook the larger campaign issues. This can be tackled by moving up a level in your evaluations.

Rather than use a single sale as the base level, why not use the campaign? And rather than judge a required response rate against experience, why not use your best estimate of a response rate and *judge whether to proceed or not on the profit likely to be generated*. You can always work out individual sales profitability from the overall campaign calculation, as the following example shows.

Campaign based budgeting

	Price A	Price B
Price	£49.50	£39.50
Item cost	£24.50	£24.50
Gross margin	£25.00	£15.00
Number mailed	10,000	10,000
Response percentage	1.75%	3.5%
Responses	175	350
Sales	£8,662	£13,825
Cost of sales	£4,287	£8,575
Gross profit	£4,375	£5,250
Cost of mailing	£3,250	£3,250
Campaign contribution	£1,125	£2,000
Contribution per sale	£6.43	£5.71

In this example, choosing the higher price would mean sacrificing £875 worth of contribution, despite the slightly higher profit per sale. The lower price has also generated an additional 175 buyers for the database. *This illustrates the classic marketing problem of whether or not to go for higher volumes at lower cost, or vice versa.*

HOW MARKETING COSTS BEHAVE

Before going on to look at budgeting and decision-making models more closely, it is important to understand costs – what they are and how they behave.

Costs in marketing, as in every area of business, fall into three basic groupings: fixed costs, variable costs and overheads. In building the cost component of a budget, you need to be concerned with the costs you will incur, whether these costs are fixed or variable, and if variable, on which elements are they dependent?

VARIABLE COSTS, FIXED COSTS AND OVERHEADS

The definition of costs changes depends on the level being addressed. Some costs may be fixed when looking at an individual campaign, but variable in the context of a year's worth of campaigns.

▷ **Variable costs** – are defined as costs which vary with the amount of a given activity. For example, the cost of a mailing list will vary according to the quantity you decide to rent. Postage will be directly proportional to the number you mail. Data capture of responses will be linked to the number of people who respond.

▷ **Fixed costs** – are costs which are not influenced by changes in activity. For example the cost of artwork is fixed at the campaign level (although it could be seen as variable at the strategic level).

▷ **Overheads** (indirect fixed costs) – are costs which are incurred whether or not an activity takes place. For example, property rental is likely to be a cost which is not only independent of the quantity mailed in any one campaign, but also independent of the number of campaigns in a given period (within reason).

THE TWO-WAY EFFECT OF QUANTITY

Some marketing costs increase with quantity. For example, overtime processing can result from an unexpectedly high response to a mailing or advertisement.

On the other hand, some costs, e.g. the unit cost of printing, can be dramatically reduced with increases in quantity – as is demonstrated by the following example for a fairly standard mailing pack. From this example, it can be seen that a straight-line extrapolation from test mailing costs would seriously distort the financial implications of a roll-out. The cost of the 20,000 roll-out mailings projected from the costs of the 5,000 test would be £8,800, rather than the £7,000 it would actually cost.

Table 9.3
Effect of quantity on print costs

Effect of quantity on print costs (C5 mailing)		
Quantity	Total cost	Cost per pack
Test – 2,000	£880	44 pence
Roll-out – 20,000	£7,000	35 pence

However, if you were to 'run on' a further 20,000 copies there might be hardly any further reduction for quantity, as you would already have amortized the set-up costs and used most of the 'economy of scale'.

Understanding the effect of quantity is important if the correct inferences are to be drawn from a test campaign about the financial implications of a roll-out.

How to handle overheads

The handling of costs is probably one of the most difficult areas of budgeting. Variable costs, by definition, can easily be allocated and do not present a problem. Fixed costs, directly related to an activity, e.g. artwork for a mailing, also do not create a problem. It is the allocation of overheads (indirect fixed costs) which causes most of the problems.

You can attempt to allocate overheads to products or campaigns, but there are problems. For example, say an assistant has planned twelve campaigns for the year, you could allocate a twelfth of their salary to each campaign.

But what if two of the campaigns take twice as much time as the others?

> *What if one of the campaigns is cancelled (after your assistant has done most of the work) or another campaign is added during the period?*

One answer is to instigate a method of decision-making that does not require overheads to be allocated to specific activities. This is the *contribution* or *relevant costing* approach.

THE CONTRIBUTION APPROACH

When looking at a campaign, the most useful level for decision-making is the contribution level. This takes into account *all the revenue and costs directly associated with an activity*, including those costs and revenues which are only incurred/generated *because* the activity is being undertaken.

If the decision to do, or not to do, a mailing does not affect the cost, then it is not part of the analysis.

EXAMPLE OF THE CONTRIBUTION APPROACH

The example opposite considers whether or not to undertake a mailing to 7,500 businesses. *Your selling price is £400 and you expect a response of 2%.*

According to this calculation the activity makes a loss. But there are two indirect costs (overheads) included, which you are going to have to pay whether or not the campaign goes ahead.

These are: staff costs and office costs. These costs add up to £9,000.

A relevant costing approach would say that the campaign generates an income of £18,750 and, as *a result of undertaking the campaign*, costs of £12,000 will be incurred. This leaves you with an income of £6,750 to contribute towards your overheads, i.e. if you don't do the mailing you will be £6,750 worse off at the end of the period.

This contribution (or relevant costing) approach, based on identifying the *relevant costs* associated with a campaign, looks to see if undertaking the campaign *contributes* towards the overheads (which will be incurred whether or not the campaign goes ahead).

EXAMPLE OF THE CONTRIBUTION APPROACH

The costs you expect are:

Cost of goods	£275
List rental	£300 per thousand
Artwork/agency fees	£4,500
Production and postage	£500 per thousand
Marketing staff handling	
ten campaigns per year	£40,000
office costs (rent and so on) allocated	£5,000
Response handling - allocated	£10 per response

Putting this together you calculate:

Mailing quantity	7,500
Response	150 responses
Revenue	£60,000
Cost of goods	£41,250
Gross profit	£18,750

List rental	£2,250	
Production/print/postage	£3,750	
Agency artwork/fees	£4,500	
Staff	£4,000	
Office costs	£5,000	
Response handling	£1,500	
Total costs		£21,000
Profit/(loss)		(£2,250)

It is important to remember, that although the contribution approach does not attempt to allocate overheads to a specific activity, they *cannot be ignored*. The contributions from all the activities which the overhead supports, must add up to more than the overheads, if the business is to survive.

The benefit of the contribution approach is that it looks at what *additional* costs will be incurred, over and above those that will have to be paid anyway, and so helps to lead to decisions which maximize profit – as the previous example illustrates.

To return to the earlier point, when you concentrate on making profit on the initial sale, you are likely to make fewer sales at this stage and you will therefore grow your database more slowly. *On the other hand, you may stay in business longer – an important consideration at any time.*

Whatever your decision regarding acquisition costings, you will want to maximize the additional business you get from the new customers you have gained. This then, requires a *retention strategy* which is dealt with elsewhere in this book.

SUMMARY

The ability to test, is one of the major benefits of direct mail. Testing enables decisions to be made from solid information, rather than hunches or vague research responses.

There are several methods of testing, but all have one or more of the same strategic objectives:

▷ To increase response
▷ To improve the quality of response
▷ To improve cost-efficiency.

It is tempting to become 'test-happy', especially with alternative versions of copy. Creative testing is quite valid, but it is not the most important element in a mailing.

The priorities for testing in direct mail, *in order of importance*, are:

▷ List
▷ Offer

> Timing
> Creative
> Response methods.

If your budgets are limited, it clearly makes sense to concentrate on targeting the right person first, thinking up an attractive offer next, then finding out when the prospect will be most interested. Only after getting these three things right, should you start to consider alternative creative concepts.

In testing, you can do only one of two things. You can either:

> Test each individual aspect, or
> Test an entire package.

To test individual aspects you need many names and large budgets, so in most cases you will take the latter course.

STATISTICS

In order for your results to be reliable, your tests must conform to the basic laws of statistics.

BENEFIT TESTING

This is really market research rather than testing, but it can be very helpful in highlighting good and bad headlines and copy statements.

EVALUATION

In order to plan properly and build your business successfully, it is essential to have a good grasp of the basic techniques of measurement and evaluation. The 'standard measures' are useful for comparing competitive quotations.

It is also vital to find a method of campaign evaluation which is relevant to your own business. The available options range from simple 'per transaction' costings, to full contribution methods. These are detailed on pages 194–203.

WHAT TO DO NEXT

Read all you can about testing – it will help you get a good feel for what is feasible, and just how much difference a successful test can make to your business. Check the reading list in Appendix 2 for details of suitable books.

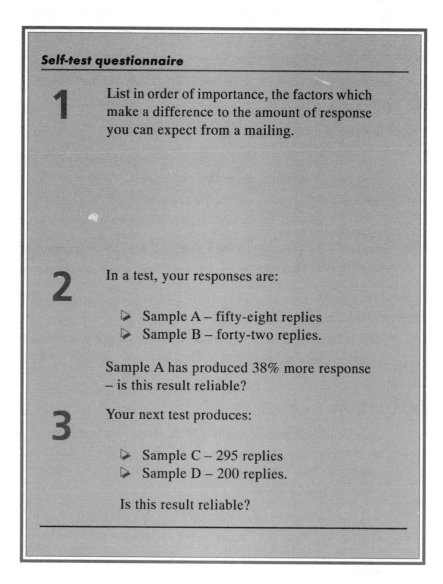

Self-test questionnaire

1 List in order of importance, the factors which make a difference to the amount of response you can expect from a mailing.

2 In a test, your responses are:

▷ Sample A – fifty-eight replies
▷ Sample B – forty-two replies.

Sample A has produced 38% more response – is this result reliable?

3 Your next test produces:

▷ Sample C – 295 replies
▷ Sample D – 200 replies.

Is this result reliable?

Check your answers in Appendix 4.

Part Four

Services

10 When to use outside suppliers and how to choose them

In the field of direct mail, there is almost no job that, given enough time, you cannot tackle yourself. You can write and print letters, address the envelopes, even produce a descriptive leaflet, all on your desktop PC.

However, an important consideration is – should you spend your time doing things that can often be done more cost-effectively or perhaps, better by others?

There are two areas to consider:

▷ Could someone else do it better and/or quicker?

▷ Could your time be more profitably spent doing other tasks?

In this chapter I will identify some of the specialist resources you may need and where these may be found. I will also cover the crucial issue of correct briefing. In a lifetime of using specialist suppliers, I have consistently found briefing to be the area where most problems are caused or avoided.

START OUTSIDE – GO IN-HOUSE LATER

By using outside suppliers in the early stages of building your business, you will also learn how to avoid many costly mistakes. When you have experienced a few campaigns you can decide whether it would be more cost-efficient in the future to do some of the tasks in-house.

YOU HAVE MADE YOUR FIRST DECISION – NOW WHAT?

Let us assume that you have made a decision to use outside resources for at least some of the tasks with which you are faced.

Among the services you may wish to consider are:

▷ Design and creative teams
▷ Mailing list suppliers
▷ Mailing and fulfilment houses
▷ Database and computer bureaux
▷ Printers.

DESIGN AND CREATIVE TEAMS

Even if you feel able to write your own mailings, you may need help with design, layout, artwork and so on. You may have a flair for this, too, but before you dismiss the idea of using an outside supplier, think of the time you will have to invest. Can you do something more productive with your time?

There is no point in saving £500 if you're taking up time that could be more productively used to negotiate a better deal with your product suppliers.

The point has been made several times that it is more important to get your targeting, offer and timing correct, than to have award-winning creative work.

So, although good creative work can make a major difference to your results, there is no doubt that the first three aspects are much more important. *You are therefore likely to get a better return on the time and effort you invest in the first three points.*

> *An important reminder – when considering creative suppliers you must ask to see what they have done for other companies in your line of business – ask what the results were, too.*

Brilliant award-winning creative ideas do not always produce huge sales – see the example opposite – they often impress other creative people more than prospects.

MAILING LIST SUPPLIERS

The subject of mailing list suppliers is discussed thoroughly in Chapter 5.

EXAMPLE

We once produced a very 'creative' mailing in response to a very specific client brief and this was highly regarded by everyone who saw it. The mailing actually won four creative awards, three in the UK and one in Europe.

When it was tested against the original control, a very basic mailing consisting of a simple letter, two-colour leaflet and reply card, it produced half the response.

An alternative test, simply adapting the original mailing and making a better offer, doubled response against control - i.e. giving four times as much as the new creative approach.

MAILING AND FULFILMENT HOUSES

If your mailing is to be sent to only a few hundred people, you may decide to carry out the addressing, filling and despatch yourself. However, if there are several thousand pieces involved, you should at least consider using an outside resource. There will be a cost involved, but again, you must consider what you might be neglecting in order to save this money.

Before choosing a mailing house you should get a couple of quotations to help you make a better-informed decision.

A good mailing house can carry out the entire job, including receiving deliveries from the printer, addressing your mailing pieces by label or computer letter, assembling and enclosing, bagging in Mailsort sequence and organizing collection by the Royal Mail. Many larger mailing houses actually have Royal Mail personnel on the premises.

CONSIDER FULFILMENT TOO

Fulfilment is the name given to all activities relating to the handling of responses from your mailings. Thus a fulfilment house may:

- Receive enquiries and/or orders on your behalf.
- Capture names and addresses and despatch information packs.
- Assemble and despatch product orders.
- Receive and bank payments by cash, cheque or credit card.
- Provide support services such as helplines and general enquiry handling facilities.

A fulfilment house can take the place of many employees – the cost will be larger per job, but for a small business, the advantages often outweigh the penalties. The big advantage is that you can turn them on and off like a tap, rather than be committed to premises and staff in the early stages of building your business.

DATABASE AND COMPUTER BUREAUX

This is another area where specialist experience can be worth its weight in gold. Although there are many good books and software packages, you still need to invest a lot of your time in getting to grips with unfamiliar concepts.

If you are concerned that you may not have the time or the expertise to develop your own database, it is worth considering a bureau. You do not need to know how a database works in order to run your business efficiently, but you do need to know what it can do for you.

A good database bureau will guide you, helping you get the best out of your data. They will understand too, that your long-term aim may be to bring the operation in-house.

Meanwhile, they can help you by providing hardware and software resources, as well as experience. They can arrange data capture, analysis and output for mailings such as labels, data for laser letters and in many cases, produce the letters for you.

Your bureau will also advise you on de-duplication, data enhancement and other specialist data matters.

PRINTERS

There are thousands of printers in the UK, but not all of them understand the precise requirements for good direct mail. There are many with the right experience however, and it will pay you to seek out the good ones. Many people leave selection of the printer until the last minute, but this is a very short-sighted approach. Like your other specialist suppliers, printers have experience that can help you to produce a better job more cost-efficiently.

They can advise you on paper weights, cost-efficient sizes and formats, artwork requirements and several other aspects.

WHERE TO FIND SUITABLE SUPPLIERS – START WITH THE DMA

A good starting point is the Direct Marketing Association whose address you will find in Appendix 2. Membership of the DMA does not guarantee that a supplier will have a greater knowledge of direct mail than a non-member, but there is a better chance that this will be so.

Your first step therefore should be to ask the DMA for its list of member suppliers in your required area. Among its members are creative agencies, mailing and fulfilment houses, list brokers, database and computer bureaux and printers.

Among the advantages of choosing DMA member companies are:

▷ They subscribe to the DMA code of conduct, so you can be assured of certain minimum standards.

▷ They are likely to know more about the special requirements of direct mailers than non-members.

HOW DO YOU CHOOSE THE RIGHT SUPPLIER?

Selecting the right supplier from a list of twenty contenders can be tricky, but the following process has stood me in good stead for many years:

1 Contact the DMA for its list of member suppliers.

2 Write to some, or all of these, asking them to tell you:

▷ what they can do for you. What experience they have in your field.

⯈ who their other clients are. You need to know that they have handled a similar requirement to yours, while also checking, before you reveal all your secrets, that they are not dealing with your major competitor.

⯈ what is their basis for charging. Where possible you should look for project fees, rather than hourly or daily rates.

⯈ why they should be given the job. Their answer will tell you how keen they are to get your business.

DRAW UP A SHORT LIST

The replies to this letter will help you select a short list of two or three 'probables'. You can then arrange to visit these to discuss your requirements more fully. You should ask each for a detailed quotation.

MEET THE WORKERS

At this stage, you should ask to meet the person who will be responsible for handling your business. Most chief executives will impress you with their knowledge and experience, but if they will not be personally involved from day-to-day this may be irrelevant, or even misleading.

MAKE SURE YOU GIVE A CLEAR, COMPLETE BRIEF

As I said earlier, a large number of supplier's mistakes were made because they did not quite understand their client's requirements. Of course they should have told you they didn't understand, but human nature being what it is, they were too embarrassed to do so.

Once the mistake is made, they will try to cover it up – even though this usually adds to the problem. *The way to avoid this is to make sure that your brief is clear, complete and totally understood.*

ASK THEM TO HELP YOU WRITE YOUR BRIEF

Odd though this sounds, your suppliers are the best people to tell you what they need to know. They have been at the receiving end of many briefs, good and bad, and can help you avoid the worst pitfalls.

There is another benefit – if they are involved in the briefing process, they have some 'ownership' and are thus more prepared to take responsibility.

Expect a rapid response

The best suppliers are the busiest, so don't be surprised if they ask for a few days to send you a full response. They should, however, acknowledge your brief very quickly, either by phone or mail. If they are too busy to pick up the phone, what will happen when they have a problem on your job?

Take up references

No reputable supplier will hesitate to give you the names of existing customers. They will, of course, normally give you details of those with whom they have the best relationships. You can choose to contact those, alternatively you could 'go it alone' and ask some of their other clients. Whichever option you choose, this is an important part of the process.

Compare the quotations

Remember, price is not everything. You need to balance the price quoted with your assessment of their capabilities. Do they impress you with their systems and their staff? Do they seem the sort of people to take problems off your hands or to present you with new ones?

While you should try to buy competitively, it is not a great idea to buy solely on price. As with many other things, you tend to get what you pay for and that £500 you saved will not be worth much, if you have to spend a lot of your precious time sorting things out.

WHAT YOUR BRIEF SHOULD CONTAIN

The brief will vary according to the job you are placing and the type of supplier with whom you are dealing. Good suppliers will be happy to help you design a briefing checklist and briefs will vary according to the type of supplier and the details of your job.

As an example of the sort of information required, here are the things I would include in a briefing to a creative team:

1   **Information**. Tell them all you know about your product, your market, the sort of people who buy it, the number of competitors you have, and so on. If you don't feel you can trust them with your secrets, you have probably chosen the wrong partners. Make sure you provide supporting material – facts, figures, testimonial statements, and so on.

2   **Brief the right people**. Make sure you talk to at least one of the actual 'creatives' i.e. the people who will do the job. You will then feel confident that your requirements have been fully understood.

3   **State a clear objective**. Do you wish to sell your product direct or generate leads for further action? If the latter, do you want 'loose' or 'tight' leads? The answers to these questions may not be clear to you at this stage, but you must make these decisions before you brief your suppliers.

> *Clearly it would be impossible for a copywriter to produce relevant copy without having a clear objective in mind.*

4   **Prepare a positioning statement**. This is an area that causes great concern, but again, without clear guidance your design team cannot hit the target. Positioning is discussed in Chapter 7.

5   **Give an idea as to budget**. You don't need to reveal the precise amount you have to spend – if you do, you should not be surprised to find they have spent every penny! But they do need to know whether this is a low-budget mailing or a high-quality prestige affair.

6   **Set a timetable**. As C. Northcote Parkinson observed many years ago, work tends to expand to fill the time available. This may not be important if you have been quoted a project fee, but it could be a major problem if your suppliers are working on hourly rates. If you have fulfilled your side of the bargain by providing all the necessary information on time, you are entitled to expect the finished job to be on schedule. If your materials were provided late, don't be surprised to find your job is also running behind schedule.

Many people new to marketing are surprised to find that a delay of say, two days in delivering a piece of artwork to a printer, can result in a delay of more than a week in final delivery. There is a very simple reason for this.

Like all good suppliers the best printers are very busy – their machines run around the clock, working to very precise time schedules. If your job misses its 'slot' in the schedule, the next job cannot be delayed, so yours goes to the back of the queue. This can easily mean losing a week.

You should, therefore, be prudent and build in a little leeway in your planning to allow for the occasional 'slippage'.

7 **Describe your prospect clearly**. A copywriter cannot write to a list – only to a person. One of the best copywriters I ever worked with used to spend half an hour writing a description of the person to whom she was about to write. This was hypothetical of course, but it helped her write believable, convincing copy. Compare the following prospect descriptions:

(a) Financial directors

(b) Financial director of a medium-sized company – probably aged thirty-five plus – has a secretary who filters the mail – is prepared to listen to an argument which shows how to reduce costs or increase revenue – probably reacts well to offers of free reports showing how companies of similar size coped with a specific problem – may need to present recommendations to a board or chief executive.

Which of these would help you write the better mailing?

8 **Define the benefits**. Make sure they are benefits for the reader and not simply attributes of the product. People do not buy lubricating oil because it is a high-tech product, they buy it because it stops a hinge squeaking.

Tell them which of your benefits is unique, or at least the most attractive to your prospects. To do this, you need to put yourself in the position of the prospect and ask yourself 'What is important?'.

If you can't answer this question, you need to talk to some prospects before you brief the job.

9 **Explain your offer**. Offers were discussed at length in Chapter 8, but you must now explain yours to the creative team. If they are not excited and *if they are typical of your prospects*, ask yourself is your offer good enough? Listen to their suggestions – they may not all be sensible or relevant, but they will often come up with a brilliant idea you hadn't thought of.

10 **Put your brief in writing**. A seemingly obvious point, but one that is often ignored, even by experienced campaigners. No-one will remember everything you said in a meeting – not even you! A well-written brief leaves nothing to chance and answers questions in your absence.

The above briefing list, while clearly targeted at creative suppliers, gives an idea of the depth of detail necessary to brief correctly.

PRODUCE A BRIEFING FORM

If you use a form, especially one which you have designed in consultation with your suppliers, you have a useful checklist of things to remember. Figure 10.1 shows a typical form for briefing a creative team.

Figure 10.1

A creative
briefing form

Creative briefing form	
Name of job: (e.g. March prospects mailing)	
Date:	
Product/service description to which this brief relates:	
Background: market situation, competitive situation, any other similar relevant comment:	
Positioning: a brief simple statement describing the overall impression you wish to leave in the mind of the reader:	
Communications objective: what are you trying to achieve e.g. attract enquiries, change attitudes, encourage trial, visit to dealer?	
Target audience: who are you talking to - large or small customers, prospects, decision makers, influencers, purchasing departments and so on:	
Media to be used - i. e. is this a stand-alone mailing, or will the same theme be used in an advertisement or an insert:	
Response mechanism: mailed coupon, telephone, fax:	
Proposition: (offer) what customer benefit does this product offer - this should be expressed very briefly - if all else fails it may be used as the headline:	
Rationale: why will this product provide these benefits?	
Secondary benefits: are there any other benefits which should be included?	
Tone of voice: authoritative, questioning, advisory:	
Executional guidelines: any wider issues to be conformed to - group standards, terminology:	
Promotional aspects: what sort of promotional offer is to be made - e.g. price, prize draw, incentive?	

A good technique is to design your own briefing form and ask your supplier to do the same – when you consolidate the two, you will probably find that you have covered all that is required.

A FINAL CONSIDERATION – SHOULD YOU USE A CONSULTANT?

In some circumstances you may consider the use of a specialist direct marketing consultant. Consultants command high fees, but if a good consultant helps you avoid costly mistakes, this can be a worthwhile investment.

Your decision should hinge on what you will gain and this is not a simple judgement to make. A consultant's charges could easily be more than the cost of hiring a full-time assistant, so you have to decide whether your primary need is for greater experience or willing hands to carry out the tasks you define.

One key factor will be how much experience you already have – or can draw on – from friends and colleagues.

WHAT WILL YOU GET FROM A CONSULTANT?

To help you decide this issue, here is a list of some services you could reasonably expect an experienced consultant to provide:

▷ Market analysis and strategic planning
▷ Targeting of prospects and sales forecasting
▷ Mailing list selection
▷ Location and selection of specialist suppliers, e.g. creative teams, mailing and fulfilment houses, computer and telemarketing bureaux, printers and so on
▷ Production of, and/or evaluation of creative work
▷ Recruitment of staff
▷ Specialized training – for yourself and your staff
▷ Product design and development.

SELECTING A CONSULTANT

To select a consultant ,you could go through a similar procedure to that outlined earlier, remembering again that, although not all good consultants are members of the DMA, this is the safest place to start – unless, of course, you have someone recommended to you.

SUMMARY

When considering the subject of outside suppliers you have to be as objective as you can.

Of course you can write the letter, but:

▷ Could someone else do it better and/or quicker?

▷ Could you use the time better doing something else?

There are many possible suppliers and you should consider the following.

DESIGN AND CREATIVE TEAMS

Apart from the question of what is the best use of your time, an outside creative team may be able to add something you would not have thought of. They are exposed to many companies, products and markets and this cross-fertilization of ideas can be very valuable. Even if you do eventually do-it-yourself, the discussions you have with potential creative suppliers will help you do it better.

MAILING LIST SUPPLIERS

Mailing list suppliers are fully discussed in Chapter 5.

MAILING AND FULFILMENT HOUSES

Here again, you can do the whole job in-house, but in this area, apart from your own time, you have other things to consider. Using a good mailing and fulfilment house can save you planning time, but also the worry and commitment of hiring people and premises before you have a clear idea of your eventual needs.

DATABASE AND COMPUTER BUREAUX

Specialist experience is always valuable, but never more so than with databases and computers. As I have pointed out, you can easily set up and run your own database, but it does require time. Also, if your business is at an early stage of development, do you *really* know what your eventual needs will be. If not you should consider a bureau as a first stage.

Most people call in their printer too late. Consulted early enough, printers can help you in many ways. They not only know which papers will suit a specific format, they will often be able to tell you how to cut your costs without sacrificing quality. For example:

▷ They can usually find an appropriate paper to suit your budget.

▷ They can show you how to reduce your artwork costs.

▷ They will advise you on cost-efficient formats – sometimes, just changing the position of a fold can reduce the cost of a job dramatically.

If you get to know your printer you may find other benefits too:

> *When I was marketing director of a mail order company I managed to get most of my internal office stationery (pads, compliments slips, and so on) entirely free by asking the printer to use up the ends and edges of paper which are normally 'cut to waste' when a job is being printed and trimmed.*

FINDING SUPPLIERS

You will find many advertisements in the pages of the trade press, Precision Marketing, Direct Response and so on. You should contact some of these for a discussion.

Don't forget that DMA members have a code of conduct which can be very reassuring to a newcomer to marketing.

You should do your first 'trawl' by letter and questionnaire – this saves your time and avoids lots of wasted discussions. Once you have drawn up a shortlist there is no substitute for face-to-face discussions.

MAKE SURE YOU GIVE A CLEAR, COMPLETE BRIEF

There is a specimen creative brief on page 219. Briefing is the point at which most mistakes originate. Get input from your suppliers – they can tell you what they need to know.

THE FINAL QUESTION – SHOULD YOU USE A CONSULTANT?

Consultants can be cost-effective, but they are not cheap. A consultant's fees can easily be as much as, or more than, the cost of an assistant.

You therefore have to decide on your primary need – do you need outside experience which you could not get from one of your other suppliers? Or is your main requirement for a pair of willing hands to carry out the tasks you know need doing?

To select a consultant you should follow the same procedure as that outlined on page 213.

WHAT TO DO NEXT

Talk to the DMA and ask for its list of member suppliers.

Contact some suppliers. Ask what they need from you to produce a complete job quotation. They may have standard forms – see if you can get copies of these.

Arrange visits to some mailing houses and printers – you'll find it's time well spent.

11 Royal Mail services to help you develop your business

Royal Mail provides a whole range of options to make organizing your mailing as easy as possible. This chapter provides details of some of these services.

If you want to discuss any of these in more depth you should call your local Royal Mail Sales Centre – for further details see Yellow Pages or your local telephone directory.

MAILSORT

When you are sending at least 4,000 letters or 1,000 packets of the same size and weight, you can qualify for a discount on the postage through Mailsort.

To take advantage of Mailsort you must either:

▷ Hold an appropriate contract with Royal Mail, or
▷ Use a mailing house which holds a mailing contract – the mailing house will pass on the postal savings to you.

To qualify for this discount you must meet the following requirements:

▷ At least 4,000 letters or 1,000 packets must be sent in any single Mailsort mailing. The minimum number falls to 2,000 if all letters are for delivery within the same postcode area in which they are posted (the postcode area is defined by the first one or two letters of the postcode e.g. B for Birmingham, EH for Edinburgh and so on).

▷ A minimum of 90% of all your Mailsort items must carry a full and correct postcode.

Mailsort works on the basis that you sort your mailing items into postcode districts before giving them to Royal Mail for delivery. In return for you doing some of the work normally carried out by Royal Mail, they will refund part of your postage charges.

Mailsort mailings must be sorted, bundled and bagged. The bags must be tied and labelled and made available for collections in line with Mailsort specifications.

It would be possible for you to sort the mailing manually, but in practice it is much easier by computer. Therefore, if you plan to send regular mailings to your own list it is worth setting up your computer to produce labels or letters in the Mailsort sequence.

Most, if not all, lists available for rental will be available in Mailsort sequence – your labels or address tapes will be produced in the correct order so you only need to keep them in sequence to qualify for your discount.

Basic rates for weights over 60 g are lower than the public tariff, and you can forget about the usual weight band restriction because Mailsort operates a special *straight line pricing* system. This means that you pay for the actual weight of your package, per gram, rather than for the weight band into which it fits.

Discounts range from 13% to 32% depending on the delivery option you choose, the volume of mail you are sending and the level of sortation you carry out. Delivery options available are:

▷ **Mailsort 1** – targeted for delivery on the next working day after posting. This is designed to ensure a first class service when you need to meet an urgent delivery date.

▷ **Mailsort 2** – ensuring delivery within three working days. Mailsort 2 offers more opportunities for saving money.

▷ **Mailsort 3** - targeted for delivery within seven working days. This option carries the maximum discounts – 25% for mailings of between 4,000 and 250,000. Larger mailings offer even more discount up to 32% for mailings of one million pieces or more.

To make sure you qualify for the best possible discount, discuss your mailing with your local Royal Mail Sales Centre.

MAILSORT LIGHT

This is a special service for lightweight packages, mainly used as 'teasers' in advance of a main mailing, or as follow-ups to boost response. Subject to certain conditions regarding quantity and weight you could qualify for a substantial extra postage discount.

PRESSTREAM

This is a sister service to Mailsort – providing a nationwide distribution service specifically geared for periodicals, magazines and newsletters.

There are two delivery options:

▷ **Presstream 1** – targeted for delivery on the next working day, and

▷ **Presstream 2** – for delivery within three working days of despatch.

Qualifying volumes are the same as for Mailsort, except that for Presstream 1 you must post at least ten times a year, and for Presstream 2 at least twice a year. Publication content must be at least $\frac{1}{6}$ editorial not related to the sale of goods or services. Maximum weight per item, like Mailsort, is 2 kg.

Like Mailsort, Presstream operates a special *straight line pricing* system. This means that you pay for the actual weight of your package, per gram, rather than for a weight band into which it fits.

Generous discounts are given for pre-sorting your publications into postcode sequence.

ELECTRONIC SERVICES

Royal Mail's electronic services provide electronic access to Royal Mail's delivery network. With over 75% of all documents now starting life on a computer, using Electronic Services can save you time and reduce your costs, allowing you to 'post' your mailings electronically, for example trading documents, direct mail and other customer communications.

Using the service

Standard documents are set up as digitized electronic templates at Royal Mail's Electronic Mail Centre. When you are ready to mail to your customers you simply transmit your database and any other personalization details to Electronic Services. Data can be sent by disk, tape, modem link, direct line or EDI over a Value Added Network.

Mailings are printed on high-quality paper using the latest laser printing technology. Company logos and signatures can be included and printed in highlight colour if required. Alternatively, you can use your own headed stationery.

After printing, documents are enclosed into C5 or DL envelopes. There is a choice of using Electronic Services' distinctive yellow envelope that has been shown to increase response rates by as much as 40%. Once again, you can use your own envelopes if preferred.

There is an option of including up to five different inserts with the mail piece, for example you can include a Business Reply Envelope or product leaflet, which makes the service ideal for direct mail applications.

Once enveloped, the mailings are transferred direct into Royal Mail's sorting system for First class delivery. The Electronic Mail Centres are located within Mount Pleasant sorting office in London and at Chesterfield. Data can be accepted by Electronic Services as late as 6.00 p.m. and mail will still enter the delivery system that evening.

The Electronic Mail Centres are secure areas, to which only authorized personnel have access, so you can be assured of complete confidentiality.

Electronic Services allows you to communicate more effectively while freeing up staff to concentrate on your core business all at a highly competitive cost.

Key benefits of using Electronic Services

▷ **Speed** – Electronic Services offers you later access to our delivery systems, up until 6.00 p.m. if necessary.

▷ **Increased response rates** – by using our distinctive yellow envelopes you could improve response rates by as much as 40%. The yellow envelope stands out from other mail ensuring that it is opened and read.

▷ **Cost-effective** – costs are competitive in comparison to internal or external resource. Using Electronic Services frees staff to concentrate on your core business.

▷ **High quality** – Royal Mail's on-going investment in the latest industrial printers and envelopers ensures that your mailing is produced to the highest standards.

▷ **Ease of use** – Electronic Services' open access policy means that customers can send their data in a format convenient to them.

▷ **Reliability** – Electronic Services' operations centres are secure areas to which only authorized personnel are allowed access. All disks are virus checked.

See the case study on page 230 for details of Electronic Services in operation.

For more information on Electronic Services call Royal Mail on 0345 950950, alternatively email us at rmes@dial.pipex.com.

ROYAL MAIL DOOR TO DOOR

Royal Mail's Door to Door offers a premium door-to-door service, providing delivery of leaflets, catalogues and promotional devices with the regular post.

Delivery is made with the morning post ensuring that your promotional material is given the same consideration as the mail. Not surprisingly this leads to increased response when compared with other methods of delivery.

Royal Mail Door to Door is the only service in this market that provides complete coverage of the UK – either on a national, regional or local bias. A Royal Mail leaflet can go everywhere the post goes, to over 24 million delivery points.

A comprehensive in-house targeting system allows geodemographic profiling free of charge so your messages are received by the right audience. For further information or advice please call your local Royal Mail Sales Centre or The National Booking Centre on 01865 780400.

CASE STUDY – OGILVY & MATHER DIRECT

Ogilvy & Mather Direct is the largest direct marketing agency of its kind in the world. Its success depends on its ability to deliver highly creative campaigns on behalf of its clients while maintaining value for money. This is achieved by using only the most cost-effective suppliers.

Objective

O&M Direct approached Electronic Services on behalf of its client *The Economist*. Direct mail had been used to generate sales of diaries. Initial campaigns were despatched in red *Economist*-branded envelopes. A follow-up campaign to non-replies was sent in the same envelope – but being so recognizable it didn't achieve the desired response.

O&M Direct needed to send out a further mailing straight away. A fast and flexible service was needed and the client wanted an increased response rate.

Trial of Royal Mail's Electronic Services

O&M Direct supplied the mailing text and database by disk. The letter was set up and faxed back for immediate approval by the agency. Once approved, the letters were printed and despatched overnight for first class delivery.

Electronic Services also recommended use of its distinctive yellow envelope to give the mailing a greater degree of urgency and impact.

Results

The trial proved to be a great success, with a response rate reaching almost 12.5%. The rapid turnaround achieved by Electronic Services drastically reduced production lead times.

Conclusion

Royal Mail Electronic Services enables Ogilvy & Mather Direct to provide a faster, more efficient, cost-effective and flexible service to its clients. Letters that used to take a week to produce are now produced overnight, effectively enabling the agency to react to events quickly and more flexibly than before.

'Hitting deadlines is a way of life in this industry and Electronic Services provides a uniquely fast turnaround – as well as a degree of flexibility when necessary.'

Janine Van Stolk, account director, Ogilvy & Mather Direct

POSTCODES AND ADDRESS MANAGEMENT

The Postcode Address File (PAF)® contains some twenty-five million addresses. It is the most complete and up-to-date address database in the United Kingdom. As a result, companies are now exploiting the potential of Postcodes through PAF® to improve their efficiency in a whole range of activities from database cleaning to retail planning.

PAF® is available in a range of formats including hard copy, CD-ROM and magnetic tape. It can be obtained direct from Royal Mail or through a number of Value Added Resellers. More information is available via the Postcode Product helpline number 0131 550 8999.

RESPONSE SERVICES

One of the key elements for success in direct mail is making it easy for customers to reply. Royal Mail Response Services offer two methods of achieving this objective.

Business Reply and **Freepost** are simple cost-effective methods of encouraging response by enabling customers and prospects to contact you at your expense. You only pay for the replies that you receive.

The inclusion of one of these services can increase the speed and quantity of response, giving you more business and, when you are sending invoices, improved cash flow.

To take advantage of these services you need a Response Services License which is available for a small annual fee.

ROYAL MAIL INTERNATIONAL SERVICES

From June 1996 (tbc) Royal Mail will have in place its new range of International Business Services to replace the existing Airstream and Printflow services.

International Unsorted requires minimal sortation into Europe and Rest of World and travels by using Royal Mail's International Priority network. The service is designed for correspondence, such as letters, invoices and statements, as well as print and for packets for which there is a special rate.

International Sorted is, as the name suggests, for those customers able to pre-sort their mail to the international sort criteria, giving large cost savings. The service is for print only including magazines, mailshots and catalogues. There is a choice of three speeds — Priority, Standard and Economy. There is a set of seven pricing zones across all three speeds giving a range of competitive prices.

The M-bag option gives cost savings for heavier items going to a single address and the structure is a reflection of the sorted service.

The entry requirement for both services is £2,500 pa spend, plus for the Sorted service the ability to meet a minimum 3 kg per selection volume — although there is a supplementary residue rate for left-overs. The maximum item weight for both services is 2 kg, 5 kg for books and pamphlets.

DIRECT ENTRY

This product offers access to the domestic services in other countries for direct mail, publications and packages. There will be cost savings for certain mailings plus the valuable feature of a *local look*. The mail has the relevant country's printed postmark and a local return address, which could improve response rates. Suitable for organizations which spend more than £250 pa on overseas mailings.

INTERNATIONAL BUSINESS REPLY SERVICE (IBRS)

IBRS is for all businesses wishing to encourage and facilitate a response from their international communications. All replies are returned by airmail to a customer's designated UK address. An IBRS licence costs £300[†] which includes the first 1,000 items returned. Items returned thereafter are charged at 30 pence per item.

A single worldwide postal design provided by Royal Mail enables you to obtain replies simply and easily from throughout the world.

INTERNATIONAL ADMAIL

With International Admail your prepaid reply devices are pre-printed with a local address. This perceived local presence can help break down any customer resistance to replying overseas and so boost your replies even further.

Now available to 13 destinations Royal Mail will supply you with the local Business Reply design specification for every country that you wish to mail that operates International Admail.

Contact your local Royal Mail Sales Centre on 0345 950950 for further information on any of these international services.

WHAT TO DO NEXT

For information about Royal Mail services, contact your nearest Royal Mail Sales Centre on 0345 950950. For help and information specifcally about direct mail, call Royal Mail on 0345 750750.

---

† All prices are correct at time of going to press

Part Five

Campaign Planning

12 Campaign planning and management

In this chapter, I shall briefly summarize the main issues in planning and running a direct mail campaign. Then we will look at an imaginary campaign and follow it through to completion.

I have included in my summary the use of outside suppliers, even though you may decide to do most of the jobs in-house. This is because the process is the same whichever route you choose.

The main elements to consider are:

▷ **Setting the objective**
▷ **Developing communications strategy**
▷ **Forecasting, costing and budgeting**
▷ **Turning your strategy into an action plan**
- ❏ selecting the right people to mail
- ❏ selecting specialist suppliers
- ❏ writing and delivering supplier brief

▷ **Campaign development**
- ❏ developing creative work
- ❏ planning for production
- ❏ computer selection and address production
- ❏ scheduling deliveries, assembly and despatch

▷ **Implementation**
- ❏ assembly and despatch
- ❏ response handling and follow-up

▷ **Post-campaign activities**
- ❏ analysis, evaluation and further activity.

As many of these topics are covered in detail in the relevant chapters, I will simply run through each step briefly to demonstrate the process.

SETTING CAMPAIGN OR COMMUNICATION OBJECTIVES

What do you want this mailing campaign to achieve? 'Sales' is the obvious answer, but how many sales, and in what way? Do you expect to sell directly from your mailing or will your prospects require more information before committing themselves? Perhaps they will expect a demonstration or at least the name of a local stockist, where they can view the product.

Sometimes your mailing objective will simply be to make your customers think more of you, or perhaps to ask them for some information enabling you to develop better products for them in the future.

SO, YOUR FIRST PRIORITY IS TO SET YOUR OBJECTIVE

At this point, your mailing starts to take shape, because your objective will, to a certain extent, define the size and shape of your mailing. As explained previously, the more you tell people, the better qualified will be your respondents.

DEVELOPING COMMUNICATIONS STRATEGY

You may feel this is self-evident, but even if you have already decided to use direct mail, you still have some thinking to do.

YOUR TARGET AUDIENCE

- What sort of people will be interested in your proposition?
- Where will you find them?
- Do you already have a relationship with the people you are planning to mail, or are you planning to compile or rent a list?
- How much do you know about their likes, dislikes, buying habits, and so on?
- Do you know enough to enable you to select the best prospects?
- What additional information do you need? This may indicate that some research will be necessary.

> Is your product a Rolls-Royce or a Ford Escort? This will have a major bearing on the style and tone of voice you use.

> Will this positioning be credible, or will you need some support from third parties?

CONTACT STRATEGIES

> Will you use a single mailing, or are you planning several points of attack? For example you may decide to send a follow-up mailing to non-respondents, or to telephone prospects before or after your mailing.

> Is timing likely to be a crucial factor? Sometimes this question is easy to answer – obviously Christmas cards don't sell well in February. At other times, you may need to carry out some basic research to answer the question.

FORECASTING, COSTING AND BUDGETING

> What response do you expect? What do you need to reach break-even?

> Do you have a contingency plan in case your results are below expectations?

> How much can you afford to spend? This calculation will be necessary before you can develop your action plan.

> What do you expect in return? Orders? Leads? Do the numbers work out?

> Have you done a cash-flow forecast? Does this require you to talk to your bank manager?

TURNING YOUR STRATEGY INTO AN ACTION PLAN

You now need to put some flesh on your skeleton plan. This may entail:

> List research and development – you defined your target audience earlier. Now you have to locate them.

- Making supplier decisions and selecting your chosen partners
- Discussions with your Royal Mail account executive
- Writing and delivering a brief to each supplier
- Obtaining quotations for each part of the job
- Planning for response handling and follow-up.

CAMPAIGN DEVELOPMENT

This is one of the most exciting phases. Now you will see your plans come to life:

- Developing and reviewing creative work
- Negotiating prices with your suppliers
- Organizing print and production schedules
- Arranging list rental or compilation
- Arranging for the production of personalized letters
- Finalising delivery arrangements.

IMPLEMENTATION

The crunch! Now you have to be especially vigilant to make sure that everything arrives on time and is despatched according to schedule. You need to think about:

- Despatching your mailing
  - ❑ who will 'fill' the mailing?
  - ❑ have you consulted your Royal Mail account executive about collection and so on?

- Planning to handle the responses
  - ❑ will you need extra staff?
  - ❑ would it be better to phase the mailing so the replies come in manageable quantities?
  - ❑ what about telephone and fax responses?
  - ❑ what are you going to send them – stock material or

something special – if the latter who is producing this and what will it consist of?

▷ What about follow-up?

  ❑ do you plan to follow-up in any event, or will this be a reserve plan in case responses are too low? If the latter, how will you implement it quickly?

POST-CAMPAIGN ANALYSIS

▷ Who will record the responses, conversions and so on?

▷ What analyses and reports will you want?

It is rare that a campaign proceeds without some problems. Your analysis and evaluation should cover not only the replies or orders you received, but also what went wrong.

EXAMPLE

Let us now go through a typical campaign, using this process.

Background

You are a small company comprising yourself and three partners. You are based in Kingston-upon-Thames and you concentrate on businesses within one hour's drive of your office. This covers most of the South-east.

Your speciality is PC maintenance and troubleshooting. Your customers are offered a range of contracts from £250 upwards, which guarantee them a fixed amount of your time. The contract price varies according to the number of PCs a customer has, their age and condition and the software they use.

You offer training in most of the main office packages and you also sell parts and peripherals such as memory, cables, and desk-top accessories.

Your basic promotional offer is a free computer health check and, as there are only four of you, it is important that you do not attract too many enquiries at the same time. Ideally, in order to allow for availability when 'same day' customers call you out, each of you wants a maximum of two new prospect appointments per week.

You have sixty existing customers at varying stages of their contracts.

YOUR OBJECTIVE

Your business plan calls for thirty new contracts to be signed in the next three months. Your target cost per new contract is £45. Based on previous experience you expect to convert three out of every eight appointments you make.

Your objective for this campaign therefore is eighty appointments. Again, based on previous experience, you estimate that you can convert four out of every five enquiries into an appointment for a health check. You therefore need to attract a hundred enquiries.

Communications strategy

> *Although in plan form, each phase is shown as a separate activity, in real-life the phases merge and overlap. The following pages show how you will dip into and out of forecasting and budgeting as you develop your communications strategy.*

Your target audience is small to medium companies with five or more PCs, but with no in-house IT function. You cannot get lists from PC companies because they wish to sell their own maintenance contracts, but you know a local office products supplier, Kingston Supplies, who does not deal with PCs and he is prepared to let you rent his list of 500 customers.

In return for an additional introductory commission of £5 for each enquiry (called a 'PI' or 'per inquiry' deal) he will also allow you to use a letter from him, recommending you to his customers. (This is called an affinity mailing and it generally creates a marked increase in response and conversion.)

Depending on your forecasts from this list, you will probably need to find some other sources of enquiries. Before you do this, it will be worthwhile estimating the likely results.

FORECASTING, COSTING AND BUDGETING

Kingston Supplies list

500 names @ response 6% = thirty enquiries; appointments = twenty-five (because of the relationship you have 'borrowed' from Kingston Supplies and the information you have about the equipment they have.)

Conversion to orders – say 50% (for the same reason) – therefore you expect to get twelve contracts from this list.

Probable costs of this mailing

▷ Rental of names – say £200 – this is quite expensive on a cost per thousand basis but you expect a good response and conversion so it should be cost-effective.

▷ Mailing materials – you will produce your own leaflets using your desktop publishing software. You will also write your own letter and order form. You will buy envelopes, with a simple message overprinted, from a specialist in small runs – there is such a supplier in Wimbledon (truly) and these will cost you around £100 for a supply of 5,000.

You must therefore think through your envelope message carefully, so it will not go out-of-date. You will defer calculation of postage until you have decided how many you will mail.

Assuming your forecasts are accurate, you will still need eighteen contracts to achieve your objective and you decide to test two additional approaches:

1 A referral offer to existing customers

2 Mailing to a rented list.

Referral offer

Satisfied customers are often prepared to recommend suppliers to people they know in other companies. These offers have various names (recommends offers, referral offers, MGMs, i.e. member get member and so on). Your referral offer will be based on a free PC virus checker in return for a converted customer, i.e. one who signs a twelve-month contract. The software has a retail value of around £50 but will cost you just £17 at trade price.

You expect to get 15% of your customers to respond – some may send two or more names (you should allow for this on your response form) and you will probably offer a small additional incentive for two or more contracts – perhaps some free screen savers?

This activity should yield around fifteen names, say six contracts.

Estimated costs would be

- Literature – allowance of £15 – no need for an overprint – assuming your standard envelope has your name on – these are your customers so they will open the envelope.

- Free software, say £120.

- Postage £15 including replies, using standard reply paid envelopes from stock.

If everything works as forecast, you will now need twelve additional contracts to achieve your objective.

Rented lists

You estimate that a mailing to 1,500 companies will produce 3% response – forty-five replies. This means around thirty-six appointments and approximately thirteen contracts.

You need to brief a list broker to find you addresses of 1,500 companies selected by size (number of employees) – you have not been able to find a list indicating the number of PCs each company owns.

An analysis of your existing customers is not very helpful as the types of company seem to be very broad – you are also very wary because the list is so small, it is doubtful whether any data will be reliable. It does seem though, that they are mainly either independent firms or parts of small localized groups. You pass on this finding to your list broker, as a possible selection factor.

Costs for this phase

▷ List rental: 1,500 @ £175 per thousand including research and selections – £262.50. Note that you could try to find these names yourself from a directory, say Kompass – you will do the costings and then decide.

▷ Mailing materials: again produced in-house though you may bring in some casual help for filling and so on. Say £150 in total, (not counting any allowance for your own time).

▷ Postage: your Royal Mail account executive offers you a small incentive – if you mail a total of 2,000 pieces he will arrange for Royal Mail to pay the postage on 300 of these.

Your postage estimate for both mailings (500 Kingston plus 1,500 rented names) is therefore 1,700 pieces @ 19 pence = £323.00

Cost summary

Lists:

Kingston Supplies	£200
	+ £150 PI charges (30 x £5)
Rented from broker	£262.50

Materials:

Envelopes	£130 (Including overprinted supply)
Letters, leaflets, and so on	50 Kingston mailing
	15 referral offer
	150 rented list mailing

Postage: £340 Including responses

Incentives: £120 Free software

Total estimated cost £1,417.50

Total new contracts – thirty-one – so cost per contract is £45.72

Developing your action plan

Your forecasting indicates that you are likely to achieve your objective at around the targeted cost. However, before you develop your action plan, there are two strategic issues still to be considered.

1 How can you phase the mailings so that you are not overloaded with enquiries?

2 What if you have been optimistic in your response or conversion estimates?

The first problem is fairly simple to deal with. You should send out the referral mailing first. Being a very simple concept (i.e. one not requiring much internal management discussion) this should result in fairly rapid response.

Your first progress check can be made after the first week's responses. If you phase this mailing over a two-week period, the bulk of enquiries will come in over a period of about three to four weeks. Assuming your response estimates are correct, this means you will receive fifteen names to follow up in these first three weeks.

The next step is to send out the Kingston Supplies mailing – again in batches. If your estimates are correct you expect twenty-five appointments, which will take you three weeks to fulfil (four people x two appointments x three weeks = twenty-four). You could probably send this out in three equal batches, starting in week three. If you have underestimated the response you will know before you mail the third batch and can hold these back, if necessary.

The rented list mailing is expected to produce thirty-six appointments i.e. four-and-a-half weeks' appointments. You can phase this according to the responses and appointments you are getting from the earlier activities – bringing it forward if you are under estimate, delaying it if you are beating the numbers.

This is good strategy for two reasons:

1 You are running the smaller more cost-effective mailings first. If these over-perform, you will have less of a problem than if you have under-estimated on the larger activity. You can adjust your forecasting based on the earlier results, before you send the larger mailing.

2 Phasing it this way means that if you do decide to adjust the programme by reducing the total mailed, your reductions will be made to the less cost-effective rented list mailing – thus saving proportionally more of your budget.

The second issue – what if you have been optimistic in your forecasting?. This will also be answered before you undertake all of your main expenditure – the despatch of the rented list mailing. You will, of course, have bought the envelopes, signed the list rental contract and produced some literature, but you will not have to pay the postage until you send the mailing.

So you will have a small reserve to be available for re-allocation, if necessary.

Briefing

In developing your action plan, you will need to identify appropriate list brokers and produce briefing notes for internal and external use – see Chapter 10.

You will also need to draw up schedules showing what material needs to be produced, by whom and when it will be required.

Campaign development

You decided early in the campaign planning phase to write your own mailings. Now you have to deliver. By referring to Chapter 9 you can get an idea of where to start – by thinking about your prospect.

Based on your contacts with existing customers you should know:

▷ The sort of people to whom you will be writing

▷ Their concerns, wants and needs.

This should help you get started. When you have drafted out your letter, show it to your colleagues and encourage them to make comments. When this embarrassing exercise is over, take control back into your own hands. It is right to ask their opinions, but good copy is never written by committee, so you have to decide how much to alter and in what way.

At this stage, you also need to start thinking about how you will physically produce the mailings. It is one thing to print letters to sixty customers and quite another to produce mailings of 500 and 1,500.

However, as you have a fast laser printer in-house, your only problem is how to get the addresses into your own computer in order to do a mail-merge .

If you are lucky, your suppliers will be able to give the addresses to you on disk and you can then simply load them and start your merge. (This is simple when you know how, but less so for the inexperienced.) As you are a computer consultant and trainer you will have no problems with this aspect. *The rest of us may well need some help.*

Implementation

As you had forewarned your colleagues (and your spouses!) your assembly team is now standing by. All you have to do is fold, assemble, fill and stick envelopes until you can stand it no more – this does not usually take long!

Your mailing however, is phased over several weeks, so you will probably manage to keep your team motivated long enough to get the mailing away.

You now have to think about who will receive the responses – if they all come by mail you should have no problem – you can do it in the evening.

What about the telephone responses and the calls to make appointments though? These have to be managed too, so you may need some temporary help.

If you do need to undertake follow-up activities the chances are you will not be too busy with appointments, so this should be easy to manage. Nevertheless now is the time to plan for it. Thinking things through now, will be far more productive than when you are in a panic later.

Post-campaign activities

We will await the outcome of the campaign before deciding what to do here!

WHAT TO DO NEXT

Design a campaign planning form to suit your own business. Note which sections you cannot fill in and refer to the relevant sections of this book for advice.

Join, or at least send for details of membership of, the numerous bodies mentioned throughout this book.

You'll find they are all very keen to help newcomers to marketing – especially direct marketing.

Good luck!

Part Six

Appendices

Appendix 1   Legal and regulatory issues

I shall not attempt to cover this subject in detail. The guidelines to the Data Protection Act 1984 run to more than 120 pages. I will, therefore, discuss the implications and direct you to sources of further information.

The main things you need to be aware of fall into two groups:

▷ **legal requirements** – legislation which must be followed
▷ **self-regulation** – industry codes of practice – rules and regulations drawn up by the various bodies involved in direct marketing. These are not generally legally binding, but members are required to conform and membership carries other benefits which are well worthwhile.

We'll deal with the legal aspects first.

THE DATA PROTECTION ACT 1984

The most important act in relation to the use of mailing lists. If you store personal data about living individuals on a computer (your own or anybody else's) you are covered by this act.

The following extract from this publication indicates the main purpose of the act:

> ...the purpose of the act is to protect the rights of the individual about whom data is obtained, stored, processed or supplied, rather than those of the data user.

These rights include the right of an individual (data subject) to find out what information you are holding, to challenge it if appropriate, and to claim compensation in certain circumstances.

The act only applies to data which is automatically processed – in other words, paper records in your filing cabinet are not covered.

'Personal data' includes names, statements of fact and expressions of opinion about individuals.

The Data Protection Act can be hard to follow and a copy of 'The Guidelines' is essential. These give details of interpretations, including examples where possible. The following summary of the data protection principles indicates the breadth and scope of this legislation:

▷ **The first principle** – the information to be contained in personal data shall be obtained and processed, fairly and lawfully.

▷ **The second principle** – personal data shall be held only for one or more specified and lawful purposes.

▷ **The third principle** – personal data held for any purposes shall not be used or disclosed in any manner incompatible with those purposes.

▷ **The fourth principle** – personal data held for any purposes shall be adequate, relevant and not excessive.

▷ **The fifth principle** – personal data shall be accurate and, where necessary, kept up to date.

▷ **The sixth principle** – personal data held for any purposes shall not be kept for longer than is necessary.

▷ **The seventh principle** – an individual shall be entitled...

(a) at reasonable intervals and without undue delay or expense
(i) to be informed by any data user whether he holds personal data of which that individual is the subject; and
(ii) to access any such data held by a data user; and

(b) where appropriate, to have such data corrected or erased.

▷ **The eighth principle** – appropriate security measures shall be taken against unauthorized access to, or alteration, disclosure or destruction of, personal data and against accidental loss or destruction of personal data.

The Data Protection Act covers all aspects of the obtaining, holding and use of personal data, whether in consumer or business lists and you are strongly advised to send for a full copy of the guidelines right away. The Registrar's address is:

The Data Protection Registrar
Wycliffe House
Water Lane
Wilmslow
Cheshire
SK9 5AF

Telephone: 01625 545745
Fax: 01625 524510

A WORD OF REASSURANCE

The Data Protection Registrar is not an ogre waiting to pounce on the unsuspecting business. The staff are considerate and helpful, especially to newcomers to business.

If you are in any doubts about where you stand in relation to the Act, a phone call to the above number will put you in touch with an experienced and helpful adviser.

Although the Data Protection Act is the law most likely to affect direct mailers there are many other acts which may affect you depending on the nature of your business. Among the most frequently encountered are:

THE GAMING ACT 1968

Unless you are planning to advertise premises where gaming will take place, or to ask readers to send money to be used in gaming activities, you do not need to concern yourself with this Act.

THE LOTTERIES AND AMUSEMENTS ACT 1976

This Act relates to the sale of lottery tickets, the running of prize draws and prize competitions and associated matters. If you plan to run a competition (where an element of skill is required of participants) or a prize draw where no skill at all is required, you must conform to the requirements of this Act.

Essentially, in a competition, you are permitted to make some purchase a condition of entry, whereas in a prize draw no purchase or other commitment can be applied. If you are in any doubt about this you are advised to consult your legal adviser.

THE FINANCIAL SERVICES ACT

This covers companies or individuals dealing with the sale or offer of 'investment' products. The advertiser (mailer) must be authorized under the Financial Services Act. Again, you are advised to seek legal advice if you are in doubt.

THE MEDICINE ACT 1968

This covers the numerous requirements for the offer or sale of medicines or related products.

THE UNSOLICITED GOODS AND SERVICES ACT

Prevents demands for payment where goods are unsolicited. Introduced to counter 'inertia' selling. The recipient of such goods will own them after six months if they are not collected by the sender.

CONSUMER PROTECTION ACT 1987 AND ADDITIONAL REGULATIONS

This replaced the previous unsatisfactory Bargain Offers Regulations. It covers prices, product liability and the rights of consumers relating to cancellation of purchase agreements.

CONSUMER CREDIT ACT

Outlines the information required in your mailing and the regulations concerning the offer of loans or credit to those under eighteen years of age.

THEFT ACT

In the context of this book, this Act covers the theft (or abuse) of a mailing list belonging to another company.

COMPANIES ACT 1985

Sets out the requirements for stationery, order forms and so on.

SALE OF GOODS ACT 1979

This relates to descriptions, warranties, fitness for the purpose described and so on.

SUPPLY OF GOODS AND SERVICES ACT 1982

An extension of the Sale of Goods Act to cover services and goods offered for hire.

UNFAIR CONTRACT TERMS ACT 1977

Further consumer protection regarding the wording and enforcement of contracts.

TRADE DESCRIPTIONS ACT 1968

Covers the use of false trade descriptions of goods and prices.

MISREPRESENTATION ACT 1967

Similar to the Trades Descriptions Act, but dealing with honest but negligent misrepresentation. Legitimate 'puffery' (obvious and harmless exaggerations) are excluded e.g. 'the best bread in Britain'.

MISLEADING ADVERTISING REGULATIONS 1988

Relating to advertising (mailing) which is misleading – it does not need to be unfair to contravene the Act. 'Policed' by the Director General of Fair Trading and the Advertising Standards Authority (ASA).

POST OFFICE ACT

This covers the items which may be permitted in mailing packages and the passing off of mailings as Government literature.

GENERAL

There are many more acts and legally enforceable regulations covering subjects such as mail order transactions, copyright designs and patents, infringement of trade marks, libel, forgery, coinage offences, discrimination, safety, foods, medicines and health products.

The laws of copyright apply to mailing lists, as they do to any other form of written matter. When in doubt about any of the above topics, you should consult your legal adviser.

SELF-REGULATORY BODIES

There are many bodies, some specific to direct marketing and others covering the advertising industry as a whole. Among the more important for direct mailers are:

DIRECT MARKETING ASSOCIATION

Its Code of Practice is a comprehensive document covering rules and responsibilities for list owners and users, and direct response advertisers (including direct mailers).

The rules cover the use of gifts, incentives, premiums and awards. The subject of prize draws and competitions is also covered in detail.

Like the Data Protection Guidelines, this booklet is essential for direct mailers. Send for your copy and all recent updates and 'practice notes' to:

The Direct Marketing Association (UK) Limited
Haymarket House
1 Oxenden Street
London
SW1Y 4EE

Telephone: 0171 321 2525

DIRECT MAIL ACCREDITATION AND RECOGNITION CENTRE (DMARC)

An independent body within the self-regulatory framework of the direct marketing industry. Accreditation means that suppliers adhere to the industry's best practices and self-regulatory guidelines. DMARC administers the Data Gatherers and Response Handlers Group. A free handbook is available from:

Direct Mail Accreditation and Recognition Centre
228 Tottenham Court Road
London
W1P 9AD

Telephone: 0171 631 0904
Fax: 0171 631 0859

THE LIST AND DATABASE SUPPLIERS GROUP (LADS)

Clearly direct mailings are harder to check by simple observation. This group was formed in 1991 under the auspices of DMARC to 'police' the British Code of Advertising Practice. Its members are the main list suppliers, mailing houses and computer bureaux in the UK.

THE COMMITTEE OF ADVERTISING PRACTICE

Sometimes referred to as the CAP Committee, this body enforces the British Code of Advertising Practice (BCAP). This code covers all aspects of advertising, but BCAP produces a special list of *Rules for Direct Marketing including List and Database Management*. This paper can be obtained from:

The Committee of Advertising Practice
Brook House
2–16 Torrington Place
London
WC1E 7HW

Telephone: 0171 580 5555
Fax: 0171 631 3051

THE MAILING PREFERENCE SERVICE (MPS)

This is a joint industry scheme allowing consumers to request that their names and home addresses be removed from, or added to, mailing lists owned or operated by subscribers to the scheme.

Update tapes are provided quarterly by MPS, allowing members to update their lists on a regular basis. This is doubly beneficial, saving irritation for consumers and reducing costs for users. Membership fees for small businesses are quite modest.

Full details of the service can be obtained from:

The Mailing Preference Service
5 Reef House
Plantation Wharf
London
SW11 3UF

Telephone: 0171 738 1625

GENERAL

In addition to the above there are numerous self-regulatory bodies such as the Advertising Association, the Association of Mail Order Publishers, and The Advertising Standards Authority (ASA).

Appendix 2 Useful addresses

ROYAL MAIL ADDRESSES

ROYAL MAIL SALES CENTRES

Contact your local Sales Centre on 0345 950950.

MAILSORT

Lois Poore
Royal Mail
FREEPOST
Streamline House
Sandy Lane West
OXFORD
OX4 5BR

Hotline telephone: 01865 780 400

Or contact your nearest Royal Mail Sales Centre.

POSTCODE PRODUCTS

Postcode Products
Royal Mail
FREEPOST
20 Brandon Street
EDINBURGH
EH3 0SP

Telephone: 0131 550 8999
Fax: 0131 550 8529

ELECTRONIC SERVICES

Electronic Services
Royal Mail
22 Finsbury Square
LONDON
EC2A 1NL

Telephone: 0171 614 7178
Fax: 0171 614 7175

Or call Electronic Mail Customer Services on: 0171 239 2487

POSTAGE PAID SYMBOLS

Royal Mail
FREEPOST EH500
20 Brandon Street
EDINBURGH
EH3 0HN

Telephone: 0131 550 8559

PACKETPOST

Royal Mail
Response Services
FREEPOST
Streamline House
Sandy Lane West
OXFORD
OX4 5BR

Telephone: 01865 780 400

ROYAL MAIL DOOR TO DOOR

Door to Door
FREEPOST
Streamline House
Sandy Lane West
OXFORD
OX4 5BR

Telephone: 01865 780 400

ROYAL MAIL INTERNATIONAL

Contact your local Royal Mail Sales Centre

PROFESSIONAL ORGANIZATIONS

Advertising Association
Abford House
15 Wilton Road
LONDON SW1V 1NJ

A federation of trade associations and professional bodies which promotes the self-regulation of advertising, runs courses, publishes industry statistics.

Telephone: 0171 828 2771

Advertising Standards Authority
Brook House
2 – 16 Torrington Place
LONDON WC1E 7HW

Publishers of British Code of Advertising Practice, Rules for Direct Marketing, British Code of Sales Promotion Practice.

Telephone: 0171 580 5555

Direct Mail Information Service (DMIS)
5 Carlisle Street
LONDON W1V 6JX

Publish research and information on direct mail usage, trends and attitudes.

Telephone 0171 494 0483

Direct Marketing Association (DMA)
Haymarket House
1 Oxendon Street
LONDON SW1Y 4EE

For information on a wide range of agencies, consultants, mailing houses, list brokers and specialist suppliers who are DMA Members.

Telephone 0171 321 2525

Direct Mail Accreditation and Recognition Centre (DMARC)
248 Tottenham Court Road
LONDON W1P 9AD

For a list of recognized agencies, mailing houses and specialist suppliers.

Telephone 0171 631 0904

Institute of Direct Marketing (IDM)
1 Park Road
TEDDINGTON, Middx
TW11 0AR

Europe's leading direct marketing educational and training centre.

Telephone: 0181 977 5705

List Warranty Register
5 Reef House
Plantation Wharf
LONDON SW11 3UF

A scheme run by the Direct Marketing
Association and the Mailing Preference
Service. A central contact point for
information about warranties offered by
registered list owners.

Telephone 0171 738 1877

Mailing Preference Service (MPS)
FREEPOST 22
LONDON W1E 7EZ

The MPS allows consumers to either
increase or decrease the amount of
direct mail they receive.

Telephone: 0171 738 1625

Office of the Data Protection Registrar
Wycliffe House
Water Lane
WILMSLOW
Cheshire
SK9 5AF

Administers and enforces the Data
Protection Act. Publishes information
packs, guidance notes, and updates on
Data Protection. Also offers free video
What is Data Protection?

Telephone: 01625 545745

USEFUL READING

ROYAL MAIL PUBLICATIONS

Royal Mail Door to Door – giving details of this valuable service.

Available from address earlier.

The Mailsort User's Guide – a step-by-step manual on using Mailsort services. Available from your local Royal Mail Sales Centre.

Despatch Magazine – Royal Mail's magazine for Mailrooms. Quarterly, free from:

> Despatch Magazine, Royal Mail
> FREEPOST, Room 108
> 22 Finsbury Square,
> LONDON
> EC2A 1NL

Explore Royal Mail – a comprehensive guide to all aspects of Royal Mail. Available free on IBM-compatible PC floppy disk, from:

> Royal Mail Retail
> Royal Mail
> FREEPOST
> 20 Brandon Street
> EDINBURGH
> EH3 0HN

> Telephone: 0131 550 8955

Postal Address Book – a hard copy of PAF, a set of 11 regional editions covering every area of the UK. Your local edition is free – other area editions can be ordered for a small charge. Available from:

> Postcode Products
> EDINBURGH – see address above.

Postcodes: the New Geography – An essential guide showing you how to exploit the full potential of the UK's most comprehensive address database.

Costs £25 from good bookshops or call Postcode Products at the Edinburgh address.

Printed Postage Impressions – an introductory brochure to this method of postage payment. Get it from your local Royal Mail Sales Centre.

DIY Guide to International Direct Mail – concise step-by-step guide to creating and implementing your own international direct mail campaign. Order forms from:

Royal Mail International
FREEPOST
Fenton Way
BASILDON
Essex
SS15 4BR

Marketing Without Frontiers – a 200-page guide to international direct marketing. One copy free to all business customers, £20 per additional copy. Order it from the Royal Mail International address above or from your Royal Mail Sales Centre.

Royal Mail International Business Portfolio – a quarterly magazine providing updates on international services and topical information on exporting and overseas markets. The magazine also features special offers and discounts. Details from Royal Mail International at the above address.

Royal Mail International Services Guide – how to send your mail overseas, with advice on packaging and mailing requirements to over 200 international destinations. Free on IBM-compatible PC floppy disk or £5 in book form. From Royal Mail International or your Royal Mail Sales Centre.

Mailroom Masterclass – Not a book but a useful one day seminar, demonstrating how to run a mailroom more efficiently. Call your Royal Mail Sales Centre for details.

OTHER PUBLICATIONS

Commonsense Direct Marketing – Drayton Bird. Published by Kogan Page

Scientific Advertising – Claude Hopkins. Published by Crain Books

Tested Advertising Methods – John Caples. Published by Prentice Hall

MaxiMarketing – Stan Rapp and Tom Collins. Published by McGraw-Hill

The Great Marketing Turnaround – Rapp and Collins. Published by Prentice Hall

Beyond MaxiMarketing – Rapp and Collins. Published by McGraw-Hill

Integrated Direct Marketing – Ernan Roman. Published by McGraw-Hill

Handbook of Direct Mail – Siegfried Vogele. Published by Prentice Hall

The Customer Service Planner – Martin Christopher. Published by Butterworth-Heinemann

Creating Successful Sales Letters – Drayton Bird. Published by Kogan Page

Database Marketing – Robert Shaw & Merlin Stone. Published by Gower

Successful Direct Marketing Methods, 4th edition – Bob Stone. Published by Crain Books

The Complete Direct Mail List Handbook – Ed Burnett. Published by Prentice-Hall

Mailing List Strategies – Rose Harper. Published by McGraw-Hill

Computer-Aided Marketing & Selling – Robert Shaw. Published by Butterworth-Heinemann

Consumer Behaviour, 5th edition – Engel, Blackwell and Miniard. Published by Dryden

The Practitioner's Guide to Direct Marketing. Published by The Institute of Direct Marketing

Direct Marketing – a monthly magazine published in the USA by Hoke Communications Inc., 224 Seventh Street, Garden City, New York 11530-5771

Appendix 3 Supporting information

CHAPTER 1 STRENGTHS AND WEAKNESSES OF THE VARIOUS MEDIA OPTIONS

TELEVISION

Type	Strengths	Weaknesses
Television Used for awareness advertising and lead generation, when we do not know the names and addresses of prospects. Will also help us establish credibility when our business name is not well known.	Large audiences – millions of viewers watch the top programmes. Rapid response – telephone responses start within seconds of a commercial appearing. Colour, sound and movement, making commercials very powerful and, sometimes, memorable. High response potential – 0.02% of 10,000,000 viewers is 2,000 people. Prestige – an advertisement on television, carries prestige for your company. Rates – although outlay is high, cost per thousand viewers is low. Rates are negotiable for 'off-peak' times. Also the greater number of commercial channels available is leading to 'softer' i.e. more negotiable rates. Regional advertising – you can run TV commercials in local regions.	Cost – because of the cost of producing a commercial, there is no such thing as a small-budget TV campaign. Short 'life' – there is no 'hard' copy, so a commercial can quickly be forgotten. Poor targeting – for most products a high percentage of viewers will not be in your market and wastage will be high. Limited time – TV is not so good for putting across complicated messages – you can't go into lots of detail in thirty seconds. Low quality of response – short commercials and broad audiences tend to produce unqualified replies – so conversion to sale can be low. Need for professional help – producing television commercials is a highly skilled job – it is therefore very expensive.

RADIO

Type	Strengths	Weaknesses
Radio Used for awareness advertising and lead generation, when we do not know the names and addresses of prospects. Will also help us establish credibility when our business name is not well known. Good for local store promotions.	Good targeting – different programmes and times of day can be used to target specific types e.g. business people in cars, housewives etc. Cost-efficiency – radio advertising can be surprisingly cheap. Strong local identity – many programmes have a strong local flavour – good for local businesses. Rapid response – telephone responses can start within seconds of an advertisement appearing. Sound – can be more powerful than printed messages. Prestige – an advertisement on local radio can carry prestige for your company. Rates – cost per thousand listeners is low and production costs can also be very reasonable. Most stations will help you make commercials. Rates are negotiable for 'off-peak' times.	Short 'life' – there is no 'hard' copy so a radio advertisement can quickly be forgotten – again, high repetition is necessary to achieve lasting impact. Poor targeting – for many products a high percentage of listeners will not be in your market and wastage will be high. Limited time – like TV, radio is not so good for putting across complicated messages. Low quality of response – short advertisements and broad audiences can produce unqualified replies – so conversion to sale can be low. Need for professional help – producing radio commercials is a highly skilled job – you therefore need help, though this will often be available through the radio station.

SPECIALIST MAGAZINES

Type	Strengths	Weaknesses
Magazines dealing with a particular interest whether consumer e.g. *Angling Times, Gardening Today,* or business e.g. *Management Today, Business Equipment Digest.* Can be very good for campaigns targeted at a specific interest group – especially where we do not know the identities of the prospects.	Good targeting – if you want to reach gardening, fishing, or motorcycling enthusiasts, magazines can be ideal. High reader interest – in advertisements as well as editorial. Long 'life' – some publications are in circulation for months or even years. Pass-on readership – some magazines have a very high 'pass-on' readership – this can give your advertisement greater exposure. Prestige – some magazines are considered to be the authority on the subject – ads in these tend to carry additional prestige.	Cost – putting an advertisement in a magazine is rarely cheap – also advertisements, especially those in full colour, are expensive to prepare. Long 'lead times' – some magazines require artwork several weeks before issue date. Professional help – again you will need the help of professional designers, copywriters etc.

NATIONAL NEWSPAPERS AND SUPPLEMENTS

Type	Strengths	Weaknesses
National newspapers Used for lead generation, when we do not know the names and addresses of prospects. Can also help us establish credibility when our business name is not well known.	Large audiences – circulations run into millions. Rapid access – you can run an advertisement at very short notice – i.e. 1 or 2 days. High response potential – 0.03% response from the *Sun*'s 4,000,000 circulation is 1,200 replies. Prestige – an advertisement in *The Times*, or almost any national newspaper carries prestige for your company. Rates – although costs seem high, rates are often negotiable for last minute bookings – especially distress space i.e. space the paper can't sell. Regional editions – in some papers you can run advertisements in local regions. Quick response – a high percentage of your replies (perhaps 80%) will arrive within the first week or so. Good test opportunities – some papers offer 'split-run' facilities, enabling different offers and creative approaches to be tested against each other.	Cost – even very small advertisements can cost hundreds of pounds. Short 'life' – today's paper is 'dead' tomorrow. Poor targeting – most readers will not be in your market and wastage will be high. Limited space – compared to direct mail. Low quality of response – short copy and broad audience tends to produce unqualified replies – so conversion to sale can be low. High preparation costs – design and artwork charges can be high. Low readership of individual advertisements – research shows that as little as 5% of 'readers' see any individual advertisement. Need for professional help – producing copy and artwork for advertisements requires skill and experience – this can be costly.

DOOR-TO-DOOR DISTRIBUTION

Type	Strengths	Weaknesses
Door-to-door distribution – leaflets and 'mailing packs' distributed door to door – usually to private households but they can also be distributed to business addresses.	Cost – they are considerably cheaper than direct mail. Credibility – well-designed packs, especially those delivered with the mail through the Royal Mail's Door to Door service, are considered with the day's post and are usually well received.	Low credibility – when delivered at other times of day they are not so well received.

Loose or bound-in inserts (leaflets)

Type	Strengths	Weaknesses
Inserts – in newspapers or magazines – both consumer and business titles carry inserts. Some are carried loose inside the publication, others are bound-in. Many local newspapers carry inserts.	Power – although critics decry them, they are very powerful – producing responses which are much higher (sometimes up to ten times higher) than full page advertisements in the same publication. Some people feel that loose inserts are less likely to be successful as they can fall out, but this does not appear to reduce their effect – in fact it may actually increase response by attracting attention to the insert. Easy to respond to – prospects can tear off a reply card, or even return the whole piece. Longer copy possible – almost no limit on space – multi-page inserts, lengthy questionnaires, and even catalogues are quite common. Flexibility – part circulations can be bought – some publications allow you to insert down to wholesaler level – economical for a small business within a local area. Economical – you can use existing leaflets. Testing opportunities – one of the best press-testing opportunities for the small advertiser.	Cost – although they tend to produce more replies they also cost more – perhaps three to five times as much as a page advertisement. Timing – unless you have a leaflet you have to produce your own before you can insert it. Professional help – needed here too.

Fax 'mailings'

Type	Strengths	Weaknesses
Fax 'mailings' – sending promotional messages via fax.	Powerful – faxes tend to be treated as urgent and are usually delivered quickly to the desk of the addressee. Fast – you can have your message delivered to your prospect within minutes. Responsive – they do create high responses, but must be used with care. Cost – cheaper than most other forms of advertising.	Intrusiveness – some recipients get annoyed because your message uses their resources – fax paper etc. without permission.

THE TELEPHONE – OUTBOUND

Type	Strengths	Weaknesses
Telephone calls Two major types – ▷ outbound – you make the call to a prospect or customer. ▷ inbound – your customer or prospect calls you.	Outbound Targeting – you can get hold of the right person and be sure they have received your message – not possible with any other medium apart from face-to-face selling. Precision – you can tailor your message and even vary it during the call, according to the reception you are getting. Feedback – you can find out how well your message is being received and adjust it, if necessary. The telephone is a good way of building up information for your database. Responsiveness – telephone calls tend to generate high responses. Speed – the telephone enables you to contact a customer immediately. Power – the telephone has proved to be a very good follow-up medium for direct mailings – generating much higher responses than mail alone.	Intrusive – some people resent the intrusion of a telephone call – especially when received at home. Non-permanence – there is no 'hard' copy, so nothing to remind people once they have put the phone down. Lack of commitment – some people will say yes to get the caller off the line – there is a higher incidence of false response compared to written responses. Cost – telephone calls can be expensive compared to other media.

THE TELEPHONE – INBOUND

Type	Strengths	Weaknesses
The telephone – inbound.	Popular – one of the most popular response media. Acceptable – although many people do not like receiving selling calls they are quite happy to make ordering or enquiry calls. Customer service can be improved by the provision of a helpline or hotline.	Cost – if you provide a toll-free number you have to pay for the calls.

PRODUCT CARDS

Type	Strengths	Weaknesses
Product cards – packs of twenty to thirty 'postcards' distributed by mail to businesses – each card carries a mini-advertisement for a product or service.	Cost – they are a good low-cost method of prospecting for leads. Responsiveness – many large companies use them regularly – this tells us they must work cost-efficiently. Targeting – they are usually addressed to a 'function' within a company e.g. financial director, office products buyer.	Low credibility – some people throw them in the bin immediately. Quality of response – they can attract low quality replies as they are so easy to reply to – leads must be qualified before arranging sales visits. Competition – your card may be one of thirty or more in the same pack.

DIRECT MAIL

Type	Strengths	Weaknesses
Individually addressed, unsolicited communications, typically mailed in bulk.	Targeting – an extremely powerful advertising medium, which uses information about individuals to select those for whom the offer will be relevant. The same information also helps us to identify those for whom the message will not be relevant – this benefits us in two ways: (1) we reduce annoyance by not mailing people who would find the message an irritant (2) we save money by reducing our mailing quantities. Flexibility – having information about individuals gives us another opportunity – we can vary the message and offer to the precise requirements of an individual person or 'cluster' of people – thus we can vary what we say according to whether we are writing to a chief executive or an office manager; a plumber or a heart specialist. Relevance – the above features make good direct mail more relevant than other forms of advertising. Retention of message – well targeted mailings have a very high impact and are remembered far longer than other forms of advertising. Creative freedom – there are almost no limits on creativity in direct mail – apart from the requirement of all advertising to be legal, decent and truthful. We can use colour, sound and movement (via tapes and videos), give demonstrations and use a variety of memorable involvement devices. Creativity – a large sample of business people, when asked which of their mailings they opened first, said 'those which are bulky or look most interesting'. Acceptability – research shows us that direct mail is welcomed by a high percentage of consumers and business people – 'providing it is relevant and interesting'. Testing facilities – direct mail is an excellent 'test-bed' enabling us to make comparisons of lists, offers, timing, creative themes, response devices (stickers, vouchers, cards, Freefone telephone numbers, fax numbers etc.).	Cost – despite the cost-efficiency of direct mail, it can be expensive to produce – costing perhaps fifty to a hundred times as much 'per reader' as a press advertisement. However, the much tighter targeting capabilities of direct mail can reduce most of the wastage and thus deliver a cost per reply or cost per order which can be lower than press. To do so, however, we need to have enough information to enable this precise targeting. Direct mail is often not the most cost-efficient way to prospect for new customers. Image – there are many people, and not a few newspapers, who deliberately decry direct mail as 'junk mail'. In fact junk mail is not synonymous with direct mail, but with badly targeted direct mail. It is true that many people receive lots of badly targeted mailings. We must do all we can to reduce this so that direct mail does not continue to receive such bad press.

DIRECT MAIL – CONTINUED

Type	Strengths	Weaknesses
	Do-it-yourself – most other media require some skill in layout and writing, especially as there is a need to catch the eye against the many competing calls for attention.	
	In direct mail this is not so important – if you can place the right message, in front of the right person, at the right time, you will receive attention.	
	This is not to say that you do not have to work hard at it – merely that this is one form of advertising which is easier to do successfully yourself.	

CHAPTER 5 THE DATABASE

As Chapter 5 explains, many people think that 'database' is synonymous with 'mailing list', but this seriously undervalues the value of a database to any business.

Figure A.1 illustrates the many business processes which can be supported by a good marketing database.

Each activity is driven by, and linked to, the database. Let us now consider each activity in detail.

Figure A.1
Showing the many business processes which can be supported by a good marketing database

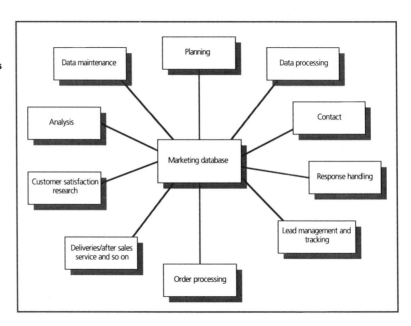

PLANNING

> ▷ **Campaign objectives** – what do you want to achieve? You must first define precise, measurable objectives. The database will help you decide what is feasible by helping you analyse previous campaigns.

> ▷ **Customers** – which of your customers will find this offer/ proposition interesting? Again, analysis of previous behaviour will help target the right people.

> ▷ **Message** – what will persuade them? How much information will they need? The database will help you decide where each customer fits on the ladder of loyalty.

Figure A.2
Identifying
communica-
tions strategies

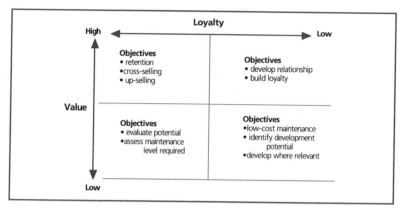

- ▷ **Timing** – when is the ideal time? Some companies send out a mailing to suit their sales requirements. A better way is to target individuals when the time is right for them. This requires analysis of their previous orders and enquiries.

- ▷ **Cost of sales and service** – by calculating the potential profit from each customer over their 'lifetime', you can 'cluster' customers into value groups and match your marketing activities to the potential returns. Figure A.2 shows how this can be done.

- ▷ **Budgeting and forecasting** – again this will be based on analysis of previous campaigns, carried out through the database.

- ▷ **Campaign management** – finally the database makes it far easier to co-ordinate and control all elements of a campaign.

DATA PROCESSING

- ▷ **Identify and select prospects** – based on the customer profiles identified in the planning phase.

- ▷ **Deliver counts for budget confirmation** – faster and more accurate than a manual system.

- ▷ **Produce output (labels, disks, tapes and so on)** – with no additional data entry required.

- ▷ **Flag selected records** – in future you will wish to know which customers received this promotion. Placing an indicator against the relevant records is known as 'flagging'.

- ▷ **Set up reports** – you need to define specific reports in advance. The database also enables you to change your mind and add or change the content and format of reports later.

CONTACT

Here the database can help in a variety of ways.

You may decide to use a mailing house. If so, you can arrange for the computer to produce a tape or disk of the names and other data needed for producing the mailing.

You may also require a hard copy of the list to be used for telephone or mail follow up.

Unless your mailing is very large, you may decide to produce it on your own computer – the mailing letter will be produced on the word-processing system and you can then set up a 'mail merge'.

▷ A mail merge – in this process a series of simple instructions is given to the computer to select the relevant parts of the name and address data from the database. This is merged with the letter copy so that you can print out the finished, personalized, addressed mailing through your word-processing system.

This is a fairly simple process and the only drawback may be the speed of your printer. If this runs at, say, three pages per minute and you intend to send out 1,500 two-page letters, the printer will be running non-stop for more than sixteen hours.

In such circumstances, it may be better to copy the merged data onto a floppy disk and get a local computer bureau to do the printing. They are likely to have much faster printers, but there will of course be a charge. You can review their quotation and decide whether you would rather pay a fee, or stand by the printer overnight refilling it with paper.

▷ **Campaign reports** – the database system will also produce pre-determined reports of the various actions taken, i.e. 1,500 records merged, 3,000 pages printed etc.

REASONS FOR CONTACT

The previous section makes the assumption that you are sending out a seasonal sales campaign. However there are many other reasons for contacting customers and prospects – many driven by the information you have in the database.

EXAMPLE

Dates   Renewals, service intervals, holidays, and so on.

Events   First purchase, moving house/job and so on.

            New premises, company acquisitions.

            Customer complaints or queries.

            Feedback from sales or customer service personnel

                e.g. competitive activity.

Need for further information

            Customer satisfaction surveys etc.

RESPONSE HANDLING

Responses are received by mail and telephone. These should be dealt with urgently, with any required follow-up literature despatched within twenty-four hours if possible.

The ideal would be to enter responses onto the system as they are received – you will have to produce some sort of despatch documentation or label, so some keying in will be necessary.

If you were able to include the customer's name and address on the reply form in your mailing, you will also have had the opportunity to include the customer's unique reference number.

Including this on the reply form makes data entry much easier. You only need to key in the URN and this will connect you to the relevant customer record automatically.

You may also want to carry out some follow-up activity. If you keep the database updated with responses each day, you will be able to produce follow-up listings automatically.

If the mailing is designed to generate leads for personal follow-up (face-to-face or telephone), it may be advisable to qualify them in some way before deciding on priorities.

Some simple questions on the response form can be helpful, e.g.

▷ When does your present contract expire?

▷ How many employees are there in your company?

▷ When does your financial year end?

The answers enable you to prioritize the leads and decide on the next action, i.e. visit, telephone call, mail details etc.

LEAD MANAGEMENT AND TRACKING

The database is the ideal way of keeping track of leads received. You can diarize follow-up dates and the database will automatically remind you to take the necessary action.

The database should automatically call for feedback if not received by the due date – this helps you manage the lead tracking process.

Follow-up materials should, where possible, be generated automatically – a simple acknowledgement letter varied according to the reply form details is easy to organize.

The lead tracking process should allow for non-converted leads to be placed into a separate file for future promotion – a non-converted enquiry is a better prospect than an outside name.

The process should allow for re-allocation of a non-converted lead into a new segment for future activity where relevant.

ORDER PROCESSING

At this stage several areas of the business need to be working closely together:

▷ **Response handling** – enter order details, produce despatch and billing documentation

▷ **Stock control** – check the product is in stock – adjust stock levels as necessary

▷ **Accounts** – response handling to notify accounts of transaction – set up credit account or process payment

▷ **Warehouse** – pick, pack, despatch etc.

The database links these functions together and keeps all parties informed through regular reports.

DELIVERIES AND SERVICE

The database provides rapid reports of despatches and enables the status of an order to be identified immediately, during a telephone call if necessary. This enables you to offer a high standard of customer service without the need for lots of staff.

A delivery or customer enquiry should also be seen as an opportunity for checking the customer information you hold.

Where a product requires regular servicing, the database can help you send reminders on time.

CUSTOMER SATISFACTION RESEARCH

As mentioned earlier, customer questionnaires are a good way of gathering additional information about customers and their needs. They can also help you keep a grip of product, delivery and service standards.

Sample research can be helpful, but if the programme covers all customers there is a major bonus – customer complaints can be identified at the individual level and tackled immediately.

One of the key factors in customer retention is how queries and complaints are handled. Customers who complain should not be viewed as a nuisance, but as people who are sufficiently interested in their relationship with you to be prepared to help you get your service right.

Several studies have shown that those who complain can be better long-term customers than those who do not.

ANALYSIS

As discussed earlier, careful analysis of previous years' campaigns, customer segments etc. forms a sound basis for campaign planning.

A key advantage of a good database system is flexibility. Therefore, in addition to producing a range of pre-determined reports at specified times, the database should permit ad hoc analysis of the 'what if' kind.

DATA MAINTENANCE

Name and address data decays at an alarming rate. One of the best ways of keeping records up to date is by frequent contact, encouraging customers to let you know when their details change.

You can also get outside suppliers to check and enhance the data. Business lists can be cleaned and enhanced by suppliers such as Dun & Bradstreet, Market Location and CCN. Consumer lists by CCN, CACI, NDL and CMT.

WHAT SORT OF DATA?

Let's look at the sort of information you might collect. This will vary according to whether you are selling to businesses or consumers and according to the nature of your product or service. Tables A3.1 and A3.2 give simple examples of the sort of data which could be useful. You should develop a matrix like this for your own business – the important thing is to have a use in mind for each piece of data you decide to store – this will avoid an overloaded database.

Table A3.1   Consumers

Consumer data	Uses	Sources
Name and address	Addressing mailings De-duplication exercises	Directories Rented or purchased lists Electoral roll Advertising responses
Household composition Number of adults Children etc	Targeting of mailings and offers	Electoral roll Lifestyle databases Rented lists
Lifestyle characteristics	Buying habits – products, holidays and so on	NDL, CMT, ICD and so on
Property types; area characteristics e.g. rural, urban, city centre and so on	Segmentation and targeting of mailings. Development of offers and messages	Acorn, Mosaic, Pinpoint and so on
Promotional responses – what sent, what responded to, how responded	Targeting and list selection	Own response data Rented lists List compilers
Enquiries – what about?	Targeting and selection	Own records Rented lists
Purchasing behaviour	Segmentation, timing and targeting	Own database Rented lists List compilers
Complaints	Development of customer panels Research Product development	Own records + customer satisfaction surveys

Table A3.2   Businesses

Business data	Uses	Sources
Company name and address Head office information e.g. subsidiary of...	Addressing mailings De-duplication exercises Pricing, support and service issues	Directories Rented or purchased lists Business database (Yellow Pages), Dun & Bradstreet, Market Location, CCN etc Advertising responses
Name, title and function of individual	Personalization of mailings Targeting of offers and messages	List Brokers, Business databases and so on
Turnover and trend data Year-end date	Targeting of messages Development of offers Sales predictions Segmentation	Companies House Dun and Bradstreet, Market Location and CCN
Number of employees, sites, vehicles, computers and so on	Targeting of mailings and offers Segmentation of customers and prospects	Companies House Dun and Bradstreet etc. Business databases Rented lists
Buying characteristics Products, quantities, frequency and so on Buying process and DMUs	Targeting of mailings and offers Segmentation of customers Development of clusters	D & B, CCN Own records
Purchasing behaviour	Segmentation, timing and targeting. Offer development	Own database Rented lists List compilers
Promotional responses – what sent, what responded to	Targeting and list selection	Own response data Rented lists List compilers
Enquiries – what about?	Targeting and selection	Own records Rented lists
Area characteristics e.g. rural, urban, city centre and so on Sector profile data	Targeting of mailings Siting of distribution points Sales force management Sales forecasting Development of offers	D&B, CCN, own research and sales force feedback
Competitor information	Research, tactical campaign planning	Own research and sales force feedback
Complaints	Customer panels Research Product development	Own records

CHAPTER 6 MAILING LIST TERMINOLOGY

There are many terms in use and the following descriptions may be helpful when you are dealing with list suppliers, computer bureaux etc.

- **Single rental** – available solely for one specified and approved use – only names who reply positively may be added to your permanent list, and then only subject to the requirements of the Data Protection Act.

- **Multiple rental** – approved for specified and approved multiple uses – e.g. multiple mailings, mailing and telephone follow-up. Again only positive responses to your mailing or telephone call can be kept on your files.

- **Outright purchase** – all data becomes user property for own use (remember the DPA), but is not available for sale or rental to anyone else.

- **Telephone use** – single/multiple rental or outright purchase of data for telephone use – conditions are the same as above.

DATA PROCESSING CONSIDERATIONS

The majority of mailing lists are supplied on magnetic media for additional processing before mailing takes place. The following points require consideration:

- **Magnetic tape format** – although certain 'standard' formats exist, not everyone conforms to them. The safest course is to ask your computer bureau what format they require and then to specify this in your official order to the broker. Some conversion work may still be required – you can keep this to a minimum by getting the specifications right at the start.

- **Address formatting** – the list owner's computer or bureau will hold the list in a certain address format. If your addressing bureau can operate their software with this format there will be no problem but this is not a formality. Your bureau may be carrying out address correction or verification, de-duplication, data enhancement or other activities, and the original data will often need re-formatting for these purposes.

It is important to keep a close eye on these matters as extra charges can mount very quickly in this area.

Appendix 4 Answers and suggestions for self-tests

CHAPTER 1

It is tempting, when faced with this question, to answer *'Rent a list of motorists'*, indeed many of my seminar delegates choose this first.

This, however, is not the right thing to do – most motorists only change their insurance once a year. Thus, to rent a list without any details of their renewal dates would be wasteful, only one-twelfth of them being in the market when your mailing arrived.

If you were able to get the renewal dates in advance, that would be different, but no competitive insurance company will rent you their names so you are faced with a critical lack of data.

The answer here, therefore, is to advertise with a powerful offer, e.g. *Do you want to save money on your car insurance?* You would choose a mass media option such as television (e.g. Direct Line), national press or posters (e.g. Churchill), inviting interested prospects to volunteer their names and their renewal dates. At this point, you can switch to direct mail to develop the leads and convert them into customers.

The question states that you have no house list of prospects, but you will, of course, have customers buying other types of insurance. During your communications about buildings, contents or other insurance you should be seeking information which will enable you to cross-sell other products.

You could also set about building a list of car insurance prospects by asking the relevant questions in a general customer satisfaction questionnaire.

CHAPTER 2

QUESTION 1

The four major benefits of direct mail are:

(a) impact

(b) relevance

(c) involvement

(d) cost-efficiency

These are explained in more detail on pages 31–33.

QUESTION 2

The five factors affecting the response to a mailing are:

(a) list quality – see page 35 and read Chapter 6

(b) your offer – see page 35 and read Chapter 7

(c) timing – see page 37

(d) creative execution – see page 37 and read Chapter 8

(e) response devices – see page 37 and read Chapter 8.

CHAPTER 5

QUESTION 1 – TEN BENEFITS OF COMPUTERISING YOUR DATA

1   Analysis of customer behavioural patterns

2   More relevant communications

3   Improved productivity of marketing expenditure

4   Better customer care

5   Development of more appropriate products and services

6   Improved forecasting and measurement capabilities

7   The ability to extend your marketing to hitherto unprofitable channels

8   More cost-effective prospecting

9   The ability to present accurate up-to-date reports to colleagues

10 Distribute your customer information to each customer contact point

You'll find more details on each of these points on pages 74 and 75.

QUESTION 2 AND 3

When you have completed your list of data items and potential usage check this against that in Appendix 3 – pages 282 and 283.

CHAPTER 6

There is no model answer for this question – the form will reflect your own product and service and the target you are seeking.

However, the creative briefing form in Chapter 10 (page 219) will give an idea as to how much detail you need to give. Re-reading the Buyer's Checklist on pages 109 and 110 may also be helpful.

The more details you give, the more completely your broker will be able to fulfil your requirements.

CHAPTER 7

Again there is no model answer – it will depend on your own circumstances. When you have developed your offers, re-read the section on the ladder of loyalty (Chapter 4 – pages 66–69).

After doing this, consider whether there is anything you now wish to change.

CHAPTER 9

QUESTION 1

No prizes for getting this right – you already did this in Chapter 2. However, for the record, they are:

(a) list

(b) offer

(c) timing

(d) creative execution

(e) response devices.

QUESTION 2

The result is not reliable (significant) – refer to the table on page 188 – with a total of one hundred replies your 'winner' would need to have achieved at least sixty replies.

QUESTION 3

This time you do have a winner. With a total of around 500 replies you would need to achieve at least 273 replies. Your 295 is comfortably past this, especially as the overall total is slightly less than 500. Your winner represents 59.59% of the total against a required minimum of 54.47%.

If you are interested in the statistical side of direct marketing, you will find the following books each have a chapter covering the topic in detail.

▷ *Successful Direct Marketing Methods* – by Bob Stone.

▷ *The Practitioner's Guide to Direct Marketing* – The Institute of Direct Marketing.

Glossary

A/B split run – See *split-run testing*.

Above the line – a term applied to traditional (i.e. non-direct response) advertising.

Acquisition (of customers) – all activities related to locating and marketing to new prospects.

ACORN – acronym for A Classification of Residential Neighbourhoods. A marketing segmentation system enabling consumers to be classified according to the type of residential area in which they live.

Added value – some additional element provided to a customer for which no extra charge is paid, e.g. a free booklet explaining how to get extra miles per gallon. Also called an *extra value proposition* (EVP).

Advance mailer – A simple mailing or postcard, mailed before the main mailing to increase awareness and response. Sometimes called a *teaser*.

Advertorial – a paid-for space in a magazine or newspaper which is laid out in editorial fashion, giving the impression therefore of being editorial rather than advertising.

Artwork – finished layout of typesetting, drawings and photographs, made up in a form which is ready for the printer to turn it into plates.

Artwork studio – place where artwork is made up from photographs, drawings, lettering and typesetting.

Awareness – advertising or other promotional activity (e.g. PR) whose primary purpose is to increase general knowledge and understanding of the company, and to make people feel more positively towards it. Also known as image activity.

Below the line – a term used to denote non-awareness activities – includes direct marketing (incorrectly), sales promotion and so on.

Benefit testing – a telephone research technique, used to establish customer comprehension of, and preference for, specific promotional statements (headlines).

Bleed – printing which carries colour up to the edge of the paper.

Block designs – a form of direct mail test matrix which reduces the number of names required.

Body copy – the main areas of text in an advertisement, brochure or leaflet, other than headlines and sub-headings.

Brief – verbal or (preferably) written instructions to a supplier, e.g. agency, mailing house, computer bureau and so on.

Bromide (PMT) – photo mechanical transfer. Laser etched black text and screened images on light sensitive paper, used to make up mechanical artwork.

Business mailing – a mailing sent to a business (as opposed to a consumer).

Business to business – direct communication from one business to another.

Caption – a brief explanation of a picture or drawing.

Cheshire labels – labels produced by a Cheshire machine which cuts up continuous stationery from a computer printer.

Cromalin – a method of proofing four-colour work chemically on photographic paper, instead of using plates and ink.

Closed face envelope – an envelope without a window.

Cold list – a list which has no affinity to the advertiser, nor any known buying history of the product or service.

Colour mark-up – specifications to a printer, showing the required colours for the item to be printed.

Communications action calendar – a detailed schedule of activities required to achieve the fulfilment of the communications action plan.

Compiled list – names and addresses derived from directories, public records, sales slips, trade show registrations and so on.

Computer personalization – printing of letters or other promotional pieces by a computer system using names, special phrases or other information based on data appearing in our database. The objective is to make use of the data to tailor the message to a specific recipient and to select only names for whom the message will be relevant.

Consumer list – a list of names and addresses of individuals at their home addresses.

Consumer mailing – a mailing to consumers at their home addresses

Contact strategy – the process of deciding the exact details of customer contact – i.e. telephone + mail, press campaign and targeted direct mail and so on.

Control (package or advertisement) – our standard (usually pre-tested or previously used) design, against which new designs and offers are tested.

Controlled circulation – distribution at no charge of a publication to individuals or companies on the basis of their title, occupation or business type.

Conversion pack – material sent out in response to enquiries from prospects, with the intention of converting them into customers – also known as a response pack.

Copy – see body copy

Copywriter – a specialist who writes copy for mailings and advertisements.

Cross-selling – using a customer's buying history to select them for related offers, e.g. a car alarm for new car buyers.

Customer database – a record of customers' buying history and related information; usually, but not necessarily, held on a computer.

Customer lifetime value (LTV) – see *lifetime value analysis.*

Customer profile – a collection of facts and characteristics about your customers, e.g. age, household composition, company size, number of cars etc.

Database – records of customer, prospect and market information. Used for many marketing, sales and business management purposes. Usually, but not necessarily, held on a computer.

Data capture – the process of keying-in (or scanning-in) data to a computer.

Data protection – legislation to protect the interests of the individual by controlling the use of personal data for marketing or other business purposes. See Appendix 1.

Decision maker – the person who makes the decision to buy, or try a product or service. With expensive products or large contracts this person would generally be a member of a decision-making unit (see next).

Decision-making unit (DMU) – a group of people within a company (sometimes including outside consultants), who discuss the acceptance or otherwise of a business offer. There can be several people involved.

De-duplication (merge/purge) – a computerized system of comparing data to identify names and addresses which appear in a list, or group of lists, more than once.

Demographics – socio-economic characteristics of customers, such as sex, age, status and so on.

Desktop publishing (DTP) – creating artwork and print from your computer. Requires special software and a fairly powerful PC (or Apple Mac).

Die-cut – a shaped cut-out in a leaflet or brochure.

Digitized (signature) – a computer-printed simulation of a personal signature.

Direct mailshot – term used to describe a direct mail promotion. Also known as a mailshot.

Direct marketing – marketing activity which is based on a direct relationship between advertiser and customer or prospect. Also known as dialogue marketing, relationship marketing and so on.

Direct response advertising – advertising carrying a response device of some sort (coupon, telephone or fax number) – the primary objective is to generate enquiries or orders direct.

Display advertising – advertising which is 'laid-out', often with illustrations, as opposed to lineage or classified advertising.

Door drops – unaddressed 'mailings' delivered by Royal Mail and other companies. Can be targeted to small areas, making them very suitable for small businesses.

Dual-purpose advertising – advertising which, whilst carrying a response device, is also intended to generate awareness of a product or service.

EDMA – European Direct Marketing Association.

External lists – mailing lists from outside sources i.e. not from within one's own company records.

Flyer – additional insert in a mailing package.

Follow-up – A mailing or telephone call made after the main mailing to increase impact and response.

Fulfilment – the processing of an order or request for information.

Fulfilment house – see *mailing house, mailshop.*

Galley proof – a proof taken before printing plates are made.

Gateholder – a member of the decision-making unit – one who has the power or authority to stop a purchase.

Gone-away – term used to indicate that a person mailed is no longer at that address.

GSM – grammes per square metre – standard measure of paper weight.

Guard book – a collection of mailings and advertisements, marked up with results information, improving capabilities for future campaign planning.

Gum strips – strips of glue applied to a mailing leaflet or envelope, enabling it to be sealed when moistened.

Hand-enclosing – assembling and enclosing a mailing entirely by hand, as opposed to machine enclosing. Also called hand-filling.

Imposition – the process of laying down artwork or negatives so that printing plates will print in the correct sequence for the finished job.

Influencer – a member of, or advisor to, the decision making unit

Initiator – the member of the decision making unit who sets the process in motion by perceiving or reporting the need.

Ink jet – a computer controlled printing process using a jet stream of ink droplets – often used to personalize leaflets or brochures with names and addresses.

Integrated marketing communications – the process of co-ordinating all our information and one or more communication media to deliver a powerful message to the right person at the right time.

Interactive – a communication method, such as telephone marketing or face-to-face meeting, where the message can be varied according to the response of the prospect, and where the respondent can become involved by discussing, asking questions and so on.

ISO sizes – paper sizes based on a square metre and internationally accepted. The dimensions are such that when a sheet is halved along its long edge, the ratio of the long edge to the short edge remains the same. Generally 'A' sizes are for printed work (e.g. A5, A4 and so on.), 'B' sizes for charts, and 'C' sizes for envelopes. Thus an A4 sheet fits into a C4 envelope and so on.

Job-bag – A large bag or envelope in which all elements of artwork, proofs, quotes and so on, are kept together for easy reference.

Key British Enterprises – published by Dun & Bradstreet, Key British Enterprises lists Britain's top companies, with additional data of interest to business-to-business marketers.

Key-coding – printing a code onto a response device to enable the source of the enquiry/order and so on to be traced.

Laser printer – a computer controlled printer which works on the same principle as a photocopier. The process of laser printing is sometimes called 'lasering'.

Layout – drawing or sketch showing the relative positions of illustrations and copy in an advertisement or mailing.

Lead generation – activity to produce enquiries (leads) which can then be followed up by telephone, salesforce or direct mail.

Leading edge – the edge of the printed piece which is inserted into the envelope first.

Lead qualification – the process of evaluating the sales potential of a lead in order to decide on the optimum contact strategy.

Lettershop – see *mailing house.*

Lift letter – an additional letter within a mailing package, often from an authoritative individual who endorses the product or service. So called because they generally increase (lift) response.

Linework – all type, lines, borders and so on that make up the finished design.

List (mailing list) – names and addresses of individuals or companies having in common a specific characteristic (e.g. SIC code), activity (workshop), or interest.

List broker – a specialist who arranges for a company to rent the list of another organization.

List building – the process of gathering names and addresses and compiling them into a list for mailing or other purposes (e.g. telemarketing).

List cleaning – the process of correcting or removing a name and address from a mailing list because it is no longer correct.

List exchange – some organizations are prepared to exchange names with other organizations who are promoting a non-competitive product or service to the same type of prospect.

List rental – the process of renting a list from a broker or, sometimes direct from the owner.

List selection – a sub-section of a list, enabling an advertiser to mail only that part of the list he considers to be more likely to respond (e.g. in a list of company directors the advertiser may select only the financial directors, or chief executives).

Literal – a misprint or mis-spelling within a printed job.

Machine fold – a process of mechanically folding printed paper.

Mailer – another name for a mailing pack or piece.

Mailing house (mailshop/lettershop) – an organization which offers a range of services to the advertiser, including; assembly and despatch of a mailing, receipt and fulfilment of responses, laser printing and other computer work.

Mailsort – The Royal Mail discount service for direct mailings. Users pre-sort the mail into postcode areas in return for discounts on postage costs.

Market profile – Selling history and other relevant information about a target audience.

Match code – a unique reference code, built from a name and address, enabling a computer to carry out a de-duplication run. See *merge/purge* below.

Matched samples – When testing various types of offer, creative treatments and so on, each test is sent to a cell made up of the same type of people or companies – matched samples – to ensure results are truly representative.

Mechanical artwork – finished layout, comprising typesettings, photographs and so on, which is ready for making printing plates.

Media – the plural of medium, i.e. advertising medium. Media therefore are carriers of advertising messages, e.g. newspapers, magazines, radio, television, direct mail and so on.

Media mix – the combination of media used in a single campaign.

Member Get Member (MGM) – a marketing device to encourage customers to introduce new customers or prospects – sometimes accompanied by the offer of a free gift. Also known as referrals or recommendations.

Merge/purge – the process of matching lists (merging) to identify duplicate listings. These are then listed and can be removed (purged) before mailing. See *de-duplication.*

Negative option – an offer where delivery to the customer is carried out unless the customer requests to the contrary within a specified period.

Net names – names actually usable after a de-duplication operation.

N'th name selection – a method used in list testing to ensure randomized sample selection, e.g. to select 1,000 names at random from a list of 15,000 we would specify 'every 15th name'. This overcomes any bias which might arise if the list is held in chronological or value sequence.

Objective – a stated requirement (usually precisely quantified) for achievement, e.g. 'to increase our number of buying customers to 200 by June 1996.' See also *strategy* and *tactics.*

OCR – optical character reading (or recognition) – a process using equipment which can 'read' specially formed characters to speed up the analysis of reports, questionnaires and so on.

Off the page – obtaining a lead or a sale directly from a press advertisement without additional follow-up.

OMR – optical mark reading – similar to OCR but reading marks or bars rather than alpha and numeric characters.

One-shot – a solo mailing, usually promoting a single product, without follow-up.

Origination – preparation work for printing, i.e. creative work, photography, artwork, typesetting and colour separation (q.v.).

Overprint – to run previously printed material through a press to print additional matter, e.g. adding the name and address to a previously (pre-printed) letter.

PAF – the Postcode Address File.

Personalization – see *computer personalization*.

Piggy-back – additional promotion in a mailing package, usually from a different advertiser to the main offer.

PMT – photo-mechanical transfer – a reproduction quality copy of an original piece of artwork.

Postcode – an alphanumeric code that defines each part of a postal address.

Pre-paid – printing a mail mark or applying a stamp to a reply device to encourage response. Using Royal Mail Business Reply or Freepost services is more cost-effective as advertisers pay only for those returned.

Printed postage impression (PPI) – A Royal Mail system enabling volume users to pre-print envelopes with a postage paid impression, instead of affixing stamps to each piece.

Profiling – selection or clustering of customers or prospects according to specific characteristics e.g. profiling may indicate that our best customers are companies with more than 200 cars, or who are in heavy engineering and so on.

Proof – a printed sample of work to be checked for errors in text, positioning or quality of colour reproduction.

Prospects – literally prospective customers who match our buying profile but have never bought this particular product from us. See also *suspects*.

Qualitative research – research which is used to assess opinions, understanding of concepts, like or dislike of concepts, creative treatments and so on.

Quantitative research – research which sets out to answer the 'how many' questions. Requires much larger samples than qualitative research.

Rate card – publisher's details of advertisement rates, copy dates, artwork sizes and so on.

Referral – See *member get member*.

Referral rate – the frequency or percentage of referrals we receive.

Relationship marketing – see *direct marketing*.

Reminder mailing – a mailing sent to a customer reminding them of a significant date such as a renewal or cut-off date.

Response rate – the level at which replies or orders are received as a result of a promotional campaign, advertisement or mailing. Usually expressed as a percentage of the number mailed or universe promoted to (e.g. newspaper readership).

Retention (of customers) – activities to increase the loyalty of customers, i.e. to make them remain as regular buyers.

Retention rate – the percentage of customers who remain 'loyal' from year to year.

RFM – an acronym for recency, frequency and monetary value – a form of analysis relating to buying behaviour.

ROI – return on investment.

Roll-out – a test mailing would normally be done to a sample of a list. If the results are satisfactory the mailing may then be 'rolled-out' to the full list.

Roman typefaces – type faces with serifs such as this one are easier to read and generally score much higher in comprehension testing than sans serif faces. See *sans serif typefaces*.

Rub-off – an involvement device where the recipient rubs or scratches off a surface coating to reveal a symbol or prize and so on.

Run-on price – price from a supplier for continuing to produce further supplies of a print job over and above the quoted quantity.

SA – abbreviation for self-adhesive (labels or envelopes).

Salutation – the addressing of a letter to an individual, e.g. Dear Mr. Brown.

Sample – a representative sub-set of a list or 'universe', used in research and testing. See *matched sample* and *N'th name*.

Sans serif typefaces – typefaces without serifs which, although they look clear and easy to read, are in fact a barrier to comprehension when used in body copy.

Seed names – names placed into a mailing list to enable the advertiser to establish when the mailing 'touches down', i.e. arrives. Also used as a control when renting lists to other organizations (enabling the renter to know whether the list has been used more than once).

Segment – a sub-section of a list which contains people or companies which have common characteristics.

Segmentation – the process of selecting and isolating segments from within a list or market.

Selection criteria – definitions of characteristics indicating segments within a list.

Self-mailer – a mailing piece where the outer envelope is an integral part of the piece. An attached, perforated response card or envelope may also be included.

Shoot – a photographic session.

SIC – standard industry classification – Government numeric classification of businesses in the UK. Direct mailers can select companies of a specific type (industry) by using this coding.

Source code – a unique coding given to an advertisement or mailing response device, enabling precise allocation of the responses to source.

Speed premium – an incentive offered for an early reply. See also *time-close*.

Split-run testing – test involving alternative creative elements or offers to be tested in newspapers or magazines. Also known as A/B split-runs.

Split-test – two or more matched samples from the same mailing list, i.e. the direct mail equivalent of the split-run.

Strategy – the route, or method by which an objective will be achieved. See also *objectives* and *tactics*.

Suppression file – a list of names and addresses that are not to be mailed.

Synergy – the working together of two or more elements (e.g. direct mail and awareness advertising) to produce an effect greater than would be achieved by the sum of their individual effects.

Tactics – the detailed actions involved in fulfilling a strategy. See also *objectives* and *strategy*.

Take one – a leaflet placed where interested prospects can 'take one'. Often in a dispenser or display stand in retail sites.

Tandem communications – the use of simultaneous multiple mailings or other communications to target more than one member of a decision-making unit with messages relevant to their specific interests.

Target group index (TGI) – Analysis of purchasing habits among consumers – covers 4,500 brands and services across more than 500 product fields.

Targeting – the precise identification of an audience or target for a promotion.

Telemarketing – telephone marketing – use of the telephone as a marketing medium. In-bound is where the call is instigated by a customer or prospect; Outbound is where the call is made by you to a customer or prospect.

Telemarketing bureau – an independent organization offering telemarketing services on a project or campaign basis.

Telephone account management – the process of managing customers by telephone, usually with the addition of direct mail. Typically used for accounts which do not warrant regular, personal calls by the salesforce.

Telesales – the use of the telephone for selling. This is distinct from using the telephone to receive enquiries, develop customer relationships and manage accounts.

Testing – the process of evaluating alternative media, creative treatments, offers, timing, response devices and so on.

Time close – an offer or special price which is said only to be open for a limited period e.g. 'for 7 days only', 'until 30 March' and so on.

Tip-ons – a one piece mailer or postcard which is attached by a dab of glue to a leaflet or advertisement.

The Times Top Thousand – A business register, giving names, addresses and general information about Britain's largest companies.

Typesetting – The assembly of body copy and headlines by keyboard, photosetting or digital means.

Typo – slang term for literal. Shortened version of 'typographical error'.

Unique selling proposition (USP) – a single proposition which sets your product or service apart in the minds of your prospects. In direct marketing it is common for USPs to be varied according to the status of the prospect within the buying process. See *decision-making unit*.

Universe – the total audience within a certain specification, e.g. the 'universe' of company car drivers – all the company car drivers in the UK.

Visual – A layout, indicating the general design, and the position of the various elements.

Window envelope – Envelope which has a portion cut out to reveal an address or other message printed on the material enclosed.

PRINTING PROCESSES

You will not need to know the technical details, but a brief word about the various printing processes may be helpful. There are basically four processes in common use by commercial printers:

1 **Letterpress**, or relief printing – the oldest of the printing processes, used nowadays only for very short runs, e.g. business cards, formal invitations. The image is in relief (it stands up off the plate), ink is applied to the raised parts and transferred directly onto the paper.

2 **Photogravure**, or intaglio printing – the opposite of letterpress in two ways – (a) it is only used for very long runs (large circulation magazines, catalogues and so on) because of the high cost of preparing the print cylinders, and (b) the image is engraved into the surface of the cylinder and the ink is held in a 'honeycomb' of cells and transferred to the paper directly.

3   **Silk screen**, or stencil printing. This is a very simple process based on the stencil method. A material with a fine open weave (the screen) is stretched across a frame – a stencil is laid on top blocking out the areas which are not required to print and ink is then squeezed across the screen forcing it through the open weave which is not covered by the stencil. Silk screen printing is used for short runs, typically posters for local events and any work which requires a particularly high density of solid colour. It is often used for window bills in retail stores. An advantage of silk screen is that it can be printed onto almost any surface – material, glass, plastic and so on – e.g. logos or messages on promotional pens or gifts are usually silk screened.

4   **Lithography**, or planographic printing, also known as offset litho – the main choice for leaflets, mailings, and so on. Depending on volume there is a choice of two offset-litho systems:
  ▷ sheet-fed – printing onto individual flat sheets
  ▷ web – printing onto a continuous reel of paper (the web).

DIFFERENCES BETWEEN SHEET-FED AND WEB-OFFSET LITHOGRAPHY

There are several important differences between sheet-fed and web-offset as follows:

Sheet-fed

▷ Usually prints on one side at a time at up to 15,000 sheets per hour.
▷ Prints from flat cut sheets.
▷ Delivers flat sheets.
▷ Ink has to dry before printing the reverse of the sheet.
▷ Paper ranges in weight from 70 to 220 gsm (grammes per square metre).
▷ Suitable for runs up to 50,000.

Web-offset

- ▷ Prints both sides simultaneously, at up to 40,000 impressions per hour.
- ▷ Prints onto a reel of paper (web)
- ▷ Can deliver flat sheets or folded sections.
- ▷ Ink is dried instantly by very hot air, giving a high gloss finish.
- ▷ Paper weights range from 52 gsm to 180 gsm.
- ▷ Suitable for runs into millions.

WHY OFFSET?

Originally in litho printing, the impression was transferred directly from the printing plate to the paper. However, the increasing requirement over the years for faster press speeds and lower grades of paper meant that the standard litho process was not able to deliver the quality of impression required. This led to the development of offset litho.

In offset, the inked impression is first transferred to an intermediate cylinder faced with a flexible 'rubber' blanket. This, in turn, transfers the impression to the paper, but because the blanket is flexible, it is able to transfer ink at higher speeds to lower qualities of paper.

WEB-OFFSET

Offset litho which prints onto the continuous reel is thus called 'web-offset'.

Offset-litho is now the main printing process for most forms of marketing material with the exception of the longest runs of mail order catalogues, which are still printed by gravure.

THE FOUR-COLOUR PROCESS

It is now time to describe briefly how full colour illustrations are produced by the various printing processes. In each case, the basic system is the same – i.e. the four-colour process.

Theoretically, any colour in the spectrum can be made up through a mixture of the three primary colours, yellow, cyan (blue) and magenta (red). In practice, black is also needed to achieve sufficient density in the darker colours and to achieve a perfect black.

CONVERTING A COLOURED ILLUSTRATION INTO PRINTING PLATES

Briefly, a colour illustration is 'scanned' through a coloured filter which allows only one of the three primary colours to pass through. The primary colours are yellow, cyan (blue) and magenta (red). A printing plate is made from each of the resulting negatives and an additional black plate is made.

To enable continuous gradations of tone the negative images are broken up into tiny dots by a mesh 'screen' – although nowadays this is achieved using laser scanners, rather than the traditional process cameras.

The full colour effect is built up by printing each colour successively, with the black providing the final density and 'key'.

Before a machine starts running the job proofs are made and there are four types:

- ▷ **cromalin proofs**. A process producing a simulated colour proof which is actually a photographic print. Needs experience to visualize the finished job. Expensive for more than one or two copies. It does, however, enable an experienced art director to check on the colour work before plates are made.

- ▷ **ozalid proofs** – a monotone proof enabling copy and positioning to be checked before the finished plates are made.

- ▷ **wet proofs** – there are two kinds of wet proofs (i.e. proofs made from plates and ink):

  ❑ proofing press proofs. Made using real plates and ink, but on a special proofing machine – corrections made at this stage, whilst expensive, are still cheaper than making corrections when the main press is ready to run.

  ❑ machine proofs. The real thing. These are proofs taken while the machine is being made ready and running up to speed. Only minor corrections are possible at this stage, without incurring major expense and time delays.

▷ **progressive proofs**. You will usually be able to see 'progressive proofs' from the proofing press – these show the impression from each individual colour plate and how they progressively build up the full colour impression.

IN-LINE FINISHING

Modern web-offset machines can offer a variety of folding, glueing, varnishing, perforating and even ink jetting of names and addresses as the job progresses through the machine. This means that on very long runs, the web or reel of blank paper goes in at one end of the press and a complete finished mailing can be delivered at the other.

LASER PRINTING

This is a totally different process, basically a sort of high speed computer-controlled photocopying system, but working from computer data rather than a solid original. In very simple terms, an electrostatic 'image' is projected onto the paper. This is then passed through a drum of charged particles of grey powder (toner) which adhere to the charged areas. The paper is then passed across a very hot wire which fuses the toner to the paper effectively 'baking' it onto the paper.

COLD FUSION LASER PRINTING

There is a newer system where this 'fusion' is brought about by gas instead of heat and this is called 'cold fusion'. An advantage of cold fusion is that brighter inks can be pre-printed onto the paper as there is no danger of them melting during the fusion process.

Laser, and other forms of computer printing such as ink-jet, are mainly used to apply 'fill-in' details to stationery which has often been pre-printed by one of the conventional methods described above.

There are special paper considerations (including size limitations) when using laser printers and it is necessary to seek professional advice at an early stage.

Index